The Practice of Leadership in Higher Education

This practice-orientated book explores the nature of leadership in higher education during three key stages of the leadership cycle: becoming, being, and leaving leadership.

Providing perspectives on leadership from a range of professional sectors, this book presents considered views on contemporary and future leadership practices in higher education from a global network of contributors. Included within each chapter are prominent questions designed to engage the reader to think about their own leadership experiences to date and leadership development needs. Key points covered include:

- the complexities of leadership in higher education in a changing world
- discussion of internally resourced leadership development frameworks and programmes currently used across the sector
- leading complex education systems
- perspectives on leadership from a range of professional sectors such as corporate, military, elite sport, and public, that can be used to improve the quality of higher education leadership
- case studies of academics' leadership practices that provide readers with authentic personal insights into discipline-specific leadership experiences from around the world.

Full of practical examples of personal leadership experiences which can be used to help inform readers' leadership aspirations, development, and legacy planning, this is the ideal read for anyone interested in understanding their identity and practice as a leader in higher education.

Kendall Jarrett is a Senior Lecturer in Higher Education Management at the University of Bath, UK, as well as a Lecturer in Higher Education at the University of Kent, UK.

Stephen Newton is a longstanding management consultant and qualified business coach.

The Practice of Leadership in Higher Education

Real-world Perspectives on Becoming, Being and Leaving

Edited by
Kendall Jarrett and Stephen Newton

Routledge
Taylor & Francis Group
LONDON AND NEW YORK

First published 2021
by Routledge
2 Park Square, Milton Park, Abingdon, Oxon OX14 4RN

and by Routledge
52 Vanderbilt Avenue, New York, NY 10017

Routledge is an imprint of the Taylor & Francis Group, an informa business

© 2021 selection and editorial matter, Kendall Jarrett and Stephen Newton; individual chapters, the contributors

The right of Kendall Jarrett and Stephen Newton to be identified as the authors of the editorial material, and of the authors for their individual chapters, has been asserted in accordance with sections 77 and 78 of the Copyright, Designs and Patents Act 1988.

All rights reserved. No part of this book may be reprinted or reproduced or utilised in any form or by any electronic, mechanical, or other means, now known or hereafter invented, including photocopying and recording, or in any information storage or retrieval system, without permission in writing from the publishers.

Trademark notice: Product or corporate names may be trademarks or registered trademarks, and are used only for identification and explanation without intent to infringe.

British Library Cataloguing-in-Publication Data
A catalogue record for this book is available from the British Library

Library of Congress Cataloging-in-Publication Data
A catalog record has been requested for this book

ISBN: 978-0-367-42365-0 (hbk)
ISBN: 978-0-367-42367-4 (pbk)
ISBN: 978-0-367-82384-9 (ebk)

Typeset in Goudy
by Swales & Willis, Exeter, Devon, UK

Printed in the United Kingdom
by Henry Ling Limited

Contents

Editors	viii
Contributors	x
Foreword	xvi
Introduction	xix
STEPHEN NEWTON AND KENDALL JARRETT	

PART 1
Realities of leadership in higher education in a changing world   1

1   Defining leadership in HE   3
    STEPHEN NEWTON

2   Developing leaders from within   20
    KENDALL JARRETT

3   Learning to be a leader   43
    STEPHEN NEWTON

    Part 1: summary   57
    KENDALL JARRETT AND STEPHEN NEWTON

PART 2A
Leadership insights: from within the sector 59

4 The influence of experience and culture on leadership 61
RICHARD L. LIGHT WITH MOHAMMAD SHAH RAZAK

5 Leading for learning: building on values and teaching expertise to effect change 71
KATHLEEN M. QUINLAN

6 Leading complex educational systems 87
KENDALL JARRETT AND JOHN BAUMBER

7 Academics in exile: a ghost chapter 102
KENDALL JARRETT AND STEPHEN NEWTON

8 Leadership legacy in higher education 105
SALLY BROWN AND PAULINE KNEALE

PART 2B
Leadership insights: from outside the sector 119

9 Lessons from corporate leadership 121
STEPHEN NEWTON

10 Military leadership 136
STEPHEN NEWTON

11 Leadership in sport 150
KENDALL JARRETT WITH VICTOR LÓPEZ-ROS, ANDY SIDDALL, SERGE ELOI, MATTHEW HOBBS, AND LUKAS MAREK

12 Leadership in the public and third sectors 166
KENDALL JARRETT WITH KARL WADDELL, CHRISTINA CURRY, REV TIM SMITH, GABRIEL MACGREGOR, AND JAN HAWKES

Part 2: summary 183
STEPHEN NEWTON AND KENDALL JARRETT

PART 3
Stories of leadership in higher education — 187

13 Becoming a leader — 189
    A. Rachel Masika — 189
    B. Emily Rumschlag Booms — 194
    C. Dave Thomas — 198

    Chapter 13: summary — 204
    STEPHEN NEWTON AND KENDALL JARRETT

14 Being a leader — 206
    A. Joanne Bowen — 206
    B. Luke Buchanan-Hodgman — 211
    C. Lisa Fedoruk — 215

    Chapter 14: summary — 220
    KENDALL JARRETT

15 Leaving leadership — 222
    A. Carlton Cooke — 222
    B. Fran Beaton — 228
    C. David Hopkins — 233

    Chapter 15: summary — 242
    STEPHEN NEWTON

In conclusion — 245
STEPHEN NEWTON AND KENDALL JARRETT

Index — 248

Editors

Kendall Jarrett's experiences of tertiary education began in Australia with the completion of two bachelor's degrees and a master's. Upon moving to the UK, he took up his first university appointment as a Senior Lecturer in Sport Pedagogy. His pursuit of knowledge took him back to Australia and then to New Zealand, where he completed his PhD at the University of Canterbury.

His development as a multi-discipline academic coincided with a move back to the UK and completion of further studies in applied educational leadership. He is currently working as a Senior Lecturer in Higher Education Management at the University of Bath, responsible for supervision of doctoral students within the International Centre for Higher Education Management (ICHEM). He also works in the Centre for the Study of Higher Education at the University of Kent and as a consultant for the newly founded International Centre for Educational Enhancement at the University of Bolton.

Stephen Newton began his working life as an Army officer, joining the Royal Military Academy Sandhurst directly from school. He was commissioned into the Royal Artillery and selected for an Army scholarship to undertake an in-service degree at Oxford University.

On leaving the Army, he started work in the investment management industry in the City of London, becoming sales director for the mutual funds business of Mercury Asset Management (MAM) – at the time one of the largest fund managers in the UK. He moved within MAM to become operations director, with a brief to reorganise its UK institutional business.

Stephen took on a similar role at Schroder Investment Management before starting his own management consulting and executive coaching business in 2001. The initial focus of that business was the implementation of strategy, working mainly with professional firms, banks, and insurance companies. However, in the aftermath of the 2008 financial crash, the work expanded to include business development (including BD strategy), client relationship management, and leadership skills development for similar firms.

Stephen has authored several books and papers that explore the topics of business development, how to start and build a successful coaching practice, and how professional services firms can create competitive advantage.

Contributors

John Baumber is Director of the International Centre for Educational Enhancement at the University of Bolton. In addition he retains his role as Director of Education for Kunskapsskolan(UK). He has over 40 years' experience of school leadership, including 27 years of headship and executive leadership in the UK/US and Sweden. John continues to support and coach school leaders across the world, from India to South Africa, Sweden to the US.

Fran Beaton is a Senior Lecturer in Higher Education and Academic Practice working within the Centre for the Study of Higher Education at the University of Kent, UK. She has led HE programmes and teacher education programmes for over 20 years. Beyond the university, she has served on the Executive Committee of the Staff and Educational Development Association (SEDA) and is currently on the SEDA conference committee and the steering group for the Standing Conference on Academic Practice.

Dr Joanne Bowen is an Associate Professor in Physiology working in the Adelaide Medical School of the University of Adelaide. She has been responsible for redevelopment of the Honours Degree of the Bachelor of Health and Medical Sciences, and researcher training through Higher Degree Coordination. She has held leadership positions in the Australian

Contributors xi

Society for Medical Research and the Multinational Association of Supportive Care in Cancer, and is passionate about the intersection between research and education.

Professor Sally Brown enjoys life as an independent consultant in Learning, Teaching, and Assessment and is Emerita Professor at Leeds Beckett University, where she was, until July 2010, Pro Vice-Chancellor (Academic). She is Visiting Professor at the Universities of Plymouth, South Wales, Edge Hill, and Liverpool John Moores, and formerly at the Robert Gordon University, Aberdeen and at James Cook University, the University of Central Queensland, and the University of the Sunshine Coast in Australia. She holds honorary doctorates from Plymouth, Kingston, Bournemouth, Edinburgh Napier, and Lincoln Universities. She is a Principal Fellow of the Higher Education Academy, a Staff and Educational Development Association (SEDA) Senior Fellow, and a UK National Teaching Fellow.

Dr Luke Buchanan-Hodgman is the Director of Undergraduate Admissions, lead outreach co-ordinator and lecturer within the School of Economics at the University of Kent. While in the role he has been actively engaged in developing the Higher Degree Apprenticeship Programme offer by Kent and participated in, *inter alia*, the Government Economic Service.

Professor Carlton Cooke is the Head of the School of Social and Health Sciences at Leeds Trinity University in the UK and also the university lead for research and knowledge exchange. Prior to this he worked for 25 years at Leeds Beckett University (LBU) and is about to return to work there. He is an experienced academic in sport-related HE, having held leadership positions related to teaching, programme development and delivery, research and postgraduate education, and knowledge exchange at the level of academic group, school, faculty, and university.

Dr Christina Curry is the Academic Director of Western Sydney University International College and a senior lecturer in Health and Physical Education within the School of Education. She is elected to represent her community on Bayside Council and has been a councillor for over seven years.

Dr Serge Eloi is the director of the Masters of Training and Optimization of Sports Performance programme at Paris-Est Créteil University in France. He has been involved in performance analysis for over 20 years, which includes being a national coach (Head of Statistics and Game Plans) for the French Volleyball Federation (FVF). He has 15 years' experience as an assistant and head coach within men's and women's professional volleyball leagues in France and continues to develop performance software for the coaching and analysis of volleyball.

Dr Lisa Fedoruk is an Educational Development Consultant at the Taylor Institute for Teaching and Learning at the University of Calgary (Canada.) She collaborates with colleagues, faculty, postdoctoral scholars, and students to guide and support post-secondary teaching and learning. As a faculty leader she is an academic leader and facilitator for programming and resource development related to the Taylor Institute's Certificates in University Learning and Teaching, and Teaching Assistant Orientation. She is a board member on the University of Calgary's Conjoint Faculties Research Ethics Board.

Jan Hawkes is an experienced commercial organization development consultant working within a large local authority in the UK. She is responsible for developing future-focused, collaborative leaders throughout the authority who can deliver mindset and behavioural change within ever-changing environments. Previous leadership experience includes responsibility as a non-executive director for a pharmaceutical company in the private sector and experience of working with schools.

Dr Matthew Hobbs is a Senior Lecturer in Public Health at the University of Canterbury (NZ). His research in the fields of physical activity and sport, geospatial and population health, and social and cultural inequity is consistently published in world-leading journals such as The Lancet, JAMA Paediatrics, Preventive Medicine and the International Journal of Obesity. In 2019 he was awarded the New Investigator Award in Public Health by the European Association for the Study of Obesity. He is the deputy editor for the Royal Society for Public Health's (MRSPH) flagship journal Perspectives in Public Health and also a member of their international advisory panel.

Professor David Hopkins is Chair of Educational Leadership at the University of Bolton and also Professor Emeritus at the Institute of Education, University College London and the University of Nottingham. Among a range of previous educational roles, he has been Chief Adviser to three Secretary of States on School Standards in the UK, Dean of Education at the University of Nottingham, consultant to the OECD, and an international mountain guide.

Professor Pauline Kneale (NTF, PFHEA, FRGS) is Emeritus Professor at the University of Plymouth, where she was Director of the Pedagogic Research Institute and Observatory and Pro Vice-Chancellor Teaching and Learning. She is Visiting Professor at Edge Hill and Anglia Ruskin Universities. Recent work includes an edited volume on teaching at master's level, projects on inclusive assessment and student engagement, and HEA-funded projects 'Evaluating teaching development in HE: towards impact assessment', and 'Learner Analytics'.

Professor Richard L. Light is a leading figure in the development of athlete-centred coaching with a focus on game sense and positive pedagogy for sport coaching. He has significant experience of leadership in sport in Australia and Japan and in full-time appointments at universities in Australia, the UK, and New Zealand. Richard has held full-time positions at the University of Melbourne, the University of Sydney, Leeds Metropolitan University, Federation University Australia, and the University of Canterbury, New Zealand. His leadership roles have primarily been in research but include being a head of school. He is currently Professor of Sport Coaching, Chair of the College Research Committee, and sits on the Academic Board at the University of Canterbury, New Zealand.

Dr Víctor López-Ros is a Senior Lecturer in Physical Education and Sports within the Faculty of Education and Psychology at the University of Girona. He is also the University's Chair of Sport and Physical Education. Prior to his academic career he was involved in elite handball teams and currently works with several elite athletes.

Gabriel MacGregor is a former Head of Corporate Law and Deputy Monitoring Officer for the London Borough of Croydon (UK). She also held the position of Acting Director of Democratic and Legal Services. Gabriel led the Council's Corporate Legal Team and provided support to councillors and senior officers, working closely with the Leader of the Council, Cabinet and CEO. She has also acted as Honorary Secretary of the Croydon Church Tenements Trust.

Dr Lukas Marek is a postdoctoral researcher with experience in research and teaching from New Zealand and the Czech Republic. He currently works within the GeoHealth Laboratory at the University of Canterbury (NZ). He also co-founded a geospatial web magazine and acted as the deputy chairman of a non-profit organisation focused on the popularisation of science.

Dr Rachel Masika is a senior research fellow in higher education learning and teaching for the Centre for Learning and Teaching (CLT) at the University of Brighton (UK). She co-leads the Higher Education

Pedagogies and Policy Research and Enterprise (HEPP) group, chairs the CLT's Research Ethics, convenes the university's annual pedagogic research conference, and is part of the CLT's management team. Outside of the university she has led consultancy projects for governments and international organisations and led teams and departments for charities and private sector organisations.

Professor Kathleen M. Quinlan is the Director of the Centre for the Study of Higher Education (CSHE) at the University of Kent (UK). She has held various leadership roles in and out of academia, including Head of Educational Development at the University of Oxford (2009–2016).

Dr Emily Rumschlag Booms is a teaching and research leader in the Department of Biology at Northeastern Illinois University (NEIU). Within higher education, she is experienced in implementing evidence-based active learning and student engagement techniques. Outside the classroom, she is a member of the University Assessment Team, promoting assessment of student learning to drive informed changes in programme curriculum and pedagogy. Beyond higher education, she serves as a reviewer for several academic journals and as vice president for a local primary school association.

Dr Mohammad Shah Razak is a Head of Department at Jurongville Secondary School in Singapore. He is an experienced PE teacher and Head of Department. He is the designated Professional Learning Community leader for a group of Singaporean secondary schools. He is a guest lecturer at the National Institute of Education (Nanyang Technological University).

Andy Siddall is Director of Cricket at Uppingham School and is a former Academy Director at Leicestershire County Cricket Club. His experiences also include leading university programmes and coaching overseas in South Africa. A Master Practitioner of NLP, Andy has worked as a leadership and personal performance coach since 2012.

Reverend Dr Timothy Smith is a parish priest in the Anglican Church of Australia, responsible for leading the process of growing authentic community within small congregations in the rural context and leading the development of volunteers for ministry within their local communities. Beyond parish ministry, he is the Pastoral Care Community Member of the Human Ethics Committee of Deakin University, Geelong. He is also Founder and Director of the charity Foundation South Sudan, providing university scholarships to South Sudanese still resident in East Africa for the purpose of establishing an educated leadership for the development of the newest nation.

Dave Thomas is an occupational therapist, public health specialist and doctoral researcher, working as a project manager on the institutionally funded Student Success Project at the University of Kent. He is a skilled and experienced diversity practitioner and advocate for social change; Dave's primary remit is in social justice. Outside of university, Dave engages extensively in providing relief to deserving persons through charity. For example, the Calabar Alumni and Friends Association, UK, where Dave is the President.

Karl Waddell is general manager of River's Gift, Australia's leading SIDS (Sudden Infant Death Syndrome) specific charitable organisation. As co-founder of the organisation, following the tragic loss of his first child (River) to SIDS in 2011, Karl's focus on leadership encompasses a strong desire to bring community together to drive fundraising activity and themes of awareness around the prevalence of sudden and unexpected infant loss. He regularly represents River's Gift and provides keynote deliveries at health industry seminars, corporate events, and community fundraisers, representing his family's story and the organisation's mission of Stamping Out SIDS.

Foreword

In the fast-changing world of tertiary-level education, where there is increasingly plurality even in what it means to be a higher education (HE) institution, leaders of those organisations are now faced with a myriad of different strategic questions, and an increasingly complex set of global stakeholders. What changes might we face to our government funding models, and how can we influence such central decision-making? How should we manage an increasingly consumer-like 'student–HE institution' relationship? Where should we strike the balance between our emphasis (and income base) derived from research, with the need to deliver value through employability outcomes and work-ready skill-sets? How can we improve access, and the diversity of our HE student body, especially if governments continue to under-resource secondary/high school education? And looking at an even more macro level, as the 'Asian Century' develops, with the long-predicted west to east shift in global centricity, how will a phase of global, geo-political competition – rather than collaboration – affect strategies for partnering internationally, student mobility, and attraction strategies?

In this maelstrom of change, the leadership role in any HE institution becomes more critical and demanding. It requires insight, breadth of vision, and skill-sets different from those needed in similar senior roles in HE institutions even 10–15 years ago.

For all these reasons, I feel that HE leaders will find it particularly timely and welcome to have a book giving practical, hands-on advice for all stages of their journey: in becoming an HE leader, being a leader, and then leaving an effective leadership legacy as they hand on the baton to their successor. Moreover, as someone who has spent the last 15 years trying to build practical, workplace-focused leadership development approaches in both HE and City businesses, I am particularly pleased to see this volume take an approach of offering *practical* guidance from peers and colleagues across the world. 'Learning by doing' stories – including examples from outside the HE sector – add immense value and can provide leaders with rich new learning from colleagues who may have experienced similar challenges, experimented with new approaches, and learned much in the process. This volume weaves a wonderfully rich tapestry of such stories stitched together from leaders with experiences from worlds as diverse as the HE, corporate, sporting, and military spheres and, geographically, from those who have held leadership roles in Europe, Australia, the US or war-torn Syria.

The structure of the book is also helpful, considering leadership from three different perspectives along the career path: the 'Pathway towards' ('Becoming'), the 'Pathway within' ('Being') and the 'Pathway beyond' ('Leaving'). All stages present challenges, and the authors discuss important issues from all these stages along the journey.

For example, there are the structural challenges of the career path 'towards', if one is to *become* an HE leader. Given the increasing shift from longer-term tenure to short-term contracts, how can we effectively build pathways in our own institutions *towards* leadership, to retain and grow the next generation? The book considers 'developing from within', critical to building the culture of an institution. But how is it possible to do this effectively if it is still hard to create a next career step beyond postdoctoral roles, enabling a viable talent pool ready to become your next deans and vice-chancellors? Again, comparison from outside the sector can be valuable, because the corporate world is also struggling with the pathways and retention of early/mid-career professionals, even if the drivers may be different. In those sectors, business models are rapidly reshaping with the advent of increasing technology and automation, and career roles and the traditional pathways are also evolving rapidly and fracturing. With the additional issue of the next generation seeking different things from work, the challenge of retaining diverse talent pools is great, and cross-sector learning is always instructive and helpful.

Looking beyond these structural challenges, the volume emphasises correctly that there are then the needs to identify potential leaders across your institution, and to give them early exposure to opportunities to learn leadership by *doing leadership*. But what type of leadership might that be? It might be leadership of the institution's global partnership strategy, or of building profile in a specific area of research (to take just two very different examples). And how does one prepare future leaders for such varied roles, especially when such positions are often new and no pre-existing 'template' exists?

The volume helps on this last question, I feel, in two important ways. First, it looks beyond the world of HE to see how organisations in other sectors are trying to develop leaders able to deal with similar (and increasing) levels of ambiguity in senior roles. Second, it allows leaders to learn from leaders, with the personal stories in the book giving specific, varied examples of how people learned to lead, what the different nature of their leadership role was – and also, looking back, what they might do differently if they had their time again. Such vignettes helpfully allow readers to draw out principles and approaches which have been tried and tested in different situations, and then to apply key learnings to their own leadership context.

As a final thought, along one's leadership journey there is often an important consideration of identity, again touched on in the volume. Senior leaders from many walks of life often report that, looking back, one of the aspects they found most hard as their careers progressed was to constantly reframe who they were at each step: recalibrating the skill-sets required to succeed in each new role, their networks and relationships, and – above all – establishing a discipline of truly 'letting go' of their previous identities through each transition. These deeply personal mindset shifts need regular attention, together with effective mentoring and coaching at the moments of change. Giving greater attention to this area of HE leadership practice will, I feel, help all generations: senior mentors will build a legacy of smoother leadership transitions by sharing with junior colleagues how they might effectively *become* or *be* a leader; and for the senior leaders themselves in their *leaving* phase, it will enable them to look forward beyond their current role, thinking about who they *could* be, and building a rewarding life beyond the institution they have led as they pass the baton on to a trusted successor.

Professor Nigel Spencer
School of Law, Queen Mary University of London
August 2020

Introduction
Stephen Newton and Kendall Jarrett

This book is about the practice of leadership in higher education (HE). As authors and co-editors, to paraphrase Baran's (2002) comments on agenda-setting, our intention is not to tell readers what to *think* about leadership, more so what to *think about* as a leader in higher education (HE). For us this distinction is important as it helps maintain a nuanced focus to discussion while at the same time allowing the exploration of the usefulness of knowledge about leadership from a range of contexts and sources. As such, the book explores and celebrates leadership experiences and knowledge from both 'inside' and 'outside' the sector. In doing so, the book directs readers at all stages of leadership in HE – *becoming a leader, being a leader,* or *leaving leadership* – to consider what they may be able to learn from a range of colleagues and contexts to inform their leadership practice.

Included in the book are perspectives on leadership in HE from academics across the globe, thus providing readers with a range of voices and contexts to help shape practice. As leaders ourselves with multi-sector leadership experience (e.g. within the military, corporate, tertiary, charity, and volunteer sectors), we have found that despite significant differences in context, the similarities of leadership are far greater than the differences; hence the learning opportunities are considerable. However, it is not only our own beliefs about the utility of leadership experience between sectors that has driven us and colleagues to write this book; it is also informed by wider comment about how to improve leadership in universities. As Alison Johns (2016) remarked when proposing five ways to improve leadership in universities:

> [A] third of governors believe leadership within the sector could be improved by increasing the number of leaders with diverse experience and expertise.

Thus, we decided to write this book because we felt that, while there is a considerable amount of academic literature available on the topic of leadership overall and some on leadership within HE, there is insufficient current literature on the practicalities of leadership in HE, internationally. We also felt that the pace of change in the field of HE is such that a practical handbook, into which readers could dip in at need, was timely.

Writing within the book acknowledges the relatively recent shift, for an increasing number of academics and other staff of higher education institutions, from long-term security of tenure in their role to short-term contracts. That of course affects the way in which leadership functions, which often means that hierarchies become inherently less stable. That in turn indicates an increased need for those in leadership roles to exercise influence rather than relying on organisational structure to achieve their aims. It also emphasises the need for willing collaboration between colleagues.

There is often a tendency by leaders to over-complicate both the results they seek and the process by which they choose to achieve those results. As such, the writing of this book was guided by our desire to keep the book simple without it becoming simplistic. Yet discussion within the book does not shy away from the complex or nuanced elements of leadership in HE, and we have sought to examine such issues accordingly. Indeed, while we acknowledge that leaders in HE must necessarily become comfortable with uncertainty (and hence flexibility of approach to delivery), we see no greater vice for a leader than the tolerance of ambiguity – whether in terms of their own self-leadership or in terms of the results they seek to deliver.

To negate the presence of such ambiguity and the typically resultant limitations of leadership practice, chapters within this book fall into three practice-oriented parts: Part 1: Realities of leadership in higher education in a changing world; Part 2: Leadership insights; and Part 3: Stories of leadership in higher education. Regardless of the nature of leadership role a reader may have (e.g. research leader, pedagogical leader, department leader, or any other formal or informal position of influence), our hope is that what is read encourages learning about leadership by *doing leadership*. As such we expect readers to dip into the book at need rather than to read it cover to cover. Chapters to *dip into* are as follows:

Part 1: Realities of leadership in higher education in a changing world

In Chapter 1, 'Defining leadership in HE', we discuss the complexities of leadership in HE in a changing world. Initially, a broad discussion of leadership is presented and informed by questions such as: What is leadership? What are the characteristics of effective leadership? What is the value of effective leadership in a changing world? HE-specific discussion of leadership is included with commentary responding to issues around the influence on leadership of changing workforce trends in academia and how academics can recognise and/or conceive of leadership opportunities in HE.

Chapter 2, 'Developing leaders from within', reports on current research in HE that focuses on how leaders are developed 'from within' the institution. Internally resourced leadership development frameworks and programmes currently used across the sector will be discussed, with the many myths and realities that influence leadership development and effectiveness in HE also considered.

The realities of learning to be a leader and the means through which individuals become a leader (e.g. being 'tapped on the shoulder', groomed for a position of responsibility, or actively 'stepping in' to avoid uncertainty) are discussed in Chapter 3, 'Learning to be a leader'. Key questions explored include: What is important when 'learning how to lead'? And, how can leadership roles be 'prepared for'?

Part 2: Leadership insights

The second part of the book contains two sub-sections. The first sub-section of chapters relates to perspectives *from within the sector.*

Chapter 4 utilises personal narrative to highlight a range of issues relating to the influence of experience and culture on leadership. Key issues discussed include the emergence of leadership inclination, leadership mobility between institutions and countries, learning to lead within academic contexts, and learning from the leadership of others.

Chapter 5 explores how educators in HE can lead learning and build on values and teaching expertise to effect change. This chapter investigates core components of a framework of leadership for student development. Three main spheres of development for emerging HE leaders to focus on are discussed: themselves, their knowledge of learning and teaching, and organisational conditions that facilitate movement toward improvement.

Leading complex educational systems is the focus of discussion in Chapter 6. The chapter includes discussion of some of the unique challenges and opportunities of multi-site and multi-institution system leadership, including hero leadership and the transition from the project champion to the sustainer, finding the balance between creativity and conformity, and responding to failure. Commentary from current leaders of complex educational organisations showcases a diverse understanding of the role of a system leader and the non-negotiable leadership practices that come with it.

What happens when you are stripped of your professional identity, your citizenship, your state? Chapter 7 was originally intended to uncover the leadership challenges of being an academic in exile. Leadership insights from academics directly affected by the Syrian conflict were to be the focus of this chapter, along with the processes required to 're-become a leader' in HE. However, the current realities of the Syrian conflict have meant a ghost chapter is presented in its place.

Chapter 8 will explore a range of topics associated with creating a leadership legacy in HE, including transitioning from the 'big role' to making the most of retirement careers. Guidance on developing the legacy you want to create and dealing with intentions vs. reality is framed within personal perspectives on academic leadership and what it is like to leave a senior role in higher education.

The second sub-section includes chapters relating to perspectives *from outside the sector.*

What lessons can we learn in HE from the failings of corporate leadership? Chapter 9 explores a range of concepts relating to failed corporate leadership and the situations to avoid in the ever-changing world of HE. Discussion includes consideration of how leaders in HE can balance the competing elements of conflict vs. resolution and the requirements for developing an agile leadership mindset.

Chapter 10 outlines lessons that can be learned from military leadership and how such learning might be used to inform leadership decision-making in academia. Requirements of military leadership such as after-action reporting and the devolution of responsibility are discussed, along with guidance on how to maintain effective leadership under stress.

Chapter 11 makes use of anecdotes from the sporting field to frame discussion around the synergies between leadership in sport and leadership in HE settings. The different contexts of leadership in sport are discussed (e.g. on-field, off-field) with commentary on the characteristics of effective sport leaders complemented by leadership stories from a range of sporting contexts around the world.

Leadership in the public and third sectors is the focus of discussion in Chapter 12. At a time when the influence of government on academia is gaining more media attention than ever before, this chapter explores the synergies between leadership in HE, leadership in public office, and leadership in the third sector. Through the sharing of micro-stories from charity and church leaders and public officials, the leadership practices of five leaders are surveyed with particular consideration given to key communication practices required when the majority of those being led remain 'unknown' to the leader.

Part 3: Stories of leadership in higher education

Case studies of academics' leadership practices provide us with authentic personal insights into discipline-specific leadership experiences from around the world. These stories of leadership in HE are presented to help inform colleagues' decision-making in relation to personal leadership aspirations, development, and legacy planning.

Chapter 13 includes colleagues' reflections on becoming a leader, with common threads of discussion intimating: a desire to understand followed by a commitment to be understood; an appreciation of the contexts within which leadership operates; acknowledgement of the benefits of other-sector leadership experience; the importance of building relationships, collaboration, and knowing thyself; and seizing the opportunity to take more responsibility.

Chapter 14 focuses on colleagues' experiences of being a leader. Attention across reflections is given to: effectively separating work from home; a desire to invest in more strategic leadership CPD earlier in career; the broadening of experience to inform leadership growth; asking oneself 'Do I have enough information?'; and giving colleagues space for blue-sky thinking.

Chapter 15 provides readers with insights into leaving leadership. Within colleagues' reflections a range of leadership experiences are shared inviting readers to consider the importance of: expectation that others contribute; not being surrounded by like-minded people; the balance of work/life/leadership commitments; the nexus between policy, practice, research; trusting others; the practice of humility; and being aware of external factors before they become acute.

Included within each chapter are prominent questions pertinent to the context of information being discussed which have been designed to engage the reader to *think about* their own leadership experiences to date and leadership development needs. We hope these questions, along with the manner in which chapters have been written, stimulate and challenge readers' to *think about* a range of contemporary, sector-diverse leadership contexts to ultimately inform their practice as leaders in HE.

References

Baran, S. J. 2002. *Introduction to mass communication: Media literacy and culture*, Second Edition. Boston: McGraw-Hill Books Company.

Johns, A. (27 Jan 2016) *article Five ways to improve leadership in universities*. Accessed at www.theguardian.com/higher-education-network/2016/jan/27/five-ways-to-improve-leadership-in-universities

PART 1
Realities of leadership in higher education in a changing world

CHAPTER 1

Defining leadership in HE

Stephen Newton

What is 'leadership?' Does leadership in higher education (HE) differ from leadership in other fields? What impact do local cultural norms have on the exercise of leadership? In other words, what are the impacts of context and culture on the practice of leadership? How does leadership adjust to changes in the structure and economics of HE that are of increasing scale and rapidity?

In this chapter, we seek to address some of these questions (culture and context are covered in Chapter 4) and to highlight the impact of change in a sector that had, for many years, remained relatively stable in terms of structures and business model.

The HE business model began to change significantly in the UK with the move from grant-funded tuition (where many students could attend university at no cost to themselves) to the current tuition fee and student loan regime. That, arguably, altered fundamentally the relationship between students and universities, with students beginning to see themselves as customers rather than supplicants, and universities and other higher education institutions (HEIs) having to operate as commercial businesses needing to recruit customers from a finite pool.

For the purposes of this book, we take the term 'higher education' to include not only universities but also colleges of further education – those institutions that focus on technical or vocational subjects. In the past, in the UK, these might have been referred to as 'polytechnics', although all of the former polytechnics now have university status. In the US, the equivalent would be community colleges; similarly, the TAFEs in Australia.

What do we mean by 'leadership'?

There is no single answer to this question and indeed there can be confusion between the theory and practice of leadership in different contexts, between the various approaches or styles of leading in any given context, and the characteristics that may define a 'good' leader. We explore such issues throughout the book, focusing on practical, actionable ideas rather than theory.

My own definition of leadership is:

> Getting things done through others, by creating a common purpose where all concerned believe that the goals can credibly be achieved and that they, individually, have the wherewithal to do so in the context of a shared culture, marked by mutual professional and personal respect.

That is somewhat complex, but in my experience, leadership is rarely simple. Key elements to consider are:

- 'Through others' – in other words good leaders generate willing followership.
- 'Common purpose' – effort of the whole group is focused on agreed outcomes and there is a greater likelihood of mutual support in achieving that purpose.
- 'Believe that goals can be achieved' and 'they have the wherewithal to do so'. These concepts are self-explanatory and critical to gaining buy-in to exert what has been called 'discretionary effort' over and above routine requirements.
- 'Shared culture' and 'mutual respect'. This pair of concepts is especially relevant in the military. It can also occur in corporates and professional firms. In the military, these attributes come together to enable individuals to trust others with their personal safety and 'look after my back'. They do not necessarily extend to liking each other, as such, although that may be the case. Both concepts remain relevant in HE (and indeed in the professions and corporates). However, the stakes are lower and therefore the intensity with which they are fostered may also be lower.

Leadership occurs in a variety of contexts. Conceptually, leadership is similar, whether in HE, the professions, or the military. The routine practice of leadership differs, however. In the HE world, it can encompass:

- thought leadership (developing new areas of specialised research)
- executive leadership (roles such as vice chancellor or head of department)
- leadership in teaching or supervision (at undergraduate or postgraduate level)
- team leadership (in research programmes for example)
- management roles.

In each of these categories, leadership can be seen in several dimensions; for example, see Figure 1.1 (Newton, 2012).

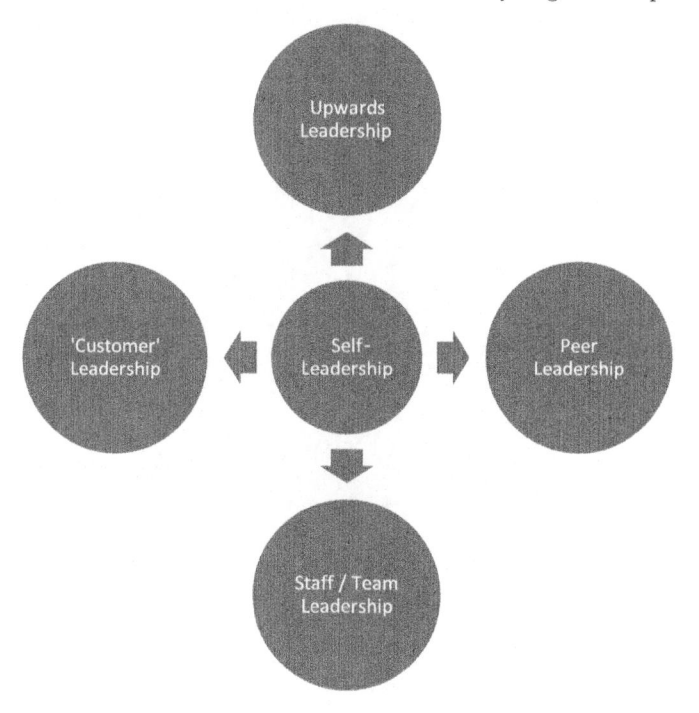

FIGURE 1.1 A model to visualise the dimensions of leadership

Variants of this model appear to work effectively on both sides of the Atlantic, in both corporate and professional firms and in the military. In most cases, the model appears to work particularly well in the context of more senior roles, where at least an element of politics is likely to be involved; hence the increased importance of upwards leadership (see below) and stakeholder mapping/management.

A variant of this model, developed for professional firms, was put forward in the book *Professional Services Leadership Handbook* by Clark, Kent, Beddow, and Furner (2017) (Figure 1.2). Aimed at managing or senior partners, this model seeks to visualise the need to balance business imperatives with those of the firm's people and clients. At the centre of this triangle, which exists in a state of dynamic tension, sits the values and behaviours of the firm's senior leader (shown as 'Self').

Self-leadership

In both models, self-leadership is the first consideration. This is about your own values and behaviours, your psychometric preferences and your personal 'style' or characteristics. It is also about your personal boundaries – things you

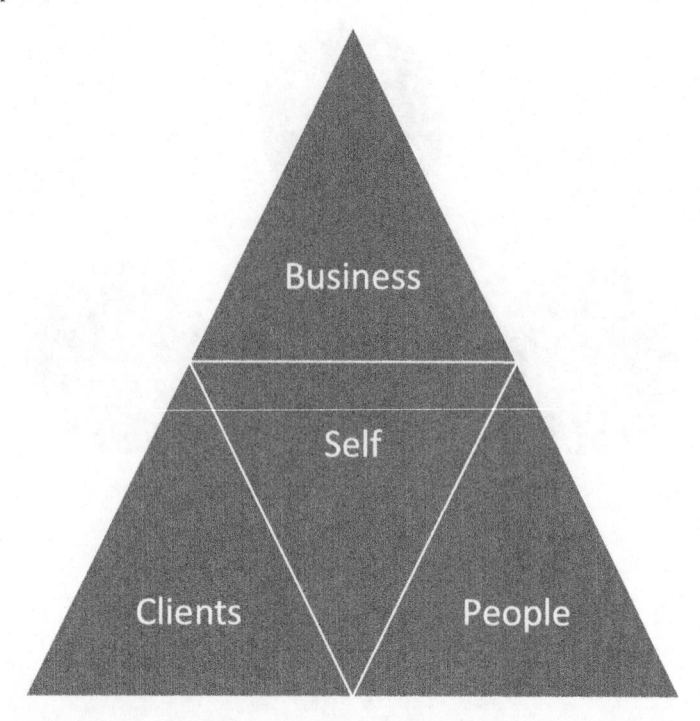

FIGURE 1.2 A leadership model for professional firms – a question of balance

will do, or will refuse to do, regardless of the difficulties you encounter as a result. In other words, self-leadership encompasses the concepts of integrity and authenticity. We explore these ideas in greater detail below.

> **Questions to consider**
> - What factors define your success as a leader?
> - How will your success be judged, (a) by you yourself, (b) by your team, and (c) by other stakeholders?
> - If these measures differ substantially, how best can you bridge the gaps?

One cannot change significantly 'who you are' simply because of taking on a leadership role. All you can be is yourself (as Oscar Wilde remarked, 'Everybody else is already taken'), and experience indicates that it would be a mistake to try to present a new face to the world. To do so tends to damage perceived credibility, without which leadership success becomes immeasurably harder.

Upwards leadership

Upwards leadership (Figure 1.1) comes second. This is about managing expectations of your boss and your boss's boss. In other words, you need to create relationships two levels up, across the range of stakeholders that impact your role. You need to manage those relationships openly and actively so that no surprises occur for anyone.

Key questions to ask in this context (and we mean ask explicitly, not implicitly) include:

- How will you judge my success?
- What factors will you measure in assessing my success and how will you measure them?
- On what basis is your own success measured?
- How can I best ensure your success? (Alternatively, 'What actions can I take to ensure your success?', which is more robust and results oriented.)
- What is my span of decision?

The first two questions are relatively common topics for discussion when one enters a new role. They are essentially context setting and they set up future conversations around goals and evaluation of performance. It is usually helpful to record the answers so that there is no room for doubt.

The second pair of questions can serve to place you in a different position in the eyes of your boss and boss's boss. Very few others will have asked them such questions. The effect is to emphasise your commitment to teamworking and collaboration, and your support for these individuals. Do not ask these questions lightly: you may be expected, by implication, to deliver against the answers you receive, unless you make it clear that you cannot or will not do so.

Question to consider

- What specific results must you deliver in order to be recognised as successful in your leadership/management role?

The last of these questions is critical to the way in which you are able to carry out your role. Many people interpret it as a reference only to budget authorisation. However, this is only one aspect of your span of decision. More important in determining your leadership success will be to understand your authority to give instructions versus your need to exercise influence. In most cases, influence is both greatly to be preferred as a leadership style and will

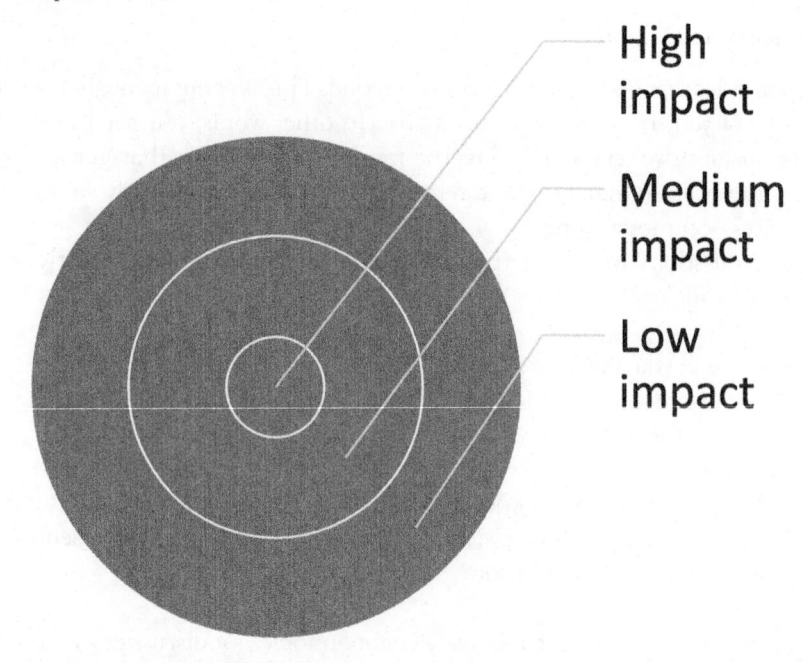

FIGURE 1.3 An approach to stakeholder mapping

usually be what is required in HE leadership situations. Occasionally, an instruction becomes necessary, especially on those occasions where you experience deliberate blocking behaviour by colleagues.

In all dimensions of this leadership model, but especially in upwards and peer leadership, it is helpful to map your stakeholders so that you can understand the various layers and complexities of relationships and competing interests more easily. We offer an approach to do this in Figure 1.3.

Customer and peer leadership

These two can be considered together in that both require the careful use of influence. That can best be achieved by first taking a genuine interest in the relevant individuals and gathering information about what drives them personally and (where practicable) at a psychological level.

This, of course, needs to be linked to their commercial/academic/career interests ('business interests' for this purpose). The key is conversation, usually one-to-one. You can direct the conversation by asking well-thought-through, pre-planned questions to elicit the information you need and at the same time establish rapport. This is the basic 'like and trust' that is essential to any successful personal, business, professional, or academic relationship. Once you have mapped their business interests and personal drivers, it becomes far easier to present your ideas in a manner that resonates with that person.

Useful questions in this context include:

- What results must you achieve in order to be recognised as successful in your current role?
- What do you feel are the most important factors that drive your success in your current role? How do you measure them?
- What issues or factors cause you friction in achieving the results that define your success?
- What do you most enjoy about your current role?
- What made you take on this role?
- What do you see yourself doing next?
- What do you feel will be your greatest contribution in your current role?

Peer leadership is relatively easy to define. In the HE context, it refers essentially to fellow academics and/or those in management or technical support roles. It could also include external suppliers (for example of technology) who provide critical infrastructure that is necessary for research purposes and other institutions with which HE institutions (HEIs) partner to deliver some learning outcomes – such as NHS hospitals in which medical students train.

The idea of 'customers' may be unfamiliar to many in HE. As most HEIs become increasingly commercial in their focus, students have come to see themselves as customers who seek a variety of results, which might include:

- a good degree leading to well-rewarded employment that justifies the cost of gaining their degree
- intellectual stimulation and enhanced interest in their subject, which may translate into lifelong engagement with it
- positive engagement with them by academic and other staff
- a positive academic and social experience during their time at the HEI.

'Customers' might also include members of a research group working under a senior academic. The term could also apply to departmental heads in relation to the executive of the HEI and to individuals or organisations sponsoring research.

Perhaps the most effective way for leaders in HE to think of customers, peers, and external suppliers and partners is as 'stakeholders'. We explore identifying and mapping stakeholders' interests below.

All of the above ideas apply equally in the professions, corporates, and the military. In a military context, the term 'customers' may cause confusion. Depending on context, it could include politicians who set the agenda of the military in terms of deployment and results to be delivered. It could also, in peace-keeping operations, include those the military seeks to protect. One might argue that the so-called 'teeth arms' (types of unit that engage the enemy directly) could be thought of as 'customers' by supporting units.

Staff leadership

This may be a misnomer but serves as a shorthand for those within the ambit of a given leader, who are more junior in the organisation and who report to that leader either directly or by way of a matrix structure (the so-called 'dotted line'). In reality, organisational structures may mean that dotted line reports may be peers in terms of hierarchy, although rarely senior.

The key points are (a) that staff too are stakeholders in the context of leadership and (b) only when the other four dimensions of leadership (i.e. self, upward, peer, customer – outlined above) are in place can a leader decide how best to lead staff.

There is no such thing as a one-size-fits-all approach to successful staff leadership. Each individual will need a somewhat different approach, depending on multiple factors, especially their overall capability and experience. This is sometimes known as 'situational leadership' (i.e. the leadership approach changes depending on the situation) and is one part of the overall context in which leadership occurs.

Once again, these concepts apply equally in HE, the professions, corporates, and the military. A key variable is organisational culture. In some professional firms and corporates, staff leadership is done by way of micro-management. In a military special forces environment, leadership is usually fungible. In other words, rank matters less in operational situations than capability.

Stakeholders

Every leader must recognise the need to take account of the varied agendas of their stakeholders. They must also be able to identify all of their stakeholders. The leadership model outlined in Figure 1.1 highlights a number of stakeholder groups. Others could include:

- the HEI executive (e.g. vice chancellor, finance director)
- local, regional or national government
- supranational bodies (e.g. the EU) that may provide funding or other resources
- employers and employer groups (who may seek to influence curriculum development, for example, in order to produce graduates with specific skillsets).

> **Questions to consider**
> - Who are the key individual stakeholders in relation to your leadership role?
> - What factors drive them?
> - How well aligned are your interests and theirs?
> - If not well aligned, what is the best way to bridge the gaps?

Each will have their own specific agenda and sometimes these agendas will conflict to some degree. One of the most important jobs of leaders at any level is to understand who their stakeholders are and to map their interests in order to be able to navigate successfully what may become complex policy and delivery issues. Stakeholders and their aims may well change over time, so this needs to be subject to continual review.

In the professional services world, it is sometimes said, 'There is no such thing as a "a firm" – only people.' Exactly the same is true in understanding your stakeholders in the HE leadership context. Every stakeholder group will be represented by one or more individuals. Your leadership success depends on understanding what drives each individual so that you can decide how best to balance their collective interests as they impact your leadership role.

Mapping your stakeholders

As the number of individual stakeholders increases, the complexity of managing their conflicting interests grows exponentially. It can be helpful to create a stakeholder map so that you can see those conflicting interests and what drives each individual in a visual format. This makes it easier to prioritise interests and make decisions about your own courses of action.

The factors that drive individuals will not normally become clear until you have conversations with them. Using the type of questions outlined above under the sub-heading *Customer and peer leadership*, you can gain a combination of explicit information (what they say in response to your questions) and implicit data (how they say it). The latter includes word choice, tone of voice, body language, and eye contact – or lack of it. Essentially, you are looking for language and other clues that help you to test your assumptions about the individual, which you should consider before arranging a conversation. This information helps you to compile your stakeholder list, as outlined below. We suggest creating one record (which could be a simple card or entries on a spreadsheet) for each person. Confidentiality of this information is obviously essential.

Stakeholder list

- organisation/department
- name of individual
- their job title and role (not necessarily the same thing)
- their impact on your role
- their likely success measures
- their likely personal drivers
- how good is your relationship with them? *(represent by traffic light: red (poor), yellow (okay), green (good); use white where there is no current relationship)*
  (a) personally?
  (b) professionally?

Compile the data for each person that impacts your role. Take four sticky note pads, one for each traffic light colour (red, yellow, green) plus white. Write each name on a sticky note. Use the colour of sticky note that represents the traffic-light colour of your relationship with each person.

On a flipchart, draw three concentric circles. The innermost circle represents highest impact on your role, the middle circle medium impact, and the outer circle low impact.

Place each sticky note in the relevant circle. If you have red or yellow sticky notes in the 'high impact' circle, or reds in the middle, 'medium impact' circle, you need to develop a plan to improve the relationship with that person. If you cannot achieve that (rarely the case), you will need to consider how to neutralise that person's impact on your role. Yellow sticky notes in the outer circle can be ignored, but reds will need to be addressed as a second priority once any high- and medium-impact issues have been handled.

Each sticky note represents a relationship you will need to manage and develop. Once you have placed all of your sticky notes, count how many are in the 'high impact' circle. Any more than half a dozen will make it increasingly complex to balance the interests of these key stakeholders. If you have more than that number in 'high impact', consider carefully whether each merits its place there. It is too easy to assume that every stakeholder will have a high impact on your role. Careful prioritisation will make your life far easier. This should not be a one-off exercise. Circumstances and roles will change over time. It is worth repeating this exercise every three to six months (or once during each academic term/semester).

Characteristics of effective leaders

Much of the literature on leadership styles is somewhat superficial. Some of it looks at leadership through the lens of stereotypes, such as the square-jawed

'Follow me!' approach portrayed in comic books of the 1960s. Leadership character is, we suggest, more subtle and varied, whether in the context of HE or in corporates, professional firms, or the military. There is now, for example, a growing recognition of the value of different leadership styles, popularised by books such as *Quiet Influence* by Dr Jennifer Kahnweiler.

We also suggest that local or regional cultural norms impact leadership characteristics as they are displayed day to day (the basis of discussion in Chapter 4). Such norms also vary by industry sector and even by service (Army, Navy or Air Force) and branch (e.g. infantry or artillery) within the military. It seems to us that leadership characteristics and leadership style or approach are not in fact one and the same, although they may often be conflated. For example, the characteristics of recognised leaders in investment banking, engineering, and law firms will likely differ as will their approach to leadership. While recognised leadership characteristics across the armed services will likely be similar, the culture of, for example, a special forces unit will differ from that of a line infantry unit, leading to a difference of leadership style and approach.

Recognised characteristics of effective leadership will also vary regionally (at least in terms of emphasis), as will the typical approach to leadership or leadership style. In this context, by leadership style, we mean, for example, hierarchical versus inclusive/participative.

A detailed discussion of these issues is beyond the scope of this book. However, Dr Mary Crossan (Professor of Strategic Management at Ivey Business School, Western University in London, Ontario) has written at length on the topic with colleagues (2012, 2013a, 2013b, 2013c, 2018).

In summary, Dr Crossan proposes that in assessing leaders, one must consider three issues:

- Does the person have the competency to be a leader (i.e. knowledge, understanding, facts, relationships)?
- Does the person have the commitment to be a leader (work ethic, engagement with others, mission orientation, etc.)?
- Do they have the character to be a good leader?

She defines leadership character starting with traits (habitual thought patterns), including:

- conscientiousness
- openness to experience
- extroversion
- agreeableness
- neuroticism.

These have come to be known as the Five Factor Model (FFM) of personality.

She then explores leaders' values (which she describes as beliefs about what is important or worthwhile to individuals) and virtues (behavioural habits exhibited fairly consistently). She lists ten virtues:

- humility
- integrity
- collaboration
- justice
- courage
- temperance
- accountability
- humanity
- transcendence
- judgement

... and proposes that character is the foundation of effective decision-making for leaders.

> **Questions to consider**
> - How do you see your own leadership character?
> - To what extent is your view aligned with the views of colleagues and other stakeholders?
> - How will you know?
> - If the gap is significant, why might that be?

What other leadership characteristics might be relevant in this context? Much of the available literature speaks to flexibility, authenticity, credibility, and effective communication skills. We suggest that the last three are in fact linked and would add a further characteristic: honesty.

Flexibility does not indicate a lack of firmness or clarity of purpose, but a willingness to recognise and adapt to changing circumstances. It is often said that no plan survives contact with reality (although the process of planning is vital). A flexible mindset enables a degree of comfort with uncertainty while not encouraging ambiguity. It is a characteristic that enables pragmatism and acceptance of ever-changing reality. We look at flexibility further in Chapter 3.

Acceptance of reality both in terms of events that are occurring and, more importantly, of one's own limitations and capabilities is a necessary first step to overcoming problems or addressing issues. It is also the starting point of your own personal development as a leader and indeed as a human being.

Failure to understand and accept reality (including root causes of issues) will normally result in failure to achieve goals or to realise potential.

Honesty, like charity, begins at home. To be brutally honest with oneself as a leader in terms of one's own capabilities and limitations will often be an uncomfortable experience. The same applies to the degree of honesty one must exhibit in evaluating performance and capability in others and having the subsequent conversations, whether difficult or not. However, such honesty is ultimately a necessary first step in one's development as a leader and to seeking the feedback of others to inform that development.

Leadership approaches/style

An understanding of leadership characteristics (in the abstract and also as they relate to your own leadership traits) is helpful in comprehending your interactions both with colleagues and with other stakeholders. To that extent it is akin to psychometric instruments, such as Myers Briggs (MBTI)®, which, among other things, offer safe, neutral language in which to discuss differences and possible causes of friction between individuals. A different perspective on leadership is the approach or style of the individual. I use these terms, 'approach' and 'style', interchangeably here, although they are arguably different.

By the term 'approach' we have in mind, for example, the servant leader versus the autocrat, which could be seen as opposite ends of a spectrum. Several contributors to this book indicate that their own approach to leadership is that of the servant leader. However, the ways in which this is described differ somewhat.

In the subsequent chapter regarding leadership in the military, we note that servant leadership is a common approach in the military – certainly in the western world. There may be a perceived dichotomy between the servant leaders who, on the one hand, look after the wellbeing of those under them, but on the other are willing to commit them to operations against an armed enemy, and hence put them in harm's way.

In my experience, the two are not at all incompatible. Military personnel in today's volunteer armed services have committed to military service in the knowledge that this may well involve active duty. They expect leaders to deploy them with due care, but injury or even death cannot be ruled out as facts of military life. One aspect of taking responsibility for the wellbeing of subordinates is ensuring that they are trained, equipped, and capable of active service and mutual protection. We explore this in more detail in Chapter 10.

At the other end of the spectrum from the servant leader is the autocrat. People in leadership roles who adopt this approach (whether by choice or by temperament) exist in most walks of life – certainly in the professions and among corporates and of course politicians. One tends not to come across many pure autocrats in the military; they simply do not last very long in modern military environments. That is not to say that there is lack of assertiveness, especially when on active service, where immediate obedience to orders can be essential both to achieve an objective and to minimise risk.

Other approaches/styles of leadership include what I term 'process driven' and 'discussion driven'. The former, predictably, relies on adherence to established processes and protocols to deliver results and minimise the possibility of errors. The latter seeks to avoid action but instead to focus on 'bringing everyone along' through the use of meetings to discuss options rather than delivering concrete results based on an already agreed plan.

Both have their place. The former can be helpful in implementing organisational change. It helps to minimise the number of variables in play and hence to speed implementation while minimising risk factors. The latter can be helpful in clarifying courses of action and comes into its own during the planning phase of any complex project. Depending on organisational culture, neither will necessarily serve the organisation over the long term and probably not in strategic leadership roles.

> **Questions to consider**
>
> - What do you see as your own key weaknesses as a leader?
> - Who among your team can best cover those weaknesses for you? How?

The key for senior leaders is to recognise the leadership temperament (i.e. preferred style/approach) of their subordinates and peers in the context of the culture and capability of the organisation, and to then establish a framework that allows each individual to play so far as possible their strengths.

Leadership and management

Leadership and management are not synonymous. Management is generally about process and control. Leadership is about purpose, influence, and ultimately enabling ordinary people to achieve extraordinary things. It is not simply to do with realising potential, but enabling individuals to realise that they have unrecognised potential and to achieve even more.

Can a good manager be a good leader? Very often, but not always, the answer is 'yes', although it is usually the case that some development will be needed: the effective manager must learn to be a leader and be allowed to practise that skill in a live environment. That does not mean being thrown in at the deep end, but entails being given opportunities to learn by experience, beginning at a small scale.

Can a leader be effective without being an effective manager? There is an element of chicken and egg about this question. In our experience, it is very hard for a leader to be fully effective without sound management capability. That does not imply that a leader needs to 'do everything'. It does mean that effective delegation is a necessary skillset and one that includes understanding the nuts and bolts of what is being delegated. That helps to ensure that what is delegated is within the capabilities of the person to whom it is delegated.

Leadership in a changing world

The scale and pace of change have arguably never been greater. That is true not only in the HE sector, but in geopolitics, the professions, and among corporates. HEIs are faced with externally imposed constraints on funding, changing demographics, increased demands from employers concerned about (lack of) employability among recent graduates, competition among HEIs for a finite pool of both student and academic talent, and increasing concern among undergraduates over the real value to them of costly degree programmes.

HE leaders need to balance the needs to:

- continue to deliver meaningful student learning and ongoing progress
- enable the application of knowledge by way of meaningful research, often externally funded
- ensure long-term financial viability of their programme/institution
- remain relevant in a dynamic and sometimes hostile industry environment.

In the professions, increasingly savvy clients are either taking more work in-house where they can and seeking more from their professional advisers for less (or at least no more) money. This 'more for less' approach is also evident among corporates. In each case, one of the approaches to square the circle has been to adapt the business model to favour the use of part-time or freelance staff with a view to keeping direct costs to a minimum. The so-called 'gig economy' now extends to academics and professionals as well as to experts in the corporate world.

Even the military has suffered from reduced funding in many countries, leading once again to the need to deliver as much if not more with a reduced budget. The military (at least in the UK) must also factor in two additional issues:

- a diminishing pool of willing recruits who also have the basic physical fitness needed for front-line service

- the huge fixed costs of many of its assets – aircraft, warships, armoured vehicles, and even the basic infantryman's rifle. Many of these assets have a lifespan measured in decades rather than years and maintenance costs can be greater over that lifetime than the original purchase cost.

Unlike the professions, many corporates, or HE, the military has not as yet made great use of the 'gig economy' approach to staffing, for a number of fairly obvious reasons. In many NATO countries (and elsewhere), however, the balance between full-time serving personnel and reservists has shifted towards the latter.

In HE, the academic workforce is increasingly freelance. The same is the case in many support roles. This represents a new and different challenge for HE leaders. Likely trends include:

- The erosion of hierarchies in favour of flat structures in which influencing skills become increasingly important.
- The development of a cadre of permanent staff in leadership roles who lead groups of freelancers, be they involved in research, teaching, or management roles. Those leaders may not always be, themselves, involved in teaching, research, etc., which in turn may give rise to the kind of 'them and us' situation one can observe in professional firms between fee-earners and non-fee-earners. Indeed, some institutions are introducing job titles that differentiate between teaching and leadership.
- It is also possible that HEI leadership and management cadres may become more professionalised, to the extent that they are the only full-time employees of the HEI; all academic and research staff being freelancers.
- A heating-up of the so-called 'war for talent', both in the form of talented students, especially those able to move into postgraduate research and teaching roles, and academics. This is already becoming a significant issue for the study and teaching of technology.
- Increasing internationalisation of the workforce and (to a degree) of students. (The impact on student numbers and calibre of issues such as migration controls and Brexit remains unclear.)

All of the above reinforces the need for HE leaders to become comfortable with uncertainty in their environment and to develop a strong sense of 'who they are' (i.e. self-leadership ability). That will include, over time, coming to understand their own leadership temperament, be it to favour autocracy or to adopt a 'servant leader' approach and the resulting impacts.

References

Clark, N., Kent, B., Beddow, A. and Furner, A. (2017). *Professional Services Leadership Handbook*. London: Kogan Page.

Crossan, M., Gandz, J. and Seijts, G. (2012). Developing leadership character. Ivey Business Journal. January/February. [online] Available at: https://iveybusinessjournal.com/publication/developing-leadership-character/ [Accessed 29 March 2020].

Crossan, M., Mazutis, D. and Seijts, G. (2013a). In search of virtue: The role of virtues, values and character strengths in ethical decision making. *Journal of Business Ethics*, 113, pp. 567–581.

Crossan, M., Mazutis Imd, D., Seijts, G. and Gandz, J. (2013b). Developing leadership character in business programs. *Academy of Management Learning and Education*, 12(2), pp. 285–305. http://dx.doi.org/10.5465/amle.2011.0024A

Crossan, M., Seijts, G. and Gandz, J. (2013c). *Developing leadership character*. New York: Routledge.

Kahnweiler, J. B. (2013). *Quiet Influence*. San Francisco: Berret-Koehler Publications.

Newton, S. (2012). The invasion game. *Business development and Practice Growth for Lawyers*, p. 172 (DLO Associates (no longer in print)).

Seijts, G. (2018). *Leadership in Practice: Theory and Cases in Leadership Character*. New York: Routledge.

CHAPTER 2

Developing leaders from within
Kendall Jarrett

> We believe that leadership development must begin early and from within the institution.
>
> Coll and Weiss (2016)

The development of educational leaders and managers *from within* can be a highly effectual way to enhance leadership and managerial capacity within any learning institution. Whether it's during times of institutional/sector austerity or in response to a growth in research funding or student numbers, an investment *in people* resourced *by those people* should be seen as a compelling *and* wholly attainable leadership development offering. The types of programmes I am alluding to here include formal and informal mentoring arrangements, peer-coaching programmes, bespoke workshops (such as *leading effective conversations*), and formal course completion (e.g. Postgraduate Certificate in Educational Leadership).

To clarify, my use of the term *from within* here does not include on-site delivery of programmes by a third party – not that there isn't significant benefit to be had from engagement in such programmes if their commissioning is seen to specifically address and/or complement existing staff leadership development requirements. My desire to discuss the development of educational leaders *from within* is based on research and peer comment suggesting that successful professional development practices are often interactive, collaborative, located in practice, typically informal, of significant duration, and self-regulated – elements we believe support an internally resourced development initiative (Coll and Weiss, 2016; Nash, Sproule and Horton, 2017; Sherwin, Campbell, and Macintyre, 2017: Griffiths, Armour, and Cushion, 2018). It is important to note, though, that the success of any internally resourced offering will be heavily influenced by the degree of existing capability within the institution as well as a commitment-to-programme made by the highest authority on campus (Coll and Weiss, 2016). Finding the right balance and justification for what can be delivered *from within* against what should be

Developing leaders from within 21

What results must we achieve in order to be recognised as successful as an organisation?
(NB these results will likely fall into a number of different fields / streams of work)

↓

How will we measure our achievement of those results?
(Alternatively, 'How will we define and measure our success?')

↓

What is our timeframe? How will we prioritise and phase the necessary work?

↓

With all of the above in mind, what resources, practical delivery skills and capabilities do we need in order to deliver those results in a timely manner?

↓

What leadership capabilities/behaviours have we determined we require?

↙   ↘

What requires investment now?   What can wait?

↓   ↓

                    What are the opportunity costs of waiting?

Do we have current capacity to deliver *from within*?

↓

Should we deliver *from within*? E.g. what are the opportunity costs of internally resourced provision as opposed to externally resourced provision? What messages do either provision give our leaders?

↓

Is current capacity sustainable? What investments are required to develop long-term internally resourced capability and capacity?

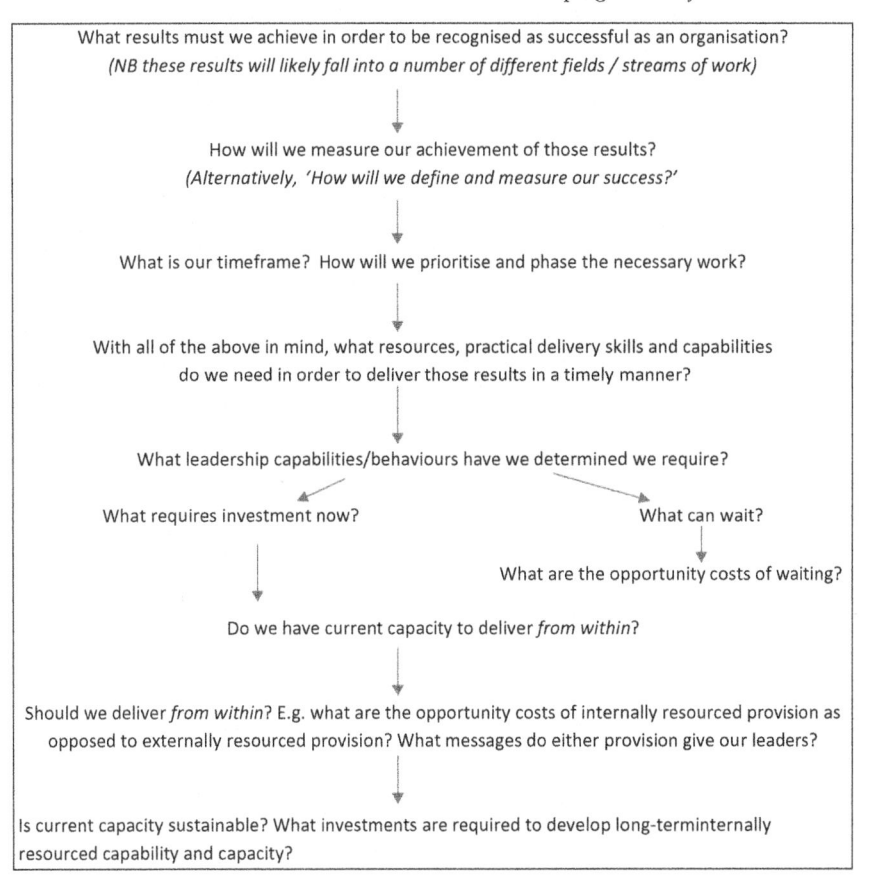

FIGURE 2.1 Questions to ask to help determine your organisation's capacity to develop leaders *from within*

externally resourced is critical to offering success. It is important then to ask yourself the questions in Figure 2.1.

Before we engage in further discussion about the structure and benefit of educational leadership development *from within*, it is important to consider the many myths and realities that exist in HE that spawn a reluctance for some academics to pursue any kind of leadership development opportunity, be it offered *from within* or by an external agency.

Myths of leadership within HE

Myth 1 – Leaders must be experts

The post-millennium global education market requires HEIs to consider radical changes in their structures, operations, and missions to stay relevant and sustainable. This means that positions of responsibility within HEIs are being scrutinised and rationalised more than at any other time in history. In their 2015 *Harvard Business Review* article 'Leading people when they know more than you do', Wallace and Creelman discuss career advancement and the likelihood that for leaders this means responsibility for areas outside their expertise. The reality here for leaders in HE is that there is a growing likelihood that those being led will know more about their work than those who lead them. The often siloed, discipline-specific work orientations found in HE help perpetuate this likelihood.

In line with the myth that leaders must be experts is the often-held conception that good leaders have all the answers. They don't. What good leaders do have in the absence of 'all the answers' is knowledge of where to look and who to engage with to find them. A leader's willingness to admit their limitations can then lead to more successful hiring and team formation practices, where the weaknesses of one are complemented by the strengths of another. A shared, distributed view of expertise can then help leaders in HE avoid single point of failure situations.

Myth 2 – Good leadership requires an absence of vulnerability

The view that a leader must be perfect at all times can be a damaging sentiment, for both the leader and those being led. According to Crouch (2016), true leadership requires both authority and vulnerability, in that a function of leadership relates to responsibility for exposing the institution, colleagues, and self to risk and in turn the possibility of loss. For a leader in HE, accepting the presence of vulnerability and viewing it as a key function of leadership can ingratiate oneself with colleagues through recognition of peers' capacities for decision-making influence. This 'shortening of the distance' between leaders and those being led can often translate into a more dynamic and successful leadership function.

It should also be recognised that leaders in HE are many things to many people, thus remain vulnerable to the ever-changing nature of opinions, relationships, and decision-making climates. The acceptance of leaders as being vulnerable in their capacities as decision-makers can then help to avoid the occurrence of blind faith followership and the range of issues such a dynamic can have on institutional culture and performance.

Myth 3 – Leadership requires authority

What authority did Swedish teenager Greta Thunberg have to lead the world's biggest international youth movement against climate change? What authority did Thurgood Marshall have to alter the tide of education access abuses in US higher education institutions? To our knowledge, neither sought permission to lead social change movements now celebrated for their local, national, and global significance. It was instead their ability to *influence* that helped them to change the thoughts, values, and behaviours of others. Accessing this informal, dynamic, and multidirectional source of power is typically dependent upon an individual's personal characteristics and attributes (Bacharach and Lawler, 1980; Bush, 2011), such as those discussed in Chapter 1.

It is important to recognise, though, that within HE establishments both *influence* and *authority* exist as sources of power. And while a vice-chancellor might 'typically have substantial *authority* by virtue of their formal leadership position' (Bush, 2011, p. 97), it is the power of *influence*[1] that shapes the success of leaders at all levels of the institution.

Myth 4 – Effective leaders need to be extroverted

Some of the world's most influential leaders have been introverts. If introversion was a barrier to good leadership, the likes of Rosa Parks, Bill Gates, and Nelson Mandela would not be the household names they are today. And although much of the research into leadership emergence and effectiveness identifies a positive correlation between extroversion and group effectiveness (Bono and Judge, 2004; Ensari et al., 2011), studies have also conversely highlighted the role that extroverted leadership can play in threatening the effectiveness of group performance (Judge et al., 2009; Grant, Gino, and Hofmann, 2011; Badura et al., 2019).

As Gibbs, Knapper, and Picinnin (2009) suggest, there is no one way to lead an educational department effectively. Thus, in HE institutions, the presence of introverted leaders, who by definition are likely to be 'more open to hearing opinions and perspectives that are contrary to their own' (Clack, 2017, p. 2), has merit as collegial models of decision-making (e.g. where power and decision-making is shared amongst faculty) remain common practice (Bush, 2003).

Myth 5 – Leaders accomplish through control

Good leadership is not about having control. Rather, control is the bedfellow of good management. An effective leader in HE, charged with developing learning communities and encouraging social change, requires 'a much more adaptive and open sense of leadership which is contrary to the hierarchical command-and-control mind-set' (Black, 2015, p. 57). In a 2009 report commissioned by the Leadership Foundation for Higher Education exploring departmental leadership of teaching in research-intensive environments, Gibbs et al. stated that good leadership 'entails personal involvement, understanding others, and getting them to work together towards a shared goal' (p. 55). What Black (2015) and Gibbs, Knapper, and Picinnin (2009) allude to here is the importance of considered delegation, the setting of parameters to shape behaviours, and the ability of leaders to remain in partnership with those they lead.

If indeed leaders do covet a wider span of control, the ramifications of such 'flatter' organisational structures can be significant. A study by Thiel, Hardy, Peterson, Welsh, and Bonner (2018) reported that the assigning of a wider span of control to leaders attenuated their influence by limiting the number of unique interaction opportunities with those they led. This in turn meant observations of a leader modelling exemplary conduct were diminished, thus weakening leader–member exchange relationships. Thus, effective leadership is less about control and 'exercising a concise set of capabilities, but rather employing different combinations of leadership practices depending on and appropriate to a particular situation' (Parrish, 2010, p. 2).

Myth 6 – Leaders are born, not made

Far removed from any singular notion that a leader is born, James George Fraser's *The Golden Bough* includes one graphic interpretation of how a leader is made. The story told relates to Diana of the Wood (or Diana of Nemi), a goddess of Italian mythology, and the violent rite of succession each sacred king who sought a place in her sanctuary on the banks of Lake of Nemi was required to partake.

> In the sacred grove their grew a certain tree round which at any time of the day, and probably far into the night, a grim figure might be seen to prowl. In his hand he carried a drawn sword, and he kept peering warily about him as if at every instant he expected to be set upon by an enemy. He was a priest and a murderer; and the man for whom he looked was sooner or later to murder him and hold the priesthood in his stead. Such was the rule of the sanctuary. A candidate for the priesthood could only succeed to office by slaying the priest, and having slain him, he retained office till he was himself slain by a stronger or a craftier. The post which he held by this precarious tenure carried with it the title of king; but surely no crowned head ever lay uneasier, or was visited by more evil dreams, than his.
>
> (Frazer, 1890/2009, p. 11)

Within this scene of 'a strange and reoccurring tragedy' (Frazer, 1890/2009, p. 9), parallels can no doubt be made by many who carry similar burdens and have trod a similar path to leadership in HE (minus the violence, we hope).

But more than this, we have included this story to reinvest in the commonly held view that leaders are made, not born. To become the sacred king in Diana's grove a set of circumstances were required; in this instance it was that only a fugitive, a man disaffected from society, who could take office. And although we recognize the role that genetics can play in the emergence of characteristics associated with leadership potential, it is the presence of these circumstances, whether happenchance or planned, that verifies the path to leadership as one which is made. This then leads to the acceptance that the skills of leadership can be learned and enhanced.

Myth 7 – Everyone wants to be a leader

Being recognised as a leader is a reluctant undertaking for some. Take the UK rapper Stormzy as an example. Upon being selected for the 2019 cover of *Time Magazine* in recognition of being included on the publication's list of 'next generation leaders', he tweeted:

> On a deeper, honest one the thought of being a 'role model' or 'leader' or whatever it is feels way way way too heavy and too overwhelming and a lot of the time I think nahhhh fuck all that I ain't no one's anything.

Realities of leadership in HE

It is all well and good to debunk the myths surrounding leadership in HE, but this in no way means leadership in HE becomes more accessible for all. The reality is that the majority of academics have their leadership aspirations quashed time and time again by systemic failings within the HE sector to tackle individual and institutional prejudices. Professor Gus John, an education campaigner, equality activist, and academic, has stated that the principal function of education is to humanise society. Yet colleagues' attempts to be developed and recognised as leaders in HE continue to be blocked by a range of incredibly divisive realities.

Reality 1 – Stereotypical assumptions about black leader incompetence still exist

Why are negative evaluations of black leaders so persistent? Carton and Rosette (2011) explored this issue by reflecting on long-standing theories related to how leaders are evaluated. Their review of archival data found that the presence of goal-based stereotyping, which is the application of stereotypes driven by a perceiver's comprehension goals, self-enhancement goals, and their motivation to avoid prejudice (Kunda and Spencer, 2003), 'may systematically bias leader evaluations against black leaders' (Carton and

Rosette, 2011, p. 1153). And according to Kunda and Spencer (2003), this activation and application of a group stereotype does not take much:

> Ordinary everyday experiences such as being criticized by a stereotyped person, having a readily available excuse for stereotype-based reactions, or being fatigued can suffice to undermine normal inhibitions on stereotype use, leading people to apply activated stereotypes that they would otherwise curtail.
> (Kunda and Spencer, 2003, p. 540)

In education, perceptions of black leader incompetence have had a significant impact on the lives and careers of many. Within his 2019 inaugural lecture for the British Educational Leadership, Management and Administration Society (BELMAS), Professor Gus John, former Director of Education for the London Borough of Hackney, shared his experience of being stereotyped as an incompetent leader. In his words:

> They [Hackney headteachers] were so adamant that this black man could not run the education service in the borough because no black person had done so anywhere in the UK that they saw the borough's payroll disaster as proof of their scepticism ... Even before I got my feet under the director's desk they were hell-bent on making Gus John, just gone ... The Hackney headteachers were acting in a wholly racist manner in the wilful attribution of the failings of the finance department to me simply because those failings provided evidence of the stereotypical expectations of incapacity and failure on my part for no other reason than that I was black and in their eyes most likely deficient.
> John (2019)

Professor Gus John's account of perceived leadership incompetence dates back to the late 1980s, early 1990s. It is beyond the scope of this chapter to explore in any great depth the step-changes in leadership perceptions (or lack of) made by societies since then, but feel it is important to add a more contemporary note to this issue. Specifically that in a 2015 study commissioned by the University and College Union (2016), the largest trade union and professional association for academics in the UK, a survey of its 7,003 black members concluded that 'racism is present in our colleges and universities' and that there continues to be 'a persistent glass ceiling for black employees across post-16 education' (2016, p. 12).

Reality 2 – 'Academia is so ableist'

To paraphrase Thomas Hehir (2007), an ableist perspective asserts that it is preferable for an educational leader to read policy and strategy documentation in print rather than braille; to walk to leadership meetings rather than access them via a wheelchair; to read a report rather than have to listen to it on tape. But as Dr Jen Leigh points out:

> Ableism in educational leadership goes beyond how able bodied and neurological the leader is (or appears). Ableism incorporates the structural issues that might stop someone from becoming a leader e.g. the prejudices and preconceptions about disability and illness, recruitment procedures, promotion and progression processes where you have to demonstrate working at the next level in order to achieve.
>
> (Personal communication)

Current research revealing falling disability declaration rates in academia (as compared with disability declaration rates found within undergraduate student populations) paints a troubling picture insofar as it suggests that 'the academy is an environment that is intolerant and non-accepting of non-stereotypical ways of working' (Brown, Thompson, and Leigh, 2018, p. 83). For academics aspiring to educational leadership positions, ableist assumptions (along with stereotyping, invisibility of role models, limited senior buy-in to strategic change, and disorganised infrastructure) represent yet another barrier to leadership access and effectiveness (Martin, 2017). Brown and Leigh (2018) have suggested a societal shift in thinking is needed and that 'rather than focusing on disabilities and illnesses, it is time to consider how ingrained the normalisations are in society' (p. 988). Alas, currently it does seem that 'academia is so ableist' (Brown, Thompson, and Leigh, 2018, p, 83).

Reality 3 – 'We don't see women as leaders'

Terms such as 'glass ceiling', 'labyrinth', 'glass cliff', and 'sticky floor' are just some of the metaphors used to describe the barriers, successes, and failures of women in leadership (Carli and Eagly, 2016). Yet their use over the years has done little to advance the dismantling of what they allude to (Smith, Caputi, and Crittenden, 2012), as demonstrated by some of the online and print media headlines created in recent years (see Table 2.1).

Research into female leadership in HE has found that women are not being identified and prepared for leadership (Morley and Crossouard, 2015) and as such are 'often located on career pathways that do not lead to senior positions' (Morley, 2014, p. 124). Further research by Shepherd (2017) has detailed that the structural inequalities limiting female access to leadership are being covered up by 'the premium that academic culture places on individual agency'. This in turn has given rise to the view that women's underrepresentation at senior leadership level is because of 'the women themselves, or rather that

28 Kendall Jarrett

Table 2.1 Select online and print media headlines relating to women and leadership

1 Jul 2019	Top firms taking 'one and done' approach by appointing token woman to board, review chief says	The Telegraph
27 Sep 2018	How do you explain the decline of women in leadership roles in higher education in Massachusetts?	Women's Power Gap
22 Dec 2017	We don't see women as leaders – and it's holding them back in our universities	The Guardian
8 Mar 2017	Why universities can't see women as leaders	The Guardian
3 Mar 2016	Where are the women in corporate leadership?	World Economic Forum
10 Feb 2015	South Asian women 'missing out on university leadership roles'	Times Higher Education

of their missing agency' (p. 84). While some HEIs have embraced more gender-balanced leadership appointment practices (e.g. University of Liverpool's Vice-Chancellor Professor Janet Beer advocating for a minimum 40 per cent leadership quota for each gender), regrettably, the pace of change in the education leadership space is still at a crawl.

Reality 4 – Promotion challenges

Post global financial crisis in 2008, a number of HEIs around the world enacted staff compulsory redundancy intentions (e.g. Glyndwr University, Western Sydney University) and promotion and/or hiring freezes (e.g. Hampton University, East Carolina University). For British universities the ramifications of Brexit have also meant significant budget overhauls and staff restructures, limiting the availability of promotion opportunities and the chance to apply for more formal leadership responsibility. The length of some academic staff probation periods (e.g. up to five years) also presents as a structural barrier for those seeking more formal leadership positions. Self-selection promotion processes, commonplace in HEIs, are also often viewed as a barrier to formal leadership opportunity, as one anonymous academic has said:

> Forcing staff to self-select is inherently biased towards those with the capacity to excel in what is essentially a self-branding exercise. Not every academic can shamelessly self-promote, or is comfortable doing so.
> (Anonymous academic, 2017)

Reality 5 – Limited awareness of leadership opportunities

Leadership in HE now operates in a multi-dimensional matrix context due to the complexities arising from an increasing number and variety of stakeholders influencing decision-making. As a by-product of this, the range and number of leadership opportunities in HE has also increased. Yet it is often the case that avenues to leadership are only seen by academics to lead to formal positions within an organisational structure. At a time of significant change in HE practices and identities, new leadership avenues relating to research, pedagogy, multi-discipline knowledge, advocacy, sustainability, and consultancy can be paved. The reality here is that an understanding of where/when these leadership opportunities exist requires an agile, adaptable, and resilient mindset which is typically suppressed by any number of realities already discussed.

A 'developing from within' framework

With no magic recipe for leadership development success, a holistic view of how academics can/should be developed as educational leaders in HEIs is required. Developing leaders *from within* provides a framework for HEIs that prioritises utilisation of existing resources as well as providing access *for all* to leadership development opportunities. At the same time, such a framework responds to previously stated requirements of successful CPD – namely, that it be interactive, collaborative, located in practice, self-regulated, and informal. This is not to say that the outsourcing of educational development programmes and/or fast-tracking of select staff based on exclusive criteria does not have its place in HE as a route to leadership capacity development. However, when the identity of such programmes reflects an inflexible and sales-driven offering, their long-term value to an individual and institution is often wasted.

Ineffectual leadership development frameworks can be the result of single or complex challenges at all levels of analyses (e.g. macro, meso and micro). Such challenges include outdated professional body leadership award policies (macro level), changes in institutional access to resources (meso level), and 'back in my day we didn't have…' sentiments held by nostalgic academics (micro level). A developing *from within* framework holds at its core the requirement that educational leadership programmes are resourced *by colleagues, for colleagues* within the same institution. This is represented by its core elements of informality, collegiality, and familiarity. Far from just a parsimonious response to the leadership needs of an institution, these core elements can function as drivers for the development of agile, adaptable, and resilient leadership mindsets capable of responding to the various challenges that leadership development programmes face. Table 2.2 provides an overview of the core elements of a 'developing *from within*' framework for educational leadership and is followed by a conceptualisation of the framework (Figure 2.2).

Table 2.2 Elements of a 'developing *from within*' framework for educational leadership

Element	Explanation
Informality	• As Spencer and Newton (2018) allude to, there is no substitute for 'high touch' with regards to leading organisational change and development initiatives. An informal peer-to-peer development arrangement promotes the idea of accessible, unstructured interaction enabling conditioned, context-specific responses to leadership challenges and opportunities within day-to-day workplace practices.
	Leads to…
Collegiality	• The sharing of insight and experience has reciprocal development benefit for all involved. The effective pairing or grouping of colleagues can also strengthen the culture of an institution and be a valuable support mechanism in times of need.
	Leads to…
Familiarity	• By maintaining consistent access to development personnel (e.g. a workshop facilitator and/or a mentor), workplace understanding and expectation is reinforced. Language and terminology common to the institution are also shared daily, limiting instances of ambiguity.
	Equates to…
Leadership development effectiveness*	• Improved utilisation of existing resource offers a practical and sustainable response to the leadership development needs of an institution. With the potential for CPD budgets to be slashed during times of tertiary sector austerity, the need for within-budget leadership development offerings is paramount. * Caveats to leadership development effectiveness relate to the impact of personal leadership aspirations and institutional leadership needs. As with any institutional programme of development, a clear understanding of how the success of the programme will be measured is required.

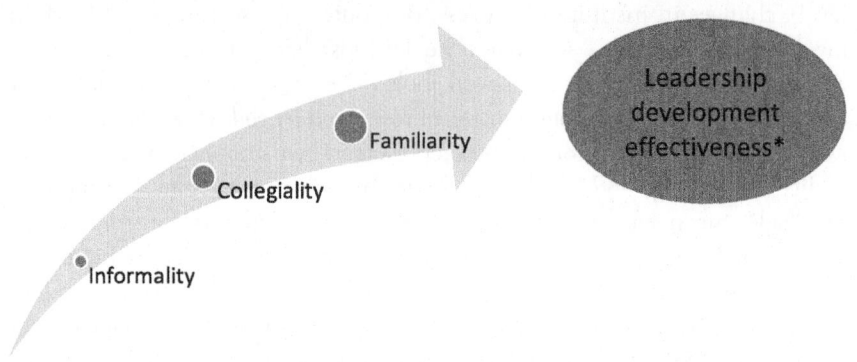

FIGURE 2.2 The 'developing *from within*' framework for educational leadership

Educational leadership development initiatives

This section provides seven examples of educational leadership development initiatives typical of a 'developing *from within*' offering.

1. Informal mentoring arrangements
   - Although seen as light touch by some, the resourcing implications of an in-house leadership mentoring programme can mean involvement of more staff, a greater focus on institution-specific leadership development requirements, and a visible commitment to staff development (e.g. a development opportunity for both mentee and mentor).
   - Alison Johns, Chief Executive of the Leadership Foundation for Higher Education in the UK, has stated that mentoring schemes can be particularly effective in improving leadership capacity in HE, with a 2016 study revealing almost nine out of ten academics who had a mentor feeling they benefitted from the relationship.
2. Peer-coaching programmes
   - The tangible and less tangible impacts that coaching can have in HE are outlined in a Leadership Foundation for HE stimulus paper by Harding, Sofianos, and Box (2018). From day-to-day leadership and teaching performance to individual wellbeing, the benefits of an effective peer-coaching offering were reported on. The financial incentives for utilising internally sourced peer coaches were discussed along with comment made that 'overwhelmingly those who receive coaching feel valued' (p. 48).
3. Bespoke workshops
   - Bespoke, targeted learning activities aimed at developing leadership skills can help individuals and institutions develop the required skills and mindsets to effect sustainable change in an institution's day-to-day practices (Spencer and Newton, 2018). Through the use of a 'design for everyone' attitude like the one used by the Centre for Co-Design & Learning in the UK, institutions can extend the benefits of bespoke learning design through involvement of attendees.
4. Formal course completion[2]
   - A range of postgraduate courses in educational leadership and education business leadership now exist in the tertiary sector. Such courses offer a nexus between theory and practice and offer opportunities to broaden education leader networks.
   - Completion of professional HE leadership courses. For example, *Aurora* (Advance HE's leadership development initiative for women), Harvard University's *Crisis Leadership in HE* short course, and the Global University Network for Innovation's *International HE and Research Leadership* course.

> **Questions to consider**
> - Currently, what educational leadership development initiatives are available to you within your HEI?
> - Which of these initiatives could you initiate involvement with yourself?

5. Field trips
    - Attracting new leaders to HE with other-sector leadership experience can provide institutions with new insights and networks when tasked with responding to sector challenges (Johns, 2016). By seeking out and engaging with other-sector leaders through leadership field trips and collaborative endeavours, similar upsides can result.
6. Peer observations
    - Use of observation to enhance leadership skills is common practice in industry, yet its place in formal leadership development programmes is often overlooked. According to Armentrout and Wiedeman (2017, p. 31), 'observing a leader during their everyday activities reveals a variety of situations, stressors and behaviors' that can assist the observer 'identify even subtle behaviors' to assist their own leadership development.
    - Frameworks such as the Leadership Observation and Feedback Tool (Oza et al., 2018) or the Observation and Feedback Model alluded to by Armentrout and Wiedeman (2017) can provide staff in HE a guide to enhance their leadership practices.
7. When do new academics first have an opportunity to take leadership responsibility?
    - Within Spencer and Newton's (2018) *Creating Competitive Advantage* series of papers exploring strategic learning and development practices in organizations, they pose the questions: 'When do new staff first have an opportunity to take leadership responsibility?', followed by 'How could you make that earlier?' The point they make is a simple one in that the *doing of leadership* by new staff as early as possible helps to accelerate the *speed to experience*, which has institution-wide benefit.

Accessing leadership development *from within*: an institutional case study

This institutional case study incorporates three separate but interwoven research projects conducted over an 18-month period. The focus of each project was to advance understanding of an institution's leadership development landscape to determine where leadership development improvements could be made.

Research Project 1: Leadership development within institutional PGCHE and HEA[3] Senior Fellowship provision

The aim of this UK-based research project was to determine the level of definition and support provided to institutional colleagues with regards to their understanding of leadership (and development as leaders) within two formal teaching and learning focused development initiatives. The first relates to completion of a PGCHE (or equivalent award).[4] The second relates to recognition as a Senior Fellow of the Higher Education Academy (SFHEA), which is a professional body award attained by academics who demonstrate that their practice meets a descriptor level of the UKPSF[5] for teaching and supporting learning in HE. For most HEIs in the UK, completion of a PGCHE (or equivalent) and attainment of a level of HEA Fellowship[6] is now considered a professional requirement.

From questionnaires completed by lead educational developers[7] from four separate UK universities (including the institution this institutional case study focuses upon), there was limited awareness of how leadership was defined by their institution. Comments ranged from 'there is no official definition from my University, but the concept is discussed in terms of being more strategic instead of operational' (Part. 1) to 'it is not something we discuss, but I'm sure there are courses run by other functions in the University around the notions of leadership' (Part. 3). Individual views on leadership were also wide-ranging and related to the act of leadership, e.g. 'it's about your sphere of influence' (Part. 2), or the process to becoming a leader, e.g. 'it is developed almost by default by lecturers as we have no formal development process' (Part. 4).

When asked to nominate the models/theories/literature (M/T/L) used to develop colleagues' understanding of leadership and to help develop their leadership capabilities, a predictably diverse range of answers were received. From Hallinger and Heck's (1998) ideas about leadership being the process of influencing that can be exercised by those not necessarily in positions of formal authority, to the use of John Adair's Action-Centred Leadership model and David Rock's SCARF model of leadership, the M/T/L used are historical and contemporary, critical and nuanced. Of note, though, was that mention of these M/T/L was solely related to PGCHE provision and not SFHEA application support. But why? When considering that the vast majority of SFHEA applicants already have a PGCHE (or equivalent), why is there such an obvious disconnect in terms of SFHEA applicants' reluctance to access leadership M/T/L they have previously been exposed to? The following participants' comments help to answer this:

> Academics developing a SFHEA claim rarely start with a sense of themselves as leaders and are not initially able to articulate clear visions or strategies – both critical elements of effective leadership. It was only through coaching that they can organise their experience of leadership in coherent ways.
>
> (Part. 4)

> For the PGCHE, the staff are not at a stage when they are leaders (they are brand new to HE and not in leadership positions).
>
> (Part. 2)

> The challenge is that leadership is less 'valued' in terms of learning and teaching so as a formal aspect it is not something that is usually of significant interest to many.
>
> (Part. 1)

From the comments above it can be argued that the disconnect seen relates to three core perceptions:[8]

1. Academics often don't view themselves as leaders.
2. Educational developers don't always view academics as leaders.
3. Some academics place minimal value on leadership as a function of learning and teaching.

> **Questions to consider**
> - To what degree do these core perceptions manifest within your institution?
> - What could you do to challenge these perceptions?

With such core perceptions no doubt arresting the development of numerous academics as leaders in HE, consideration is needed as to how leadership development in HE is serviced by existing initiatives and what leadership development frameworks are in place to contribute to a more defined, aligned and fit-for-purpose institutional offering.

Research Project 2: Evaluating the effectiveness of professional development of educational leaders through participation in the Route to Recognition for Experienced Staff (HEA RRES)

In 2017, the University of Kent gained accreditation from the HEA to assess claims for Fellowship and Senior Fellowship of the HEA. At that time a new HEA Route to Recognition for Experienced Staff (HEA RRES) initiative was developed to coach and mentor academics ahead of claim submission. A key component of an SFHEA claim is recognition of teaching and learning leadership with a requirement to demonstrate 'successful coordination, support, supervision, management and/or mentoring of others (whether individuals and/or teams) in relation to learning and teaching'. As such, the aim of this research project, led by Julia Hope and Silvia Colaiacomo, was to investigate the impact of participating in the HEA RRES with a particular focus on applicants' development as educational leaders.

From the transcribed interviews of those who participated in the research project,[9] the following composite dialogue has been developed (e.g. a selection of questions asked and responses given) to showcase different experiences and views on leadership and leadership development in relation to the HEA RRES programme:

Q: What did you learn about you as an educational leader going through the SFHEA claim process?
A1: To be honest with you it was stuff I think I already knew. I didn't learn anything radically revelatory about myself.
A2: When I first began, I thought 'I'm not quite sure that I can show any leadership'.
A3: I learnt there's a lot of leadership in my role whereas before I didn't think I had any because of my job title. I understand now my impact on learning and teaching more.

Q: When writing your claim, what indications were you given as to how leadership was defined?
A1: I don't remember leadership being defined. I suppose the key is to come up with your own examples of it, to not be bland and generic.
A2: It was clear that [leadership] was the defining feature of the whole claim. I totally understood that you had to show leadership in teaching in your field, but I don't remember any [coaching] session where we looked specifically at that.
A3: What was really interesting were the ways [my coaches] were talking about leadership. As a result, my claim encompassed way more than I thought it would in the first place.

Q: Did anything change in terms of your leadership as a result of the claim writing process?
A1: Not particularly, I would say it just enabled me to reflect on what I do well, and to carry on doing that probably, but I wouldn't say it changed the way I do anything.
A2: Thinking of things as leadership rather than just 'doing my job' and 'helping people out'. It's made me think a bit more that I *can* do it.
A3: I just have an EAP (English for Academic Purposes) Tutor job title and my boss didn't recognize any leadership element within my role. [Since attaining my SFHEA] my boss has been giving me extra responsibility when previously he wouldn't have done. He now knows what I'm capable of.

36 Kendall Jarrett

> Q: In terms of your leadership development, what was meaningful about the claim writing process?
>
> A1: It made me think about what leadership is. It did make me rethink the way that I approach day-to-day life as an academic.
>
> A2: It's added a sense of confidence or legitimacy [to my work] because I'm not currently in a [formal] leadership role as such. I'm not someone's line manager or anything like that. But the leadership that I do is of people on the same level or even senior to me … it's helped me to think that what I do actually counts as leadership for a start and that 'I can do it and should do it'.
>
> A3: I think it came at the right time. I'd been in my post for seven years and I knew I'd achieved a lot, but I didn't really have any recognition for it. Also at that point, I was doing my job but there were elements of leadership creeping in which weren't necessarily part of my job description, so it's really helped me to identify how much I was taking on and doing within that role.
>
> A4: I think the SFHEA has been good because it's helped me highlight the leadership aspects of my role, so now I can go for that additional salary award which gives me progression where I didn't have it before.

The composite conversation above gives rise to the need for further consideration of how institutional development programmes can be used to reveal and recognise the leadership impact that academics (at all levels) can have on peers and learning alike. Of significance within the conversation was the relevant lack of definition given to what leadership is/means in an institution and how that lack of definition, or even lack of definition discussion, means some academics are undervaluing their outputs as leaders of teaching and learning.

Research Project 3: Use of design thinking (DT) to inform the development of a postgraduate applied educational leadership module

Building on our[10] understanding of the challenges colleagues faced in first being recognised as leaders in academia, and second finding means *from within* the institution to further develop their leadership capabilities, the development of an applied educational leadership module was commissioned mid-2019. When tasked with designing a series of leadership development experiences with internal validity and external utility, it was agreed that a design thinking (DT) approach would be utilised to guide module development.

Developed by professionals in the design industry, DT is an approach to innovation and problem-solving that embraces radical thinking and innovative solution-finding in a user-/learner-centric manner with a bias towards action (Brenner, Uebernickel, and Abrell, 2016). The five key principles of DT used to frame a non-linear design journey are typically known as empathise, define, ideate, prototype, and test, although variations in principles exist. Further conceptualisations of these principles often include reference to 'inspiration, ideation, implementation' stages or a 'problem space' and a 'solution space' (Charosky et al., 2018; Dam and Siang, 2019).

Phase one of the curriculum design process (the problem space) was completed in spring 2019. As part of this phase, a focus group of five academics and one senior administrator from the team that would deliver the module were recruited to contribute to a 'blue sky thinking' session. This session, which included discussion of focus questions and activity completion, was replicated with one current student and one external from industry with a professional background in leadership and negotiation training. A second focus group meeting was completed in summer 2019 and aimed at developing an ideation 'response cloud'. This session was all about turning design thinking into design doing. With a statement of success agreed (e.g. our learners need a way to become better, more attuned leaders so that they lead with confidence, understanding, and purpose), the group completed a big idea activity (see Raja, 2018) and then considered how we can turn good ideas into great ideas.

At the time of writing this chapter, phase two of the curriculum design process (the solution space) was still under way. Within this phase, a series of focus groups and informal design exchanges were being used to prototype and test aspects of the designed curriculum. Looking ahead, the inclusion of 'future students' as co-curriculum designers will be pivotal during this phase as questions emerge, problems (re)framed, and ideas discussed 'until the best answers are evident and chosen' (Mickahail, 2015, p. 69). The aim of this prototyping and testing will be to develop and finalise a range of intended learning experiences suitable for all learners on the module.

Whether or not use of a DT approach will result in a 'better' development experience will not be known until the leadership practices of graduates are analysed. What is known, however, is that phase one of the design process yielded an array of visions and ideas about the nature of educational leadership and what it means to different people at different stages of their career. Of significance, though, was the belief that access to mentors and exposure to leadership in other sectors/industries should have a strong presence in module learning experiences. The latter point is a pivotal focus in Chapters 9, 10, 11, and 12 in this book.

Notes

1 It is important to recognise that influence occurs at all levels of an organisation and beyond the structures of hierarchy, not merely at senior levels. This is also discussed further in Chapter 5.
2 For further discussion of formal leadership training, see Chapter 3.
3 Higher Education Academy (now known as Advance HE) is a UK organisation supporting strategic change and continuous improvement of individuals and institutions of higher education.
4 A Postgraduate Certificate of Higher Education (PGCHE), also known as a Postgraduate Certificate in Academic Practice (PGCAP), is a teaching qualification for university lecturers.
5 The UK Professional Standards Framework (UKPSF) is a nationally recognised framework that details a set of professional values and guidelines used to benchmark and enhance practices in HE teaching and learning support (www.heacademy.ac.uk).
6 HEA fellowship is offered in four categories: Associate Fellowship (AFHEA), Fellowship (FHEA), Senior Fellowship (SFHEA), and Principal Fellowship (PFHEA). At both the Senior Fellowship and Principal Fellowship levels, an emphasis is placed on awardees demonstrating qualities of peer and programme leadership.
7 In the UK, educational developers are typically part of an internally facing academic or professional service function whose remit is to develop the pedagogical practice of institutional colleagues. Support for the attainment of HEA Fellowships is usually provided by an educational development function.
8 These three core perceptions relate to many of the myths and realities of educational leadership identified earlier in this chapter.
9 All participants in the study had experience of completing the HEA RRES.
10 An institution's teaching and learning development team responsible for the development of colleagues' pedagogical practice.

References

Anonymous academic. (2017). Want to get a promoted in a university? Learn the art of self-branding. Available at: www.theguardian.com/higher-education-network/2017/nov/24/want-to-get-a-promoted-in-a-university-learn-the-art-of-self-branding [Accessed 7 June 2020].

Armentrout, J. and Wiedeman, T. (2017). Using an observation and feedback model for leadership development. *Training Industry Magazine – Experiential Learning*, 10(4), pp. 30–32.

Badura, K. L., Grijalva, E., Galvin, B. M., Owens, B. P. and Joseph, D. L. (2019). Motivation to lead: A meta-analysis and distal-proximal model of motivation and leadership. *Journal of Applied Psychology*. Advance online publication. Available at: http://dx.doi.org/10.1037/apl0000439

Bacharach, S. and Lawler, E. (1980). *Power and politics in organisations*. San-Francisco: Jossey-Bass.

Black, S. (2015). Qualities of effective leadership in higher education. *Open Journal of Leadership*, 4, pp. 54–66.

Bono, J. E., & Judge, T. A. (2004). Personality and Transformational and Transactional Leadership: A Meta-Analysis. *Journal of Applied Psychology*, 89, 901–910. http://dx.doi.org/10.1037/0021-9010.89.5.901

Brenner, W., Uebernickel, F. and Abrell, T. (2016). Design thinking as mindset, process, and toolbox. In *Design thinking for innovation: Research and practice*, W. Brenner and F. Uebernickel, eds. Springer: Cham, pp. 3–21.

Brown, N., Thompson, P. and Leigh, J. (2018). Making Academia More Accessible. *Journal of Perspectives in Applied Academic Practice* [Online] **6**. 82–90. Available at: https://doi.org/10.14297/jpaap.v6i2.348

Brown, N. and Leigh, J. (2018). Ableism in Academia: Where are the disabled and ill academics?. *Disability and Society* [Online] **33**, 985–989. Available at: https://doi.org/10.1080/09687599.2018.1455627.

Bush, T. (2003). *Theories of educational leadership and management*. 3rd edn. Sage: London.

Bush, T. (2011). *Theories of educational leadership and management*. 4th edn. Sage: London.

Carli, L. and Eagly, A. (2016). Women face a labyrinth: An examination of metaphors for women leaders. *Gender in Management*, 31(8), pp. 514–527.

Carton, A. M. & Rosette, A. S. (2011) Explaining bias against black leaders: Integrating theory on information processing and goal-based stereotyping. *Academy of Management Journal*, 54, (6), 1141–1158. https://doi.org/10.5465/amj.2009.0745

Charosky, G., Leveratto, L., Hassi, L., Papageorgiou, K., Ramos Castro, J. and Bragós Bardia, R. (2018). Challenge based education: An approach to innovation through multidisciplinary teams of students using design thinking. In *Proceedings of the Technologies Applied to Electronics Teaching Congress* Universidad de La Laguna, Tenerife, Spain: 20-22 June 2018. Institute of Electrical and Electronics Engineers (IEEE), pp. 1–8.

Clack L. A. 2017. Examination of Leadership and Personality Traits on the Effectiveness of Professional Communication in Healthcare. *Journal Healthc Communication*, 2(2). 1–4. DOI: 10.4172/2472-1654.100051

Coll, J. and Weiss, E. (7th January 2016). Rethinking leadership development in higher education. AAvailable at: https://evolllution.com/managing-institution/operations_efficiency/rethinking-leadership-development-in-higher-education/ [Accessed 7 June 2020].

Crouch, A. (2016). *Weak and strong: Embracing a life of love, risk, and true flourishing*. Intervarsity Press: Brentwood.

Dam, R. and Siang, T. (2019). 5 stages in design thinking process. [online]. *Interaction Design Foundation*. Available at: www.interaction-design.org/literature/article/5-stages-in-the-design-thinking-process [Accessed 01 March 2019].

Ensari, N., Riggio, R. E., Christian, J. and Carslaw, G. (2011). Who emerges as a leader? Meta-analyses of individual differences as predictors of leadership emergence. *Personality and Individual Differences*, 51, pp. 532–536.

Frazer, J. G. (1890/2009) *The Golden Bough: A Study in Magic and Religion: A New Abridgement from the Second and Third Editions*. Oxford: Oxford University Press.

Gibbs, G., Knapper, C. and Picinnin, S. (2009). *Departmental leadership of teaching in research-intensive environments*. Research and Development Series. Leadership Foundation for Higher Education: London.

Grant, A., Gino, F. and Hofmann, D. (2011). Reversing the extroverted leadership advantage: The role of employee proactivity. *Academy of Management Journal*, 54(3), pp. 528–550.

Griffiths, M., Armour, K. & Cushion, C. (2018) 'Trying to get our message across': successes and challenges in an evidence-based professional development programme for sport coaches. *Sport, Education and Society*, 23(3), 283–295, DOI: 10.1080/13573322.2016.1182014

Harding, C., Sofianos, L., and Box, M. (February 2018). Exploring the impact of coaching in higher education. Stimulus Paper.

Hehir, T. (2007). Confronting Ableism. *Educational Leadership*, 64(5), pp. 8–14.

Hallinger, P., & Heck, R. H. (1998). Exploring the Principal's Contribution to School Effectiveness: 1980-1995. *School Effectiveness and School Improvement*, 9(2), 157–191. http://dx.doi.org/10.1080/0924345980090203

John, G. (2019). Inaugural annual lecture for BELMAS, Institute of Education, University College London, October 7th 2019. Available at: www.belmas.org.uk/Latest-News/watch-the-inaugural-annual-lecture-online

Johns, A. (2016). *Five ways to improve leadership in universities*. Available at: www.theguardian.com/higher-education-network/2016/jan/27/five-ways-to-improve-leadership-in-universities [Accessed 7 June 2020].

Judge, T. A., Piccolo, R. F. & Kosalka, T. (2009). The bright and dark sides of leader traits: A review and theoretical extension of the leader trait paradigm. *Leadership Quarterly*, 20(6), 855–875. http://dx.doi.org/10.1016/j.leaqua.2009.09.004

Kunda, Z. and Spencer, S. (2003). When do stereotypes come to mind and when do they color judgment? A goal-based theoretical framework for stereotype activation and application. *Psychological Bulletin*, 129(4), pp. 522–544.

Martin, N. (2017). *Encouraging disabled leaders in higher education: Recognising hidden talents*. Leadership Foundation for Higher Education: London.

McKenna, M. (27th September, 2018). How do you explain the decline of women in leadership roles in higher education in Massachusetts? Available at: https://womenspowergap.org/higher-education/margaret-mckenna-one-and-done/

Mickahail, B. (2015). Corporate implementation of design thinking for innovation and economic growth. *Journal of Strategic Innovation and Sustainability*, 10(2), pp. 67–79.

Morley, L. (2014). Lost leaders: Women in the global academy. *Journal Higher Education Research and Development*, 33(1), pp. 114–128.

Morley, L. and Crossouard, B. (2015). *Women in higher education leadership in South Asia: Rejection, refusal, reluctance, revisioning.* British Council: London.

Nash, C., Sproule, J. & Horton, P. (2017) Continuing professional development for sports coaches: a road less travelled, *Sport in Society*, 20:12, 1902–1916, DOI: 10.1080/17430437.2017.1232414

No author. (2015). South Asian women 'missing out on university leadership roles'. *Times Higher Education.* 10 February. Available at: www.timeshighereducation.com/news/south-asian-women-missing-out-on-university-leadership-roles/2018426.article [Accessed 7 June 2020].

Oza, S., van Schaik, S., Boscardin, C., Pierce, R., Miao, E., Lockspeiser, T. et al. (2018). Leadership observation and feedback tool: A novel instrument for assessment of clinical leadership skills. *Journal of Graduate Medical Education*, 10(5), pp. 573–582.

Parrish, D. (2010). Effective leadership in higher education: a circle of influence. Paper presented at the Australian Association for Research in Education (AARE) 2010 conference Melbourne, Australia 29 Nov-2nd Dec: AARE. 1–17.

Raja, N. (2018). Design thinking activities. *Educate and Iterate.* 26 February. Available at: https://educateanditerate.com/category/design-thinking-activities/ [Accessed 7 June 2020].

Schreiber, U. (2016). Where are the women in corporate leadership? *Weforum.* 3 March. Available at: www.weforum.org/agenda/2016/03/where-are-all-the-women-in-corporate-leadership/ [Accessed 7 June 2020].

Shepherd, S. (2017). Why are there so few female leaders in higher education: A case of structure or agency? *Management in Education*, 31(2), pp. 82–87.

Sherwin, I., Campbell, M. & Macintyre, T. E. (2017) Talent development of high performance coaches in team sports in Ireland, *European Journal of Sport Science*, 17:3, 271–278, DOI: 10.1080/17461391.2016.1227378

Smith, P., Caputi, P. and Crittenden, N. (2012). A maze of metaphors around glass ceilings. *Gender in Management: An International Journal*, 27(7), pp. 436–448.

Spangsdorf, S. (2017). We don't see women as leaders – And it's holding them back in our universities. *The Guardian.* 22 December. Available at: www.theguardian.com/higher-education-network/2017/dec/22/we-dont-see-women-as-leaders-thats-why-so-few-are-university-chiefs [Accessed 7 June 2020].

Spencer, N. and Newton, S. (2018). Leading strategic change. *Strategic Learning and Development Series.* Said Business School, University of Oxford. Available at: www.meridianwest.co.uk/leading-strategic-change/

Stormzy. (2019). *Twitter*, 10th October. Available at: www.instagram.com/p/B3b-xdsJVdt/, [Accessed 17th October 2019].

Tickle, L. (2017). Why universities can't see women as leaders. *The Guardian*, 8 March. Available at: www.theguardian.com/higher-education-network/2017/mar/08/why-universities-cant-see-woman-as-leaders [Accessed].

Thiel, C. E., Hardy, J. H., III, Peterson, D. R., Welsh, D. T., & Bonner, J. M. (2018). Too many sheep in the flock? Span of control attenuates the influence of ethical leadership. *Journal of Applied Psychology.* Advance online publication. http://dx.doi.org/10.1037/apl0000338

Turner, C. (2019). Top firms taking 'one and done' approach by appointing token woman to board, review chief says. *Telegraph*, 1 July. Available at: www.telegraph.co.uk/news/2019/06/30/top-firms-taking-one-done-approach-appointing-token-woman-board/ [Accessed 7 June 2020].

University and College Union. (2016). The experiences of BME staff in further and higher education. Available at www.ucu.org.uk/media/7861/The-experiences-of-black-and-minority-ethnic-staff-in-further-and-higher-education-Feb-16/pdf/BME_survey_report_Feb161.pdf [Accessed 7 June 2020].

Wallace, W. and Creelman, D. (2015). Leading people when they know more than you do. *Harvard Business Review*.

CHAPTER 3

Learning to be a leader
Stephen Newton

There is an age-old, chicken-and-egg-type debate about whether leaders are born or can be made. In other words, can leadership be learned – and, by implication, can it be taught? If not, are we limited by genetic makeup to be either a leader or a follower? If we are a 'born leader', can our innate leadership skills and characteristics be developed further? If so, how?

Our experience indicates that leadership can indeed be learned (and therefore, of course, taught). If that is not the case, the production of a mass of leadership literature and the leadership courses offered by many business schools represent a colossal waste of effort. The military around the world will also have wasted vast resources on selecting and developing future leaders. In short, it can, we believe, be done.

That said, our experience also indicates that, as in sport, some people are better equipped for leadership success than others. Whilst it may, for example, be helpful to be tall and have long arms to play basketball well, the lack of these attributes does not necessarily indicate a lack of capability to play at a high level.

There is a growing body of research into the characteristics of successful leaders and what traits indicate effectiveness (we mentioned the work of Dr Mary Crossan and her colleagues in Chapter 1). A study undertaken by Brodbeck et al. (2000) examines cultural variation in management/leadership behaviours across Europe. That study indicates these behaviours do indeed differ across Europe (and by implication therefore more widely). That may add a further dimension to the results of Dr Crossan's research.

It may also serve to reinforce the idea that leadership varies according to context. Context we suggest includes geography, the psychological makeup of the individual, and the culture of the organisation in which the leader operates. One might also therefore suggest that what leaders need to learn in preparation for leadership should also vary according to context. However, experience indicates that most effective leaders rely on a limited repertoire of skills that are widely applicable and that variations in their application are quite nuanced.

Research, starting with the work of Harvard Professor of Psychology William James, and outlined in his book *Principles of Psychology* (1890), indicates that behavioural traits are well formed and relatively hard to alter to any extent by the age of 30–35. Dr Steve Glowinkowski explores the nature of predispositions among leaders and their impact on both leadership performance and organisational success in his book, *It's Behaviour, Stupid* (2009). Characteristics and behaviours are linked although not quite the same thing. Glowinkowski's research reinforces the view that although behaviours can be modified, (a) there is a tendency for them to be repeated over time and (b) that behaviour can be a predictor of performance.

Overall, therefore, it appears that if leadership is to be learned, and if traits, characteristics, and behaviours are likely to need some adjustment, it is best to start early in preparing individuals for leadership. That, in turn, implies the need for some means to identify leadership potential within an organisation or to spot it externally and then hire in the necessary talent.

> **Questions to consider**
>
> - What do you see as your key leadership traits and characteristics?
> - How do friends and colleagues describe you at work and at home? If these differ, why?

The latter might appear to be an easier approach. In reality, especially in professional firms, it seems that external hires can all too often come up against embedded cultures that militate against change. To bring in a leader from outside who has a track record of overcoming such barriers can cause significant disruption to the organisation without necessarily achieving meaningful progress. It is a decision that current leaders and other stakeholders (for example shareholders and NEDs in the case of corporates) should not take lightly.

Some professional firms still have a policy that they will not hire externally at partner level. Others (based on previous difficult experiences) have decided not to appoint anyone to roles such as head of a practice group, managing partner, or senior partner who has not previously worked as a partner in the firm. This approach tends to perpetuate the cultural status quo. We explore preparation for leadership roles in professional firms and in the military context in greater detail below.

One of the key issues regarding leadership in HE and in the professions is that the role of leadership is not always sought actively by senior people or by those aspiring to promotion based on professional expertise. We look at this in more detail in the professional firm context below. The military differs in that leadership is one of its core competencies, whether for officers or for enlisted personnel aspiring to promotion to NCO. A key criterion for promotion is leadership capability – something routinely tested. Development in this area is therefore both commonly delivered and actively sought.

Preparing to be a leader

Anecdotally, formal preparation for leadership in HE is mixed, as is early identification of leadership potential. In part, this may reflect the fact that the HE workforce is increasingly freelance, with many contracts of employment being short term in nature and with many academics holding roles at more than one HEI.

As a result, future leaders do not always receive much by way of leadership skills development prior to their appointment. One former Master of an Oxford College indicated that he simply applied common sense to the way in which he carried out that role, as he had done in his several previous leadership roles, both within and outside HE, in which he was, apparently, very successful.

For those who aspire to take on leadership roles, it is of course possible to seek out training in leadership for oneself, whether from a business school, a professional body, or from one of the training providers operating in this field. These providers will not necessarily focus on the practice of leadership in HE, unless courses are offered by specialists such as Harvard Institutes for Higher Education, UCL's London Centre for Leadership in Learning, or Advance HE (formerly the Higher Education Academy).

Questions to consider

- To what extent do you feel you would benefit from formal leadership training?
- What opportunities exist for you?

By contrast, leadership selection and preparation in the military starts at the earliest stages of a career path for officers. Selection and training for promotion to NCO or warrant officer ranks also begins as soon as potential for leadership is identified. We explore this in more detail below.

In the professions, leadership, like management or administration (both sometimes conflated with leadership), can be seen as something actively to be avoided, as it will likely detract from winning work, looking after clients and racking up billable hours. The latter activities are seen, in varying degrees, as the nexus of power and control within the firm. The combination of high levels of billable hours and being recognised by colleagues for professional excellence ('A fine lawyer…') can be seen as the acme of professional success. To be recognised as an effective leader does not necessarily carry the same perceived kudos among peers, even if it is recognised as necessary for the overall success of the firm.

With this in mind, not all professional firms invest in leadership training and development to any extent. Those larger firms that do so may opt for courses run by business schools such as Judge or Said (at Cambridge and Oxford Universities respectively in the UK) or at Harvard in the US. Some firms may ask these same business schools to build an executive development or leadership programme for them on a bespoke basis. In all cases, it can be hard to ensure that those nominated for such courses actually participate fully. If there is a clash with demands from a client, these will often trump attending a course module.

Other approaches include the use of mentoring and coaching. The former is often regarded as part of the remit of partners within the firm, and their diligence and effectiveness in such a role can be mixed. Some firms have built a cadre of internal coaches (sometimes retired partners) to minimise the direct cost, recognising that an effective third-party coach can cost as much per hour as a senior fee earner. Mentoring and coaching programmes that are started around leadership development will often extend to areas including business development skills, client relationship management (e.g. key accounts), and the economics of the firm's business.

With many medium and smaller professional firms, leadership development is often by way of mentoring – much of which may be carried out informally – with individuals who aspire to leadership seeking role models either within their own firm or elsewhere. This mirrors what is beginning to happen in other areas of L&D in the professions.

Given that younger professionals in particular are increasingly mobile and willing to move to a new firm if they feel it will aid their career development or that there may be a better cultural fit, some firms now pay only for basic technical training. Individuals are encouraged to seek further development and may receive advice as to what may be of benefit to them. However, if they wish to receive development, especially in non-technical so-called 'soft skills', they must often cover the cost themselves.

In HE and in the professions, therefore, learning to be a leader can be a somewhat hit-and-miss affair. The position among corporates tends to vary by size of firm, with larger firms tending to invest more in L&D (as one might expect) with a view to building an in-house talent pool – something smaller firms, for the most part, cannot afford.

In the field of HE, it appears that there is a growing segregation between those who lead and manage institutions and those who prefer to focus on teaching and research. It is arguable that this may lead to the development of a professionalised group of leaders and managers within HE. However, there could be obvious unintended consequences. In the professions, as noted above, there can be a 'them and us' barrier between fee earners and others (so-called 'support staff') regardless of seniority. It would be perverse to encourage the creation of a similar barrier in HE.

How do individuals become leaders?

Higher education

In HE, appointment to a leadership role can occur in a number of ways. The process is governed by regulation in some countries and by tradition elsewhere. Often the appointment will follow an application by the individual for an advertised role and an interview process: indeed, this approach may be mandatory for what are considered to be public sector appointments.

Sometimes, an individual may be asked to put their name forward, especially for a role within their own institution. This can result from recognition in teaching, research, thought leadership, or management capability. To be asked to apply does not obviate the interview or other selection process, nor does it guarantee appointment (not least because many HE appointments are covered by regulations requiring that they be advertised and open to public competition). However, it may help to ensure inclusion on a shortlist.

Sometimes, an individual's leadership potential (and/or management capability) may be recognised at an early stage in their career. If they are fortunate to have at least one mentor in a relatively senior position within their HEI, it is possible that they may be groomed for eventual succession. That is more likely to occur at departmental level or within a research team. In our experience, this is less common now than it may have been in the past, due to the increasingly peripatetic nature of staffing within HE.

Even more rarely, an individual may find leadership thrust upon them – for example, if their immediate boss suffers an unexpected and serious illness. That will tend to be an interim situation, although success in the interim role may lead to eventual confirmation in it.

The professions

As outlined above, leadership tends not to be sought after in the professions. Promotion to partner appears rarely to be based on leadership capability, but instead on technical ability and/or effectiveness in client relationship management. That said, promotion to partner inevitably brings with it an element of management responsibility and eventual leadership roles, whether leading a team carrying out a large piece of work for a client or leading a practice group or department. Individuals who are seen to be successful in such roles may well be asked to put themselves forward for roles such as managing partner.

In most professional firms, leaders are elected by the partners, from within the existing partnership, rather than simply appointed. Candidates may be asked to present a 'manifesto' to their partners outlining how they propose to run the firm (or their part of it) during their term, and their targets, be it for growth, profitability, or changes such as merger or acquisition. In most cases, roles such as managing or senior partner are for a fixed term, often four years, with a maximum of two terms being served by any individual.

As with chief executives of corporates, there is a case for appointing managing partners when they are in their early 40s. Energy levels tend to be higher and there is some evidence that performance (as measured by profit growth and/or shareholder value) of the firm can be higher, by comparison with firms led by older individuals.

In the professions, that can lead to a question of 'What next?' for a managing partner who has completed their maximum of two terms by their early 50s, having largely given up client work for the previous eight years. Some move to another firm at this point. Others move within their current firm to take on a role as senior partner or more commonly one of mentoring younger partners and associates approaching partnership. This issue is examined in the fourth Paper in the Strategic Learning and Development series, co-authored by Dr Nigel Spencer and Stephen Newton (see Spencer and Newton, 2018) (also referenced in Chapter 15).

The military

In the military, officers are typically appointed to leadership roles or to roles such as staff appointments from a pool of candidates previously identified. Those candidates will have met specific threshold criteria such as passing staff college exams and may also require specific training or experience, depending on the role. Appointments will typically be for one tour of duty, i.e. two to three years, with the rotation ensuring that there is continual renewal within the relevant organisation. The military is also adept at learning by experience and documenting such learning to ensure it is not lost as individuals move on to new roles. We examine leadership in the military in more detail in Chapter 10.

Self-awareness

In Chapter 1, we put forward a leadership model that placed self-leadership at its centre. Whether in HE, the professions, corporates, or in the military, we believe that self-knowledge combined with acceptance of 'who you are' are critical to leadership success.

As mentioned above, research from the field of psychology indicates that behaviours are largely hard-wired by the age of about 30–35, i.e. before most people will have the opportunity to gain significant leadership experience. Understanding yourself and also your own traits and characteristics in relation to your interactions with others is vital to minimise friction as a leader.

Some organisations and individuals seek to make that understanding more objective through the use of psychometric instruments. These can be helpful in providing safe language to use in discussing character traits and how these may be perceived by others in light of their own psychometric preferences. It would be a mistake to think that the outputs of psychometrics are wholly 'right' and that the results are absolute. They can best be thought of as indicative and results will be subject to some change over time and also under stress.

Commonly used psychometric instruments include:

- Myers Briggs (MBTI) ®[1]
- DISC ®[2]
- VIA (Values in Action) ®[3]
- Gallup Strengths Finder ®[4] ('Clifton Strengths')
- The Hogan suite ®[5]
- Keirsey Temperament Sorter ®[6]
- Thomas-Kilmann Conflict Mode Instrument (TKI) ®[7]

Each psychometric instrument has a distinct focus, although some may be closely linked. In most cases, even where a free-of-charge version of an instrument is available online, the detailed feedback available from a qualified practitioner will usually pay dividends. Nonetheless, the free, online versions can give useful pointers. The key here is not simply to understand your own psychometric preferences but how they may interact with those of others: for example, the friction that may occur between a person with a high introversion preference in Myers Briggs terms versus a colleague who is a high extrovert. (Very broadly, the former tends to prefer quiet reflection and the latter active discussion – something that has been described as being 'battery powered' versus 'solar powered'.)

Other approaches to understanding oneself in relation to others include 360-degree feedback and (if they are done effectively) feedback from periodic evaluations. For psychometrics, the value is maximised if the entire team goes through the same process and the results are shared. This sharing of information about one's own psychological preferences can be a starting point to build mutual trust and hence speed up the building of a strong team. 360-degree feedback can be used as the basis for coaching or mentoring, but the feedback results may well not be shared team-wide.

Many feedback approaches focus on identifying weaknesses to be fixed rather than strengths to be fostered. Psychometrics such as VIA and Gallup focus on strengths. It is typically far more difficult to address an area of weakness than to develop further an existing strength. What defines strengths and weaknesses will vary depending on context. However, in general terms, one's greatest strengths, taken to excess, can become weaknesses.

Questions to consider

- Might it be helpful to use a psychometric instrument for yourself / your team?
- Which seems most appropriate?
- What other opportunities exist (e.g. 360-degree feedback)?
- Might these make you feel exposed? Why?

Regardless of context, a key leadership skill is credible communication, which translates to an ability to influence others. That does not necessarily indicate a need to be a great orator. It does mean understanding the perceptions you generate when you communicate, especially verbally. Working with senior clients in a coaching context, I have found it helpful to use the power of video to enable individuals to see themselves (and how their verbal communication changes) under different levels of stress.

The client decides which of the various subtly different personas they see is the most effective. In almost every case, they feel that the person who is visibly 'being themselves' is markedly more credible than the rest. That credibility is based on a combination of eye contact, delivery, tone of voice, word choice, and a number of other factors. Simply giving oneself permission to 'be yourself' is a significant step forward in effective leadership communication.

Adaptability and resilience

Throughout this book, we emphasise the impact of change in HE and its increasing scale and rapidity. Another key leadership skill is therefore adaptability and, linked to that, becoming comfortable with uncertainty and willingness to be flexible in terms of approach if not in terms of desired results. Resilience in the face of change is a necessary and closely allied characteristic of effective leadership. A key element of resilience that is linked to self-awareness is personal wellbeing: not only giving yourself permission to be yourself but to look after yourself. That does not mean undue self-absorption; simply taking a common sense approach to sleep, exercise, and eating is an excellent foundation.

The list of leadership skills to be developed could be lengthy. The leadership characteristics identified by Dr Mary Crossan (see Chapter 1) is a good starting point. However, in the interest of brevity and focus, we will add only one more here: the ability to generate respect, personally and professionally.

Respect

Respect is linked to likability and to being perceived as both genuinely interested in the people around you and also able in your field of work. It is also, in our opinion, linked to a perception that you will stand up for members of your team no matter what the circumstances. The latter is, in other words, loyalty. If you seek loyalty and respect from others, you must be perceived as first giving both to them: loyalty is certainly a two-way street and respect is earned over time by one's actions, not as of right.

If we look beyond HE to consider what leaders need to learn, the list will probably vary in terms of emphasis but the same skill sets will feature to a greater or lesser extent, regardless of whether we consider the professions, corporates, or the military.

Influence

Professional partnerships differ from corporates and many other organisations in that the partners are by definition not only senior participants in the business, but its owners. This participant/owner tension can lead to conflicted points of view – for example on issues such as long-term investment, with partners close to retirement seeking to maximise profit (i.e. minimise costs), whilst those who are more recently promoted may be willing to trade short-term profit reduction for long-term gains.

Even an elected managing partner has to rely to a degree (sometimes to a large degree) on influence when dealing with recalcitrant colleagues who are also partners – hence the often-used description of leadership in professional firms as 'herding cats'. Influencing skills are necessary in most leadership roles, even in the military. As one senior officer put it, 'When I joined the Army, I told a man to pick up a chair and he did it. Now I have to tell him why he should pick up the chair.' That altered dynamic of engagement with more junior colleagues applies across the board, and especially in organisations where the stock in trade is knowledge/information.

How do individuals outside HE prepare for leadership?

Military

In the military, leadership is a core competence, so leadership development, testing, and evaluation is an ongoing process throughout the career of an individual. We examine this in more detail in Chapter 10.

Selection for leadership is undertaken at a very early stage, with most commissioned officers going through a selection process before they join the service, either on leaving secondary education (although that is rare nowadays) or on graduation from university (now far more common). University graduates may well have gained some military experience during their undergraduate course by way of a cadet scheme (such as ROTC in the US or University Officer Training Corps (OTCs) in the UK).

Selection for promotion to non-commissioned officer starts at an early stage following basic training. In most cases, after initial training and a little experience, individuals are expected to be able to carry out the role of their immediate superior. That is developed and tested under training exercise conditions by temporarily 'taking out' selected seniors from the group so that others have to step up. That is of course only reflecting the real possibility of casualties on operations. However, it allows juniors to gain experience of carrying out a more senior role and has proved to be an effective way to evaluate leadership potential.

Leadership training in the military is both progressive and selective/competitive. An initial 'induction training', typically lasting 6–12 months for officers, leads to commissioning as a junior officer, at which point a selection of service branch (e.g. infantry or artillery) is made. That induction training is designed to be both mentally and physically testing in order to weed out those who may not operate well under stress in the future. It may also influence choice of service branch.

The next point of selection is for promotion to major or the equivalent – typically after around nine years of commissioned service. This involves selection for a course at staff college, which is usually by a combination of examination, recommendation through previous annual evaluations, and interview, whether formal or informal.

Corporates and the professions

In both corporates and professional firms, leadership selection and development can be far more random, based at least in part on 'getting along well with the boss' and being perceived to shine in terms of routine technical performance. Most corporates and professional firms now try to give more junior staff who are perceived to be 'hi-pots' (or individuals with high potential) some exposure to leadership or management roles by way of project-based work. Sometimes that is preceded by relevant training, but by no means always.

The 'learning by doing' approach has been identified as one of the most important ways in which learning can be achieved (the so called 70/20/10 model of skills development). To gain maximum value, however, it requires both appropriate preparation (training) and follow-up (learning by example) and to become part of a process of continuous improvement. In this context, it also requires support from more senior individuals in a coaching/mentoring role to maximise the positive impact.

Factors impacting leadership effectiveness

Leadership effectiveness in HE, as in the military, is arguably as much about the perceptions of those being led and of those observing the leader in action as it is about delivery of agreed objectives. Even in a professional firm or a corporate, where other, more objective measures may be seen as paramount, such as growth of the firm (top-line revenue, profitability, entry to new markets, etc.), perceptions are still paramount.

Factors that influence positive perceptions include:

- loyalty and respect (both professional and personal), which we examined above;
- likability of the leader;
- consistency and fairness by the leader in dealing with others at all levels;
- effective delegation (which means, among other things, ensuring that the task is within the capabilities and span of decision of the person to whom it is delegated);
- clear, unambiguous, and unequivocal communication;
- avoidance of micro-management but openness to provide guidance where required.

Dealing with the shock of leadership ('immersion')

Regardless of prior leadership experience, any new leadership role carries with it what has been called 'the shock of immersion'. In one sense, this is no different from any other significant change, such as moving to a new house. Where the business of leadership is unfamiliar to an individual, the shock of immersion is greatly increased – hence the need for prior preparation if possible.

Other ways to deal with immersion include consulting widely and deeply with stakeholders before actually starting in the new role. The volume of information to be absorbed may prove to be daunting and of course many of the views expressed will be in conflict. It is worth setting aside time not only to get to grips with the data but to understand the cultural nuances and personal frictions of the organisation and considering how to respond.

As Eisenhower remarked, 'Plans as such are useless because no plan survives contact with the enemy, but the process of planning is vital.' Simply making a plan for your first (say) three months in the role will usually help to generate a greater sense of being in control and may help to highlight some key 'unknowns' to be addressed. In addition to mapping stakeholders and their interests, considering possible cultural and personal frictions and making plans, it is worth spending time considering whether, and if so how, you wish to adjust your own leadership approach and style.

> **Question to consider**
> - How will you prepare yourself for 'immersion' into leadership?

As we observed above, credibility as a leader involves giving yourself permission to be yourself. Within that, you can decide to turn up or turn down the dial on certain characteristics in order to fit more readily into the organisation you are to inherit or that you have been asked to build. If you decide to make such adjustments, it is essential that you can do so consistently and comfortably for the duration of your time in the role.

Moving into leadership in HE 'temporarily'

Given the rapidity and scale of change within the HE field, an increasing number of roles at all levels are filled on short-term or freelance contracts. That may include leadership roles. The temporary nature of many such roles can be a two-edged sword. On the one hand, it enables aspiring leaders to gain experience and decide whether they feel suited for leadership roles in the future. On the other, a perceived failure in a short-term role can damage chances of appointment to similar roles in the future. Either way, planning and preparation will be valuable prior to applying, including spending time to consider the role in the context of your own strategic career aspirations.

The fact that you may be offered a role does not necessarily mean that you should take it. It may be that, whilst leadership, and especially a short-term role, appears attractive, it may not necessarily serve your strategic ends. As in most aspects of business, deciding what not to do is often a more valuable exercise than deciding to do something. It is also preferable to direct your career in ways that play to your strengths as opposed to requiring frictional effort on your part.

Mapping leadership style to organisational needs

We have already noted the need for leaders to 'be themselves' in order to engender credibility, especially when they communicate. It is also clear that, after the age of about 30–35, behaviour patterns are largely hard-wired and not easily changed (although they can be adjusted). To alter one's natural leadership style to fit perceived organisational needs can, therefore, become counterproductive.

We suggest looking at this issue through the other end of the telescope: identify organisational culture and needs first, then decide whether your leadership approach and style (adjusted if need be) can fit. If you decide that it does not, it may be preferable to decline the relevant role or to seek adjustments to the responsibilities and structure so that you have a greater chance of success. Once again, this is an area for deep self-knowledge and brutal honesty.

Notes

1 MBTI – Available at: https://eu.themyersbriggs.com [Accessed 8 February 2020].
2 Everything DISC. Available at: www.everythingdisc.com/Home.aspx – [Accessed 8 February 2020] Copyright John Wiley & Sons.
3 McGrath, R. E. (2019). Technical report: *The VIA Assessment Suite for Adults: Development and Initial Evaluation* Revised Edition. Cincinnati, OH: VIA Institute on Character.
4 Clifton Strenghts (Gallup) Available at: www.gallup.com/cliftonstrengths/en/home.aspx [Accessed 8 February 2020].
5 Hogan suite Available at: www.hoganassessments.com [Accessed 8 February 2020].
6 Available at: www.keirsey.com [Accessed 10 February 2020].
7 Available at: https://kilmanndiagnostics.com [Accessed 11 February 2020] – see also www.themyersbriggs.com [Accessed 11 February 2020].

References

Brodbeck, F., Frese, M., Akerblom, S., Audia, G., Bakacsi, G., Bendova, H. et al. (2000). Cultural variation of leadership prototypes across 22 European countries. *Journal of Occupational and Organisational Psychology, 73(1), pp. 1–29.*
Glowinkowski, S. (2009). *It's Behaviour, Stupid.* Cornwall: Ecademy Press.
James, W. (1890). *Principles of Psychology.* New York: Henry Holt & Co.
Spencer, N. and Newton, S. (2018). *Creating Competitive Advantage: Strategic Learning and Development Series.* Said Business School, University of Oxford. Available at: www.sbs.ox.ac.uk/programmes/custom-executive-education/creating-competitive-advantage. [Accessed 3 February 2020].

PART 1

Summary

Kendall Jarrett and Stephen Newton

Chapter 1, written by Stephen Newton, sets out our stall for the focus of the book. Through discussion that exercises caution when defining leadership based on its complexity as an act and as a means to facilitate change, recognition is given to the variety of contexts where leadership can be practised. An initial exploration of the concept of self-leadership, which Stephen says encompasses personal boundaries and takes heed of the concepts of integrity and authenticity, stems from the sharing of frameworks that conceptualise the different dimensions of leadership. Consideration of upwards leadership, peer and customer leadership, and staff leadership follows, culminating in a focus on recognising the need to take account of the varied agendas of stakeholders.

Questions posed throughout the chapter direct the reader to consider how a leader's results and success will be defined, the impact of key stakeholders on a leader's decision-making, and an exploration of leadership weakness. Leadership and management are discussed, with readers asked to reflect on whether a good manager can be a good leader and whether a leader can be effective without being an effective manager. Stephen also reflects on the spectrum of different leadership approaches/styles utilised across all sectors, from servant to autocrat, process driven to discussion driven. One of the underlying messages from the chapter is the need for HE leaders to become comfortable with uncertainty in their environment and to develop a strong sense of 'who they are' in a rapidly changing HE landscape.

Chapter 2, written by Kendall Jarrett, provides a focus on the enhancement of leadership capacity *from within* the institution. Utilisation of existing capability translates into investment *in people* resourced *by those people*, and this chapter provides a framework for decision-making when developing an internal leadership development offering. The myths and realities of leadership and leadership development in HE are presented as a backdrop to discussion, with a chapter appendix enabling readers delve deeper into why, for some academics, there is a reluctance to pursue certain leadership development opportunities.

A framework for developing institutional leadership capacity *from within* is presented with the elements of informality, collegiality, and familiarity used to justify improved utilisation of existing resource. Leadership development initiatives are presented to assist readers in considering questions such as, 'When do new academics first have an opportunity to take leadership responsibility?' and 'Are there opportunities for leadership being "lost" or "missed" at the start of academic careers?' The chapter concludes with discussion of three interlinked research projects which are brought together to form an institutional case study of leadership development opportunities. Aspects of the research that may resonate with some readers are perceptions that academics don't always view themselves as leaders and that some academics place minimal value on leadership as a function of learning and teaching.

Chapter 3, written by Stephen Newton, focuses on the learning and teaching of leadership. Different approaches to learning how to lead are presented – from coaching and mentoring to formal course completion to being handed the keys and told 'get on with it'. The idea that leadership varies according to context is reinforced through discussion of the many paths to leadership experienced across the sectors. Yet within discussion, the prevailing notion that it is best to start early in preparing individuals for leadership holds firm.

Of prominence within the chapter is the belief that preparation for leadership should vary according to context. Interestingly, these comments are followed by the suggestion that effective leaders rely only on a limited repertoire of skills. Of note, though, is that such skills are widely applicable, with the skill itself being their nuanced application. It is suggested also that understanding yourself as a leader helps minimise friction as a leader, with some organisations seeking to understand this more objectively through psychometric analysis. Stephen offers the reader poignant commentary on the shock of leadership, how individuals outside HE prepare for leadership, and the critical evaluation of whether or not a leadership opportunity should be taken up.

It is our intent that each chapter in Part 1 has provided readers with a signposting to the realities of leadership in higher education. We are also mindful that the ways in which we define leadership, how we learn to be a leader, and how we are developed as leaders are of significant importance in our identities as leaders and how we engage with the numerous leadership insights shared in Part 2.

PART 2A
Leadership insights
From within the sector

CHAPTER 4

The influence of experience and culture on leadership

Richard L. Light with Mohammad Shah Razak

When invited by Kendall and Stephen to write a chapter that considered the influence of the different cultures I have lived and worked in on learning to lead in academic settings, I immediately decided to adopt a personal experience narrative approach to tell my story because of the power of stories in conveying meaning and insight into individual experience. To inform the writing process, I thought back to: (1) relevant experiences and contexts that contributed to developing a positive disposition toward leading; (2) the styles of leading I had adopted; and (3) how these two points interacted with other experiences and culture on my life journey that predated my academic career. Thus, the academic leadership experiences I tell of in this chapter are not just formal position of responsibility roles such as Head of School (HoS), but also more short-term research leadership responsibilities such as convening an international conference.

Personal experience narrative approach

I have long been aware of narrative inquiry as an effective methodology, but it was not until my use of it in a recent study exploring the journeys of Indigenous Australian athletes that I realised the opportunity it offers for the participant to express themselves and convey deep and insightful understanding of human experience. The stories the participants told us and our telling of their stories in print (see Light and Evans, 2018) allowed me to live their experiences, have empathy with them, and gain the deep subjective understanding that I have searched for in much of my research. Hence, my use of it here aims to make accessible my journey in learning to lead and my development of a desire to lead.

The narrative I present here identifies a sequence of experiences from well before I became an academic and how these events shaped my approach to academic leadership. The stories shared hold within them a focus on the influence of socio-cultural context on experiences of leadership from around the world, including Australia, Japan, England, and New Zealand. As is common when using a personal experience narrative approach, my story is told in chronological order to link my past experience to the present and is written in the form of lessons learned to help analyse, link, and evaluate sections of the narrative (Akinsanya and Bach, 2014). Three chronological stages are identified:

1. the emergence of leadership inclination and early learning prior to entering academia;
2. learning to lead within academic contexts;
3. my experiences of leadership in senior academic positions.

The emergence of leadership ability

Martial arts in Australia

As a child and teenager I avoided the responsibility of leadership. I didn't want to be class captain in primary school nor to be captain of any of the many sporting teams I was a member of. It might have been because it was not 'cool' or due to a lack of confidence, but I can't remember. However, I do remember finding myself in a leadership role that I thoroughly enjoyed and one that changed my life trajectory – teaching martial arts. What I learned during this time proved to be pivotal to my career development in academia and academic leadership.

Prior to my introduction to martial arts, I worked as a teacher in one of the last one-teacher schools in rural Australia. At this school, I taught 33 children from the age of five to fourteen as well as drove the school bus to pick them up every morning and drop them off every afternoon. Soon after my appointment, I joined a karate club. I developed a real passion for karate and over a three-year period worked my way up to the last grade before black belt. I then resigned as a teacher to train in Hong Kong, earn a black belt and return to make my living teaching karate. I loved teaching (and still do), yet the three years of setting and achieving goals in karate helped build my belief in myself to succeed.

My martial arts business grew to include four clubs in four different towns. Teaching so many students – from five-year-old children to karateka and national champion kickboxers – and organising a range of regional events, saw my leadership inclination to emerge and my ability begin to develop. Reflecting from where I am now, I see how I had become a mentor and leader for my students, many of whom I still keep in contact with.

> **Question to consider**
> - Thinking back to experiences in your life not directly related to academia, how significant were certain situations in terms of your development of skills or dispositions toward leadership?

This was my first taste of substantial leadership and I enjoyed it. As a boy and teenager I felt that I had often disappointed my father. Several years later, however, I overheard my father boasting to a friend about what a great leader I was as head of a chain of martial arts schools, and remember very well how good it made me feel. My experience as a leader in martial arts encouraged me to run other major sporting events and set up a security business. All the events I staged required a great deal of help from my martial arts students, their friends and their families, all of which required good relationships and mutual respect. I learned how to treat people well and create a strong sense of belonging and loyalty, instead of just using them or telling them because I was *sensei*.

Rugby coaching in Japan

After eight years I left my martial arts business and took up an opportunity to work as a professional rugby coach in Japan. When I arrived I was a little short on high-level rugby coaching experience, could not speak Japanese, and did not have an interpreter, but was able to clumsily communicate and develop my Japanese. The confidence generated by my belief in my leadership ability helped me face an immensely challenging task. Not only did I have to coach over 100 players, en masse, and learn to communicate in Japanese, but also how to lead as a coach in a very foreign country, learn how decisions were made in Japanese organisations, and how power operated.

I continued karate training in Osaka, which helped me understand how leadership was enacted and how influential language and the vertical hierarchical structure of society (*joge kanke*) was for all interactions. I also learned the pivotal importance of maintaining *tatemae* (a social facade used to maintain harmony and agreement) and not be selfish by allowing *hone* (your real feelings) to disturb harmony. I read a great deal of anthropological, sociological, and historical literature in my quest to understand the cultural environment I was working in. As my language skills improved, I was able to engage in more meaningful exchanges as a rugby coach. I learned to be patient, listen intently, and try to understand what the speaker's real feelings were instead of focusing on finding opportunities to speak, which is typical of verbal interaction in Japan. This was quite a challenge for an Australian, who are considered to be blunt and direct by some. However, my success in gaining agreement to take a large squad of about 60 players to Australia for matches and training sessions with high-profile Australian players suggested to me I had begun to adapt to my environment. I felt that the key was to work in the background and avoid claiming any major part in the organisation as well as respecting the 'old boys' who largely funded the trip. Above all, I saw the benefit of working as a collective instead of as an individual.

Question to consider

- Can you remember a sports coach you liked and respected whose approach could be applied to higher education leadership?

Rugby-wise, we had a great first season of my tenure as coach, which encouraged me to progress the subtle and (up to that point) successful changes I had been making. However, the varying degrees of resistance I encountered inevitably began to slow progress. I should have been more patient and satisfied with slow but steady progress and knowing what was possible, and what was not. With the knowledge I now have of Japan and Japanese rugby, I would not have made such mistakes, but I learned a great deal about myself as a leader from the experience.

Learning to lead in universities

Convening an international conference at the University of Melbourne, Australia

My first appointment at the University of Melbourne in 2000 provided me with my first significant academic leadership experience. In 2001, I attended the first International TGfU[1] Conference in Plymouth, New Hampshire, and absolutely loved it. During the town meeting at the end of the conference the convenor asked if anyone was interested in organising a second conference, but I was only a lecturer at the time so, despite my interest, I did not put my hand up. Upon returning to Melbourne, I reconsidered and applied to convene the second international conference.

I knew convening the conference would be a big challenge for a novice who had only attended half a dozen conferences, but with my previous experiences of leadership success (e.g. coaching Japanese rugby and running my own martial arts business in Australia), I was confident I could do it. I had many problems to deal with and no shortage of anxiety, but deep down I never doubted that it would be a success. The patience I had learned in Japan, along with an ability to develop productive relationships with people, meant the conference was considered by many as a success. This experience gave me immense satisfaction and confidence in my ability to take on and succeed in academic leadership. Since then I have convened numerous conferences and mentored peers through the same process.

Senior academic leadership positions

Director of Research at Leeds Metropolitan University, UK

In 2009 I took up a position as Professor in Sport and Physical Education Pedagogy at Leeds Metropolitan University in the UK. I was director of the Centre for Studies in Sport and Physical Education Pedagogy, and when the Director of Research in my faculty was seconded, I volunteered to take over. Stepping up so quickly as a newcomer to the UK and the university into a role that was totally new to me was a challenge that I was looking forward to, but not without some anxiety and hints of self-doubt. The challenge was intensified when a university restructure under a new vice chancellor saw our Faculty of Sport and Education grow to have a student population of 6,000 with 150 PhDs, 400 staff and, from memory, 14 full professors. I was suddenly director of the Sport and Physical Education Pedagogy Research Centre, Director of the Carnegie Research Institute, Chair of Readers and Professors, Chair of the Research Committee, and a member of the Faculty Leadership Team. I did have doubts about my ability to meet the administrative challenges of this position, but the excellent administrative support really helped.

The challenge of stepping up into a senior leadership role at a time of such major changes across the university was made more difficult by my lack of institutional and cultural knowledge. With such a confronting task in front of me, I took more of a management position instead of a leadership position (by this I mean my adoption of a different approach to leadership, which I saw at the time as being crucial to success both personally and for the university). I talked with a range of colleagues in leadership positions to develop an understanding of the university culture and how things worked. In these early stages of my leadership I did more listening and watching than talking and doing. This included seeing how the dean, Gareth Davies, who had extensive leadership experience in business and sport, led so successfully with no prior academic leadership experience. The way in which he led also made me think about how effective leadership tends to have common features, whether in sport, business, schools, or universities. Now, as I reflect to write this chapter, I think there were also similar elements of my own leadership experiences in

Australia and Japan, in and outside universities. In 2014 Gareth was appointed Chairman of Welsh Rugby, but from his time as Dean of Faculty, his most effective skills or strengths in leadership were:

1. his calmness (while being firm), honesty, and integrity;
2. his ability to communicate clearly and concisely, and to listen;
3. his empowerment of staff (particularly senior staff) through delegation;
4. him being accountable and, while empowering staff, holding them accountable as well.

> **Question to consider**
> - What have you learned from mistakes made in leadership situations?

I also learned from the mistakes I made as Director of Research. I was new to everything and in hindsight now realise I should have sat back to watch, listen, and learn before I decided on trying to implement any changes. My enthusiasm got the better of me, as it has a few times over my career. While I recognised my lack of institutional knowledge and the need to keep things calm, I could also see opportunities to initiate change for the future. For example, I wanted to reduce the number of research centres in the Institute to increase the efficiency of each one and get better value for our investment. After discussions with different research centre directors, I was confident I would get agreement, but as it turned out I had misread the mood of those involved. I felt frustrated that my plans had been quashed, but learned valuable lessons about the context of decision-making and about being more thorough and careful at times when people feel they are losing something.

Head of School at University of Canterbury in New Zealand

In previous leadership appointments, culture had always played a significant part in shaping my experiences of leadership. The culture of Japanese society and Japanese rugby, and the culture of Yorkshire and working at a British university, had complicated my leadership experiences, but I had anticipated that. However, when I moved from Australia to New Zealand in 2014 to take up the position of Head of School (HoS) at the University of Canterbury in New Zealand, I was not prepared for the cultural difference due to how similar I thought Australian and New Zealand cultures were. These differences were amplified by the situation I was in as an HoS who wanted to make significant change, was an enthusiastic leader with a vision for the future of the school, and who was very goal oriented.

I took my time at first to get a feel for my new environment, interviewed every member of staff on a one-on-one basis to get to know them and listen to their experiences, aspirations, and expectations of me. I then formed an advisory group that met once a week to discuss relevant issues and formulate ideas and possible solutions that I then discussed with all staff at our monthly staff meetings. There were some very capable and promising staff prepared to engage in change, but others with a far more conservative outlook who opposed change. There was a general division between those with PhDs who had come more recently and supported me, and those who had been in the school longer and without PhDs who opposed me.

These tensions are evident in the reflections of one of my mature age PhD students from Singapore, Mohammad Shah Razak, which I include here:

> In 2015 I was asked by my then Head of School to spearhead a conference abstract review committee (ARC), whilst also being tasked with preparing a programme for the two-day international event. As I already had 18 years of experience in organising and leading events as a Head of Department in schools in the Singaporean secondary education sector, I saw this as an opportunity for continued leadership growth in the tertiary sector. However, I felt unprepared for the reactions shared by some academic colleagues as they responded to me being assigned the abstract review committee leadership and conference planning roles.
>
> Despite these challenging responses, I persisted with my task of being impartial in reviewing abstracts in the manner set by the ARC, as well as setting out the two-day conference programme. However, at an initial review committee meeting, disagreements were had over the wording of a session chair's responsibilities. This disagreement culminated in one colleague 'tearing up' the document in front of me. I was taken aback by this reaction and at the time felt acutely aware of cultural differences amongst the group.
>
> Although the conference went well and I received commendation for the professionalism I had shown in my role, at various times I became aware that my effectiveness as a leader was being influenced by colleagues' perceptions of experience and culture. That said, by having the opportunity to view and respond to these challenges, I have no doubt that I have become a better leader.

From my experience as an outsider, the culture in the school and the college more broadly was one in which there was a great deal of talking aimed at reaching consensus with decision-making avoided and often passed upward. From my experience, there is also a cultural expectation to appear humble and, as a small country, a tendency to look inward. The changes suggested and made, however, were too many and too soon. Indeed, I was warned by the Pro Vice-Chancellor, who said she thought I was moving too fast. I had let the heady experience of undertaking rapid and consistent change and getting immediate results like a 150% growth in enrolments in my first year, mix with my enthusiasm to blind me to the unease of colleagues and the reality of what was possible. It was also made difficult by my lack of knowledge of the history of the school and the power of existing networks and connections that a previous HoS used very effectively.

Eventually, I stepped down as HoS. I saw my stint as HoS as a failure that left me with negative feelings about myself and my environment, which encouraged deep reflection after I finished blaming people. However, as I have written about since (see Light and Harvey, 2019), mistakes are essential for learning, and from this perspective, my experience as HoS was not a failure. Over time, I learned from my mistakes of letting my passion and enthusiasm for rapid progress overpower my inclination to be more careful and recognise the danger signs that were there. A year later, I was asked to chair the College Research Committee by my PVC and I accepted on the proviso that I would not just maintain the status quo but would look to improve its operation. 'That is why you are being asked,' she told me.

Chair of the College Research Committee, University of Canterbury in New Zealand

In my first year as Chair of the Research Committee I worked with the members of the committee to design and implement a radical change in how we funded conference attendance to help improve research culture and performance as a college. The outputs-based conference funding model involved paying staff for published outputs and making these funds available for them to attend conferences. I don't have the space here to go into detail, but this was initially quite confronting for less research-active staff. It initially created anxiety and opposition for many, but this time I was more careful and controlled the pace of change while ensuring that all staff in the college understood that it was a very fair and supportive model.

As a committee leader I have seen fit to delegate responsibilities when appropriate and have enjoyed seeing staff on the committee develop as academic leaders in their own right. My experience as Chair of the Research Committee has been so radically different from my experience as Head of School due to a number of reasons, among which is how I altered my perceptions of leadership and how I endeavoured to better understand and adapt to my environment. At the time of me writing this chapter, the funding model has been accepted by all staff and is beginning to have positive effects on research culture, the development of individual research careers, and on college output.

Finding leadership

Moving overseas with a family is a very big challenge – especially when your child or children are of school age. My daughter, Amy, moved from the middle of her final year at primary school in Sydney to the end of first year in a private secondary school to be confronted by exams in subjects like British History and Latin. However, the biggest problem for my family and me was my wife's visa. It was in fact a nightmare for all of us and made me regret taking the job. In the application for her visa I submitted our marriage certificate from the church when I should have submitted the one from the government, and it was not possible to directly communicate with the British consulate. To cut a long story short, I lived alone in Leeds with my poor wife and daughter moving from one apartment to another in Sydney and changing the departure dates for their flights for four months. The education system in England was also different from what I had understood it to be before I arrived and really had no choice but to put my daughter in an elite independent school where she had her own problems adjusting, but received an excellent education.

For anyone reading this with an eye toward taking a leadership position overseas, I first suggest taking the time to check on all visa requirements and processes for anyone going with you. In terms of leadership, there is a limit to how much you can come to understand about cultural context and how the institution you will be working in operates. Upon arrival, get to know your environment – as much as you can. Take your time to understand both key and peripheral operations as well as the workplace and geographical cultures before making any significant changes. Proceed with confidence but with caution. Have vision, but be patient. Listen, look, and learn to be aware.

Reflection

In my story I reflect on experience shaped by the interaction of the external and objective environment and my internalised experiences as a learner (Dewey, 1963). Formal learning experiences of leadership, such as seminars or formal study in tertiary institutions, can contribute toward developing into a good academic leader, but prior experiences of leadership will shape and influence this formal learning and the sense we make of it in ways that are both conscious and non-conscious. Dewey (1997) suggests that the experiences we learn through are neither isolated nor restricted to formal education settings such as schools or universities but, instead, part of an experiential continuum. What we have learned, and the inclinations developed through this learning, shape current learning experiences that, in turn, shape our future experiences and learning. That is to say that all learning is shaped by prior experiences and shapes future experiences as part of a continuum that promotes the ongoing human growth of the individual. All individuals move through different situations, but some learning is always 'carried over' as an 'instrument of understanding' (Dewey, 1963, p. 44), which enables dealing with following situations and experiences in a process that continues as long as life and learning do. Accepting we are different and in different situations but with the globalisation of the world in mind, I encourage readers to give consideration to applying for overseas leadership positions.

Note

1 Teaching Games for Understanding (TGfU) is a learner and game centred model used by physical education teachers and sport coaches to teach and coach games.

References

Akinsanya, A. and Bach, C. (2014) Narrative analysis: The personal experience narrative approach.In:*Proceedings of ASEE 2014 Zone I Conference*, University of Bridgeport, Bridgeport, CT, USA, 3–5 April 2014. Available at: www.asee.org/documents/zones/zone1/2014/Student/PDFs/21.pdf.

Dewey, J. (1963) *Experience and education*. 2nd edn. New York: Collier Books.

Dewey, J. (1997) *Democracy and education: An introduction to the philosophy of education*. New York: Free Press.

Light, R. L. and Evans, J. R. (2018) *Stories of Indigenous success in Australian sport: Journeys to the AFL and NRL*. London: Palgrave Macmillan.

Light, R. L. and Harvey, S. (2019) *Positive pedagogy for sport coaching*. 2nd edn. London and New York: Routledge.

CHAPTER 5

Leading for learning
Building on values and teaching expertise to effect change

Kathleen M. Quinlan

In my model of leading for holistic learning in higher education (Quinlan, 2011, 2014),[1] I present three main dimensions of leadership to which educational leaders need to attend: (1) personal characteristics; (2) knowledge of teaching and learning; and (3) organisational conditions. These three dimensions, set within a wider social context, provide a development framework to help academics who are becoming educational leaders. This chapter illustrates and extends this model based on a project documenting the leadership experiences of newly recognised Senior Fellows of the Higher Education Academy (SFHEAs).[2]

Overview of the model: leading for holistic learning

This tripartite model of leading for learning was initially developed based on a review of literature on the elements of leadership shown to create environments supportive of holistic student learning and development in higher education (Quinlan, 2011). Initially, I argued for the importance of knowledge about learning and teaching in leading teaching for learning (Quinlan, 2011, 2014) and later applied the model to explain how programme leaders successfully led the development of two different complex, interdisciplinary master's programmes (Quinlan and Gantogtokh, 2018). In this chapter, I draw out the lessons this model offers for emerging leaders.

First, educational leaders already have their own identity, values, and purpose upon which to create a vision for modules, courses, or programmes. Through commitment and consistency around those values, they inspire others. It is important to consider how you can draw out the values that are already guiding your practice and use them to support you in acting authentically and intentionally (see Quinlan, in press, for more detail).

Second, effective educational leaders draw on expertise about teaching and learning and a scholarly approach to education to realise those visions with colleagues. If you are reading this book, you likely already have a wealth of expertise in learning and teaching. This knowledge is a vital foundation in educational leadership. Finally, to support planning and implementation, leaders also attend to the organisational conditions in which students and teachers are embedded. This third area is often new for academics shifting into leadership roles.

The project

This project involved interviewing 15 newly recognised SFHEAs about their understanding and experiences of becoming a leader in HE, as well as reviewing documents they wrote about their experiences. These data sources were read and discussed with two colleagues[3] alongside the model of leading for learning (Quinlan, 2014) to see how the model works in practice in a typical, contemporary UK university. Based on the data, I wrote short narratives relating to each aspect of the model. The project received ethical approval from the University of Kent (UK) and participants gave consent for their materials to be used under pseudonyms.

I start with a story of Luisa and will return to Luisa's story – and others – during the chapter to illustrate the model (Quinlan, 2011, 2014).

Questions to consider

- As you read this summary, consider: Is Luisa a leader? If so, how? Why do you deem her a leader?

Luisa is an academic in a UK university whose specialty is Catalan – a minority European language spoken in Catalonia, a region in northeast Spain. When she talks about her work, one can hear the passion and energy that underlies her academic practice. She writes: 'My love of languages and my pride in belonging to a very small diaspora [of UK-based Catalans] ensure that the students get the benefit of having direct contact with someone who has become an ambassador for her own native culture. This not only offers me the chance to put a stop to the othering of my people, but empowers students to … apply those insights to any other minority culture in which they become interested.' She has published on modern Catalan and Castilian poetry and theatre and its connections with other art forms. As part of this small diaspora of Catalans in the UK, she has also served as external examiner for many of the UK's programmes in Catalan. Over a six-year period, she 'organised and motivated a productive staff team' to develop the Department of Hispanic Studies from a language supplier (offering a Catalan options course as part of the Spanish programme) to one that offers its own honours degrees, MA programmes, and a doctoral programme. To support that growth, she managed, trained, and mentored visiting lecturers funded by the Catalan Autonomous government. She has used her contacts to develop exchange programmes and collaborations with both Catalan and Valencian Autonomous Governments, bring in guest speakers, and organise study tours.

Defining leadership

As alluded to in Chapter 1, we often think of leadership in managerial terms and reserve the term 'leader' for people who are in formal positions of authority. In the brief summary above, I have said nothing about Luisa's formal roles. As it happens, Luisa is now the Associate Dean for Education in her faculty. On the way to this position she served in various other formal leadership roles, both in her department and in her faculty. But her leadership neither rests in nor depends upon those formal roles. Instead, it is rooted deeply in her values, which have motivated her to build relationships, identify and exploit opportunities, and create conditions in which others – both students and teachers – can grow and develop.

Thinking of leadership in managerial terms, many academics distrust the concept and may be reluctant to call themselves leaders. This hesitation seems to be more than mere modesty. Higher education has a tradition of collegiality, self-regulation, and autonomy, which is usually set in contrast to managerialism (Tight, 2014), which is rising in higher education (Deem and Brehony, 2005). Leaders acting as managers who direct others or impose their will seems to contravene these traditional academic values of collegiality and autonomy.

Some formal definitions of leadership and many popular conceptions of leadership also tend to reinforce an impression of a heroic figure at the top, which is far from the traditional 'first *among equals*' conception of academic leadership. Many models of leadership, even those adopted formally by academic organisations, can also emphasise too strongly *planned* change in which leaders are 'driving' toward a clear set of predetermined outcomes. For example, '[Leadership is] agreeing strategic direction in discussion with others and communicating this within the organisation; ensuring that there is the capability, capacity and resources to deliver planned strategic outcomes; and supporting and monitoring delivery' (HEFCE, 2004, p. 35).

The HEFCE definition seems to assume a leader is in a formal role sanctioned by the organisation. In contrast, the notion of 'distributed leadership' focuses on influence and direction (not necessarily with predetermined strategic outcomes agreed) (Spillane, Halverson and Diamond, 2001). This kind of leadership, then, also encompasses intellectual leadership, role-modelling, mentoring, advocacy, being a guardian of academic values, or an ambassador of the university, which have all been associated with professorial leadership (Macfarlane, 2011). Distributed leaders are people located across an organisation who are having good ideas, engaging colleagues with those ideas, and using networks to stimulate debate and change. Thus, it involves many people interacting with each other, rather than a select few at the top.

Let's look at another definition that stretches this idea of distributed leadership even further. Alis Oancea described her role as a then-Research Fellow coordinating a Research Staff Forum in her department which raised awareness of the career development needs and concerns of post-docs and other early career researchers:

> This work exemplifies 'leadership', as research-driven, and built up from the ground. Collaboration, networking, and personal and collective investment of time into championing the relevant issues ... are key ... in this area of work ... aims are open to deliberation, and the grounds for authority are always shifting.

She concludes:

> what seems to matter in such activity is not 'leading' people towards given objectives, but: actively engaging with colleagues in a process of critical questioning of common values, customs, perceptions, and evidence; mobilising the knowledge, practices and resources available; and enabling the generation of new and creative developments.

Thus she casts the key activity of academic leadership as 'research-led' and 'actively engaging with colleagues in a process of critical questioning' (Oancea, 2011, p. 4).

Following from the notion of distributed leadership, I define leadership broadly as having a vision and bringing others along toward that vision through a set of actions. In Luisa's case, her vision is to 'put a stop to othering' minority cultures. By rallying others around this inspiring vision, they might, together, agree some ways they can realise that vision. Likewise, Oancea also emphasises 'championing the relevant issues'; that is, having and advancing a vision of creating a supportive environment in which postdoctoral researchers can grow and flourish.

> **Question to consider**
> - In what ways are you exercising leadership in your work?

These inclusive notions of leadership allow us to recast the core parts of academic practice as involving leadership, acknowledging the leadership activities of academics and professional services staff regardless of formal line management responsibilities or job titles. When researchers write a paper, they are putting out a thesis to be read by others with the hope of influencing future research. Researchers choose the actions for doing so: the research questions, the methods, the process of analysing and interpreting evidence that provides a thesis or answer to a question. That is, they have a vision and use a series of actions to bring others along with their vision, thesis, or conclusion.

Teachers in HE have authority, often making choices about who to teach, what to teach and what not to teach, how to teach it, what assessment standards and criteria to set, and how to assess whether students have met those standards. Teachers are – whether they are aware of it or not – role models for their students. Day after day, teachers stand up in front of 30, 50, 200, 500 young people who are in critical stages of building their own identity. Teachers show students new perspectives on the world and teach them new ways of making sense of that world. Thus, teachers are necessarily leaders, having an influence on many others.

Across their roles, academics have a vision, invite others to share that vision, and work toward it through a series of actions. Those actions are likely to involve, as Oancea (2011) argues, quintessentially academic activities such as critical questioning, and mobilising knowledge and other resources to generate something new.

Leadership actions also take place at various levels. One can exercise influence at the micro level through, for example, leading a class seminar or chairing a meeting with colleagues. At the meso level, one can design curricula for a whole module or course or lead or orient other members of the teaching team to the module or course goals. Or, at a macro level, leaders might influence a whole school, faculty, university, or field. Thinking about leadership at multiple levels also helps broaden the definition of leadership.

Model of leadership for student learning

In this section, I walk through a model of educational leadership (see Figure 5.1) I developed from a synthesis of research on leadership, particularly in higher education (Quinlan, 2014, 2011).

76 Kathleen M. Quinlan

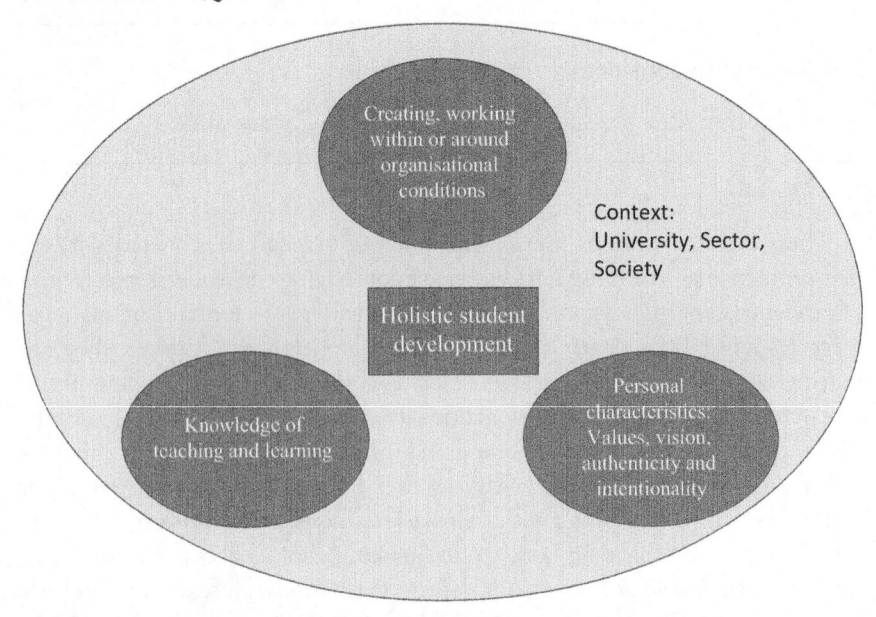

FIGURE 5.1 Dimensions of educational leadership
(Adapted from Quinlan, 2011)

In the centre of the model is the goal of student learning. Learning in this model is used in its broadest sense: not just acquiring knowledge or building skills, but helping students in their process of becoming as a person, building their own sense of identity and purpose. I have called this learning holistic student development (Quinlan, 2011). The model represents the three foundational pillars for enabling this kind of holistic student learning in higher education. These three pillars are situated, of course, within wider external conditions.

Personal characteristics: leaders' values, vision, and authenticity

I start here with the leader as a person. Academic work is a highly values-based activity (Harland and Pickering, 2011; Quinlan, 2016, 2019), so our actions as researchers, teachers, mentors, and leaders are based in our values, which are central to our identity and serve as guiding principles in our life (Schwartz, 1994). These values underpin our sense of purpose, allow us to create visions as leaders, and fuel intentional, sustained, autonomous commitment.

This sort of intentionality and authenticity is also vital in bringing people along willingly. No matter where leaders are situated in the organisation, they must be credible, demonstrate clarity of values, build unity of vision among the community, and hold these values intensely themselves (Kouzes and Posner, 2011). In higher education, academics most value personal integrity and trustworthiness in their leaders (Bolden, Petrov and Gosling, 2008). Fullan and Scott (2009, p. 102) concluded 'the ideal way to change a culture is for a critical mass of key leaders – centrally and locally – to intentionally model in their daily behaviours the attributes and capabilities they want the university to develop.'

> **Questions to consider**
> - Reflect on emotional episodes in your practice to uncover your values. Why did you feel that way? What values were being fulfilled or thwarted?

So, how can academics clarify their own values so they can authentically and intentionally lead with that sense of purpose? Emotions provide us with a good compass (Quinlan, 2019). Values and emotions are closely related insofar as positive emotions arise when people are able to act in accordance with their values to fulfil a moral purpose and negative emotions arise when people are thwarted from pursuing what matters to them. Emotions also play an important role in motivating people to act morally (Prinz and Nichols, 2010, p. 5). Thus, academics can look at aspects of their academic practice and consider emotional episodes, asking, 'What makes me angry or resentful? What makes me excited, proud, triumphant, fulfilled?' These feelings are clues to uncovering the values and purposes that motivate us. Looking back at Luisa, we hear her love of languages, her conviction about being a 'cultural ambassador', and her appreciation for the richness of minority cultures.

Catherine is another example:

> Catherine becomes excited as she talks about the importance of experiential learning as a way of supporting students' transformative learning. She has implemented a programme in criminology in which students learn about criminal justice in a local prison, alongside classmates who are prisoners there (15 university students; 15 inmates of the prison). It is structured as an exchange in which both students and inmates learn from and with each other. She talks animatedly about how students' conceptions of the criminal justice system are challenged by listening to inmates' experiences of and perceptions of the system. For Catherine, it is this process of seeing a social institution from another perspective that enables students to change. Prisoners are not just numbers or passive objects of public policy, but are able to formulate critiques of the system in which

they are caught. The programme treats them as experts from whom traditional students can learn. Their humanity is restored.

Catherine is expressing a powerful vision not only for education, but for how the prison system might work, which is revealed when we listen, not just to her words, but to the feelings of excitement and pride in which her words are wrapped. Both Luisa and Catherine are examples of how a deep love of their subject, what Anna Neumann (2006) called 'passionate thought', compels their actions.

Academic values, while seemingly individual, are often tied to disciplines, which have their own values embedded in them (Quinlan, 2016), as reflected in the UK's Quality Assurance benchmark statements for each discipline. Like the proverbial fish who doesn't know what water is, these values are often tacit for academics. It can be useful to discuss these benchmark statements across disciplines to expose what is special about a given field and to help in articulating these implicit values.

In articulating values, educators can also turn to various frameworks of professional ethics, such as the UK Professional Standards Framework (UK PSF) (Higher Education Academy, 2011), the Staff and Educational Development Association Professional Development Framework and Values (Staff and Educational Development Association, 2019), or the Society for Teaching and Learning in Higher Education's ethical principles (1996). In fact, formal recognition through the Higher Education Academy, which has become increasingly popular not only in the UK, but other parts of the world, requires engagement with the values stated in the UK PSF. These value statements are necessarily broadly defined so as to address teaching in a wide range of disciplines and institutional contexts. As such, they are unlikely to have the power or immediacy that internally generated, personalised statements of values are likely to have (Quinlan, in press). Nevertheless, one's personal purposes can often be fitted into or matched to the more generic frameworks of professional ethics. In Catherine's case, her motives, though expressed in different language, are clearly consistent with 'promoting participation in higher education and equality of opportunity for learners'.

Question to consider

- What are you most passionate about in your teaching, research, or service?

Instructional leadership: knowledge of learning and teaching

Having a passion, a purpose, or a vision is foundational. But effective implementation to support students' holistic learning and development also requires knowledge about learning and the teaching methods that support student learning and holistic development (see Quinlan, 2011).

> Question to consider
> - How are you building on what is known about promoting learning?

In the primary and secondary school leadership literature, scholars have debated which leadership types produce enhanced student outcomes. A transformational model of leadership, emphasizing personal characteristics such as those in the previous section, is assumed to work by creating positive relationships and environments (Leithwood, 2006). In contrast, instructional leadership focuses on instruction itself more than people and relationships (Robinson, Lloyd and Rowe, 2008). A meta-analysis of 27 studies showed that the instructional leadership model is three to four times more effective than the transformational model (Robinson, Lloyd and Rowe, 2008). Educational improvement is most likely to occur when department heads get involved in instructional development activities alongside teachers in their schools, taking part in professional development opportunities, visiting classrooms, and reviewing data about student performance. Therefore, to create an environment for student learning, educational leaders need to understand something about learning and teaching and must work alongside other members of the team, especially those who are closest to students, reviewing data and evidence and learning and supporting teachers in implementing solutions that address performance gaps. While necessary, it is not sufficient just to be a credible person with an inspirational vision (Robinson, Lloyd and Rowe, 2008).

Ned provides a good example of applying best practices to design an innovative teaching approach, illustrating an instructional leadership model (Robinson, Lloyd and Rowe, 2008):

> Ned is a historian who led the redesign of a second-year undergraduate course in American Studies. A major challenge of American Studies is making it truly interdisciplinary. He explained a process of backward educational design which started by thinking about what is core to American Studies, clarifying the key learning outcomes: 'I think in terms of what American Studies should be delivering, so students working with skillsets in different disciplines in film, music, history, literature.' He framed his job

as module leaders as 'trying to blend those [different disciplines] together effectively within the confines of a 12-week term'. Continuing through backward design, he noticed that there had been an over-reliance on traditional essays, and 'there hadn't been a lot of creative thinking or application of best practice in terms of mixing up the assessment or assignment balance'. He introduced new assessments focused around 'reputations' in which students chose an American person or place and used multiple sources to explain how it gained its reputation: '[students] can pick individuals, you can pick famous presidents or unknowns, you can pick places like the Grand Canyon or Wall Street, and you can get students to think about how their reputations had evolved. And in the process of doing that, almost inherently, you have to access different disciplines and different media [ensuring] the teaching can be genuinely cross-disciplinary.' He goes on to acknowledge that he was asking a lot, not just of students, but of colleagues, 'by insisting that the lecturers and the seminar tutors have to fully immerse themselves, they can't just straightforwardly teach their discipline and then claim that the students are being inter-disciplinary. ... You're constantly in this dance of trying to cajole people, seduce people in to kind of co-deliver a module.' He set up the module so that each lecturer, regardless of discipline, had ownership of that week and then he 'really work[ed] hard with them to make sure that that week is inter-disciplinary and that the readings are appropriate and that we're not submerging students in material'.

Ned used a process of backward instructional design, transforming the assessment requirements to leverage changes in teaching and learning. He then worked intensively alongside teachers to help them re-align their teaching with those outcomes and assessments, creating a truly interdisciplinary experience. In sum, to enact their values, educational leaders need knowledge of teaching and learning.

Creating organisational conditions

The third dimension of the educational leadership model focuses on creating organisational conditions for these kinds of rich teaching methods to flourish. While the second dimension focuses on specific teaching practices that promote learning, this third dimension shifts to the organisational environment within which that teaching and learning occur.

For this final dimension of the model, there is more research on the macro level of university leadership than there is at the meso (programme) level. Based on case studies of universities where holistic student learning is a central purpose, Braskamp and his colleagues (2006) found that there was intentionality in aligning culture, curriculum, co-curriculum, and a sense of community. In terms of culture and community, these campuses had a strong sense of shared, institutional mission evident in the repetition of key phrases across the whole community to describe who they are and what they do, such as, 'Enter to learn, depart to serve,' 'We exist for students and for learning,' 'Living and learning in community,' and 'We challenge and support our students.' These campuses also promoted culture and community through programmes of induction and ongoing professional development for academics and by structuring learning environments to promote interactions among students and between students and staff, both in and outside of classes. Curricula offered learning experiences such as first-year seminars or final-year projects or seminars. The co-curriculum was designed to support students to engage in supplemental or non-credit-bearing activities that connect and extend their classroom learning.

There is less research on programme leaders and course or module leaders, where many educational leaders in higher education begin their leadership journeys. In the example above, Ned created organisational conditions through the way he designed the 12-week course. He structured it so that each lecturer had ownership of a week-long unit and charged them with addressing educational outcomes he had set. This structure promoted buy-in by enabling each academic the freedom and creativity to design something that respected their expertise, while also contributing to larger course aims.

As Ned's case suggests, the line between instructional leadership and creating organisational conditions blurs as one gets closer to the coal face of teaching. Nevertheless, this dimension of the model prompts one to think not just about the design of teaching as experienced by students, but also of the ways design features are experienced by members of the teaching team. Ned might have used other structures, such as team-teaching throughout each unit, to ensure interdisciplinary learning experiences. Instead, he designed this particular structure to build buy-in of colleagues through week-by-week ownership, while concentrating minds on a common set of interdisciplinary learning outcomes and assessment tasks. As such, he was manipulating the organisational conditions of teaching, not just the curricular design for learning.

In a study of interdisciplinary master's programmes in a research-intensive university in the UK (Quinlan and Gantogtokh, 2018), successful programme leaders created organisational conditions in a variety of ways. They lined up and supported the right people to lead particular modules and courses, set up communication structures, encouraged pilot studies and created forums for sharing the results of those pilots, created forums for cross-course collaboration and professional development, sought evidence on what was working, and, when matters couldn't be resolved by consensus, they took difficult decisions. They worked very hard at creating a 'learning culture' within their teams, taking a non-defensive attitude, involving all staff and emphasising collaboration and human processes. So, at the meso level in a research-intensive, collegial university with new programmes, a key role of leaders was to create the organisational conditions that would support teaching and learning innovation (Quinlan and Gantogtokh, 2018). These leaders, though, were in the position of creating entirely new courses. Thus, they were working with relatively blank sheets of paper and were also supported strongly by heads of department who had invested a great deal in the success of those new courses.

> **Questions to consider**
> - You have a great idea for innovating teaching in your programme, department, or faculty. What systems, processes, or procedures need to be changed (or worked around or through) in order to implement it? Is the perceived barrier *really* a barrier?

Creating supportive organisational conditions may be more difficult in environments where one is trying to make a change in an existing course, in situations that are bureaucratic and tightly constrained, or where the leader does not already have the official sanction of leaders higher up in the organisation. In these cases, leaders' autonomy is more restricted, making it more difficult to manoeuvre. It may be more of a case of 'working with' and 'working around' organisational constraints than designing new organisational conditions. For example, Ross discussed bureaucratic constraints at some length in his interview:

> Ross is an academic in political science who has held a variety of service and leadership roles in his department, including Director of Education. He has designed an innovative, award-winning module on resistance that asks students to experiment with acts of resistance. He applies his disciplinary expertise to an analysis of the higher education context, expressing commitment to resistance in his educational leadership role. He observes that over the past 20 years, 'there was a change of culture in higher education' from a group of colleagues working together in an 'insular' environment to being 'providers of services where we have customers and clients and targets and so on and are subjected to all kinds of audits ... I think in terms of leadership, I've always tried as much as possible to hold onto the old values.' He wishes he had developed

more 'self-understanding' as a young teacher, rather than being 'so overwhelmed by short-term targets and aims which were externally given, and maybe not particularly meaningful'. In mentoring junior colleagues, he now aspires to help them gain greater control over their personal development as teachers and scholars. He reflects on how he might harness and direct younger colleagues' personal aspirations and ambitions, turning their complaints about the system into action, sometimes through forms of creative resistance. He explains that, because the bureaucratic system emphasises technicalities, such as submitting the right form to the right place to the right deadline, there's 'a huge space for creative subversion. Because as long as you fill out the form correctly, you can pretty much do what you want.' Although it requires work, effort and a bit of courage to experiment within those bureaucratic boundaries, 'there's really no excuse for not looking for these opportunities.' In short, he sees room for manoeuvring within organisational constraints and his job as looking for ways to exploit that wiggle room.

In another example of exploiting the spaces-in-between, Luisa, who is on a teaching-focused contract rather than a teaching and research contract, is not expected or supported to do research as it is traditionally understood. She agreed to these contract terms on the condition that she would still be able to take study leave. However, when she then applied for study leave to do some research overseas, her request was denied. She felt as if she was working in a no-win situation. However, when she reframed her study leave to show the benefit to her *educational* role, the study leave was then granted. While this example may not be 'subversive', it involved seeing opportunities within organisational constraints.

Wider environmental context

Ned's case example highlights that much of what leaders do in higher education depends upon the larger context in which they are operating. Highly managerial and marketised university contexts can sometimes create value conflicts for individual academics, making it more difficult to develop academic identities (Archer, 2008; Clegg, 2008). This model of leadership (Quinlan, 2014) does not deny these wider contexts; rather, it focuses on how leaders can exercise agency and increase their spheres of influence within their wider contexts. Reflecting on one's core values (Quinlan, in press), together with critical analysis of those contexts, can help identify wiggle room within organisational rules. Grounding oneself in one's own values and purposes, while building knowledge of teaching and learning, also enables educational leaders to take actions that challenge those rules and constraints.

Conclusion

In sum, this model of educational leadership (Quinlan, 2014) presents three main spheres that emerging higher education leaders can focus on developing: themselves, their knowledge of learning and teaching, and a critical and creative approach to setting up organisational conditions that facilitate movement toward improvement. The narratives in the chapter show how these three dimensions play out in practice and offer points of departure for readers to reflect on their own practice.

Notes

1 I have concentrated on educational leadership in explicating this framework. However, the same general categories might be easily adapted to research leadership by shifting the focus from instructional leadership to research leadership. The central aim then shifts from holistic student learning to high-quality or impactful research. Exploring this application to research leadership is beyond the scope of this short chapter.
2 Senior Fellows of the Higher Education Academy (SFHEAs) have met a set of criteria defined by the UK Professional Standards Framework (UKPSF) for teaching and supporting learning in higher education. Senior Fellows are recognised in the HE community as professionals committed to enhancing teaching, learning, and the student experience: www.heacademy.ac.uk.
3 I thank Julia Hope and Silvia Colaiacomo for sharing their data and insights.

References

Archer, L. (2008). Younger academics' Constructions of 'Authenticity', 'Success' and Professional identity. *Studies in Higher Education*, 33(4), pp. 385–403. doi:10.1080/03075070802211729

Bolden, R., Petrov, G., and Gosling, J. (2008). Tensions in higher education leadership: Towards a multi-level model of leadership practice. *Higher Education Quarterly*, 62(4), pp. 358–376. doi:10.1111/j.1468-2273.2008.00398.x

Braskamp, L. A., Trautvetter, L. C., and Ward, K. (2006). *Putting students first: How colleges develop students purposefully*. Boston, MA: Anker Publishing.

Clegg, S. (2008). Academic identities under threat? *British Educational Research Journal*, 34(3), pp. 329–345. doi:10.1080/01411920701532269

Deem, R. and Brehony, K. J. (2005). Management as ideology: The case of 'new managerialism' in higher education. *Oxford Review of Education*, 31(2), pp. 217–235. doi:10.1080/03054980500117827

Fullan, M. and Scott, G. (2009). *Turnaround leadership in higher education*. San Francisco, CA: Jossey-Bass.

Harland, T. and Pickering, N. (2011). *Values in higher education teaching*. Abingdon: Routledge.

Higher Education Academy. (2011). *UK professional standards framework for teaching and supporting learning in higher education*. York: Higher Education Academy, Guild HE, Universities UK.

Higher Education Funding Council of England (HEFCE). (2004). *HEFCE Strategic Plan 2003-08 (Revised April 2004)*. London: HEFCE.

Kouzes, J. M. and Posner, B. Z. (2011). *Credibility: How leaders gain and lose it, why people demand it* (Vol 203). San Francisco, CA: John Wiley & Sons.

Leithwood, K. (2006). *Seven strong claims about school leadership*. Washington, DC: Department for Education and Skills, National College for School Leadership.

Macfarlane, B. (2011). Professors as intellectual leaders: Formation, identity and role. *Studies in Higher Education*, 36(1), pp. 57–73. doi:10.1080/03075070903443734

Neumann, A. (2006). Professing passion: Emotion in the scholarship of professors at research universities. *American Educational Research Journal*, 43(3), pp. 381–424. doi:10.3102/00028312043003381

Oancea, A. (2011, Hilary Term). *Illuminatio: From the Oxford learning institute*. Oxford: University of Oxford.

Prinz, J. J. and Nichols, S. (2010). Moral emotions. In J.M. Doris ed. *The moral psychology handbook*. Oxford: Oxford University Press, pp. 111–146.

Quinlan, K. M. (2011). Developing the whole student: Leading higher education initiatives that integrate mind and heart. Leadership Foundation for Higher Education Stimulus Paper. Available at: www.lfhe.ac.uk/en/research-resources/publications/index.cfm/ST%20-%2001

Quinlan, K. M. (2014). Leadership of teaching for student learning in higher education: What is needed? *Higher Education Research and Development*, 33(1), pp. 32–45. doi:10.1080/07294360.2013.864609

Quinlan, K. M. (2016). Developing student character through disciplinary curricula: An analysis of UK QAA subject benchmark statements. *Studies in Higher Education*, 41(6), pp. 1041–1054. doi:10.1080/03075079.2014.966069

Quinlan, K. M. (2019). Emotion and moral purposes in higher education teaching: Poetic case examples of teacher experiences. *Studies in Higher Education*, 44(9), pp. 1662–1675. doi:10.1080/03075079.2018.1458829

Quinlan, K. M. (in press). Teaching values: Ethical and emotional attunement through an educational humanities approach. *Educational Developments*.

Quinlan, K. M. and Gantogtokh, O. (2018). Lessons in programme leadership from two cases of designing new interdisciplinary master's programmes. In J. Lawrence and S. Ellis eds. *Supporting programme leaders and program leadership: SEDA Special 39*. London: Staff and Educational Development Association, pp. 15–19.

Robinson, V. M. J., Lloyd, C. A., and Rowe, K. J. (2008). The impact of leadership on student outcomes: An analysis of the differential effects of leadership types. *Educational Administration Quarterly*, 44(5), pp. 635–674. doi:10.1177/0013161X08321509

Schwartz, S. H. (1994). Are there universal aspects in the structure and contents of human values? *Journal of Social Issues*, 50(4), pp. 19–45. doi:10.1111/j.1540-4560.1994.tb01196.x

Society for Teaching and Learning in Higher Education. (1996). Ethical principles. Available at: www.stlhe.ca/awards/3m-national-teaching-fellowships/initiatives/ethical-principles-in-university-teaching/ [Accessed 29 February 2020].

Spillane, J., Halverson, R., and Diamond, J. (2001). *Towards a theory of leadership practice: A distributed perspective.* Chicago, IL: Northwestern University Institute for Policy Research Working Article.

Staff and Educational Development Association. (2019). The SEDA-PDF and values [online]. Available at: www.seda.ac.uk/seda-values-and-pdf [Accessed 30 November 2019].

Tight, M. (2014). Collegiality and managerialism: A false dichotomy? Evidence from the higher education literature. *Tertiary Education and Management,* 20(4), pp. 294–306. doi:10.1080/13583883.2014.956788

CHAPTER 6

Leading complex educational systems
Kendall Jarrett and John Baumber

The actions of educational leaders are often viewed by those who they serve within a continuum of effectiveness: from purposeful and charismatic trailblazing to systematic corruption of educational ideals. For leaders of complex, multi-site educational institutions, or *systems*, there is the added pressure of having leadership effectiveness viewed at multiple points concurrently on that continuum. For educators tasked with leading a system of multiple educational institutions or sites, a 'treasure trove of talent, cultural diversity, ideas and innovation' is available to build a legacy of educational success (Groenwald, 2017, p. 140). Yet prior to such successes, an appreciation of the complexities of system leadership is paramount, along with an understanding of the unique challenges that such a responsibility presents.

The multi-site and multi-institution (system) landscape

There are various types of multi-site institutions and multi-institution systems currently in operation in education contexts. A multi-site institution (e.g. more than one campus) could be the result of a voluntary or forced merger, a partnership or alliance, a growth opportunity in response to demand (e.g. the development of a satellite campus), or an entirely new multi-site institution being built (Groenwald, 2017; Pinheiro and Nordstrand Berg, 2017). A multi-institutional system (e.g. State University of New York or University of London) is composed of a number of institutions, 'often with each having multiple campuses, yet all under one overarching (system-wide) authority' (Pinheiro and Nordstrand Berg, 2017, p. 6).

There are a number of benefits aligned to multi-site and multi-institution systems. As Lee and Bowen (1971) stated nearly five decades ago, a multi-campus institution has an opportunity to enhance specialisation, promote diversity, and showcase coordination. A decade ago, in an analysis of emerging expansion trends in US universities, Moody's Investors Service (2011)[1] stated that the geographic spread of sites can assist economies of scale and enhance brand recognition. In recent times, however, articles published by Times Higher Education[2] in the UK (e.g. Grove's (2015) article 'Has the multi-campus university had its day?') and by EvoLLLution[3] in the US (e.g. 'The future of multi-campus institutions') provide a more balanced view of the multi-site and multi-institution landscape. At a time of significant change in the higher education 'product' that is being made available to students, such a balanced view should be coveted by those responsible for the leadership and decision-making that influences multi-site and multi-institution planning and effectiveness.

Unique leadership challenges

With a number of HEIs having expanded campus footprints, both domestically and/or internationally, maintaining and enhancing an institution's educational charge across multiple sites presents a unique range of leadership challenges. Yet there exists limited commentary exploring multi-site leadership challenges in modern-day tertiary settings. In Groenwald's (2017) summary of the unique challenges multi-site leaders in HE face, leader autonomy issues were reported to be at the forefront of tensions – and with good reason, as autonomy and centralisation are often considered opposing forces (Timberlake, 2004). Indeed, 'relocating power and resources to a different entity can be fraught with difficulty and can lead to fractious power games' (Fraser and Stott, 2015, p. 80). Furthermore, across any multi-site system of education, there is an increase in the risk of 'inconsistent teaching, academic outcomes, and interpretation and implementation of policy' (Groenwald, 2017, p. 139).

Question to consider

- Through what means do leaders in your institution 'shorten the distance' between themselves and colleagues they lead?

It is of vital importance then to 'develop governance that accommodates the likely tensions between the central office and campuses, the main campus and satellite campus, or among campuses in a constructive manner' (Groenwald, 2017, p. 197). Increased leader distance, additional layers of administration and communication, the pursuit of uniformity without consideration of context, and a lack of consensus around a common vision and strategy can all have a significant impact on academic outcomes, campus identity, and institutional reputation. Thus, as previously intimated in this chapter, leadership practices at all levels across a multi-site institution or multi-institution system 'necessitates a fine balancing act' (Fraser and Stott, 2015, p. 82).

System leadership

In the UK, since the early 2000s, there has been significant growth in the number of executive headships[4] operating in primary and secondary schools across the country. The prevalence of such positions was initially brought about by a change in mainstream educational policy that encouraged formal cooperation between schools (Hopkins et al., 2014; Morrison, 2013). More recently, the need for such leadership structures has been amplified by reported individual school funding shortages – a trend, though, not as common in multi-academy trusts.[5] This growth in 'system leadership' is summarised in a 2015 Department of Education report:

> Evidence on the growth and diversity of system leadership suggests the notion of school leadership is shifting from the traditional concept of institutional leadership, whereby the headteacher is responsible for a single school, to educational leadership, implying a much broader sphere of responsibility encompassing multiple schools and educational well-being across wider geographical boundaries.
>
> (Armstrong, 2015, p. 3)

As Hopkins and Higham (2007) and Fullan (2004) discussed over a decade ago, the emerging need for system leadership in primary and secondary settings helped to respond to the need for system transformation and improvement. So, what of system leadership in higher education? With the offering of HE courses run on multiple campuses (e.g. multiple domestic campuses such as Deakin University or a combination of domestic and international campuses such as University of Nottingham), or across a network of providers (e.g. Ulster University quality-assuring the delivery of their academic courses across a range of external providers), there is a degree of synergy in leadership requirements. With limited empirical research available exploring the requirements of system leadership in HE settings (see Gerald, 2014; Groenwald, 2017; Stringer and Hudson, 2008), we advocate for the sharing of system leaders' perspectives drawn from primary and/or secondary collaborations to inform understanding.

Being a system leader

By John Baumber

To be able to draw ideas and learning from my own journey as a system leader, I need to first give some context. When I first became a head teacher in 1988, the UK Government were just thinking about local management of schools and heads had little autonomy over budgets or school structures. Over the next two years the whole system changed radically (based on a political decision to reduce the impact and control of local education authorities), giving leaders and their governors the opportunity to significantly shape their schools through new executive and strategic decision-making powers.

Mine was a secondary state school in proximity to another, a regally named ex-grammar school. Although that distinction had long passed, it had not in the perception of parents. I quickly decided that this perception was more than just about our schools but actually about the community, so we set about creating an active partnership between the schools (primary, middle, and high) and the local community (churches, voluntary groups, and businesses). We wanted a proud community that saw its future in their own hands.

The success of this network after ten years was plainly evident. The school had a rising roll; it was named as one of the five most successful schools by the Chief Inspector of Schools, we built an arts centre, and developed a thriving music and drama tradition. To cap it all off, the Queen came to visit for a day. We[6] called our strategy Proud to be Prudhoe, and the success and raised expectation went through every school.

But in this rapidly changing culture for schools we made mistakes and, when reflecting on the task of leading a network of education institutions, should have done some things differently.

Ten years on, I became head of Rivington and Blackrod High School in Bolton. A school established in 1564, at the heart of a community but also one of the biggest schools in the country with nearly 2,000 students. Big enough, you would think, to be enough of a job. But four years on we established a hard federation with a neighbouring high school that had been deemed to be consistently failing to improve. I had to close the school and reopen it in partnership. At the time, there was no guiding legislation on partnership schools nor multi-academy trusts (e.g. a formalised partnership of a group of schools, including both primary and secondary). My role as executive head teacher did not exist in local authority structures or job descriptions. Along with other parallel professionals, we made it up as we went along. A year later, another school joined the partnership.

In the first year of my headship I attended a leadership residential; it was fascinating for a new, young head teacher to have some sight of what the job he'd been appointed to might be and what skills he'd need to develop. But one thing really resonated with me: you have to move forward on a wide range of fronts. School development is not sequential, but complex, and operates in a frustratingly chaotic environment. My job was to clarify what was important and communicate the direction. But I also took this to mean you should not become an island cut off from other communities, and other thinking.

> **Question to consider**
> - How often in your practice as a leader or when aspiring to lead do you consider an international perspective to inform your decision-making?

So, we took advantage of a new initiative from the National College of School Leadership – the Networked Learning Community project. We built a partnership across four school communities of primary and secondary schools. We also embraced two other international school networks in Sweden (Kunskapsskolan) and South Africa (Atteridgeville Outreach). This international dimension gave us an opportunity to think and reflect on practice freed from local or national constraints and why in very different cultures they achieve outcomes in totally different ways. Thus, our aim was to make sure that we continued to learn and reflect on our own practice as we developed the effectiveness of our own organisation. Often, schools who face challenging times 'hunker down' and close down external links and opportunities. For me such links have always fuelled progress and ideas, and brought energy and excitement to the faculty.

After another ten years, I moved to Sweden to work as a head teacher inside a group of 38 free schools.[7] This was a very different network, where all schools followed the same curriculum and pedagogical approach. The network was managed centrally with a range of common services from finance to HR, marketing to site management. From this I moved to be CEO of a new multi-academy trust (MAT) sponsored by Kunskapsskolan with four academies.

I promised to do this for three years and then moved to a more relaxed part-time position. Very quickly I found myself managing a network of over 20 schools that were inspired by our pedagogical approach. This, in a way, completed a circular journey from building communities of independent schools who come together to share benefits and expertise through to hard federations and MATs, then back again to a partnership who share common values and support for one another.

So, what is there to learn from these experiences of system leadership? It is important to recognise why people and learning institutions come together in the first place. This can be because:

1. Educational institutions have huge delegated responsibilities and some, especially smaller institutions, face reduced service allocation and limited professional capital to manage all aspects of learning management. Partnering with other institutions allows for shared services and

economies of scale. This has been especially important since the UK Government's austerity measures in 2010 and its impact on school budgets. Partnering with successful institutions is a way failing institutions can be supported.
2. It is now more likely to be considered the 'norm' that new educational institutions begin life as part of a partnership rather than trying to work independently.

Embodied in each of the two reasons above, though, should be the desires to learn from one another, learn with one another, and learn on behalf of others. So, a third reason is less about school management and hard alliances, but more about institutional partnerships that share a common vision and practice. It is also vitally important that the underpinning foundation of system leadership remains school improvement, rather than just organisational efficiency and sustainability.

System leaders generally have roles that keep them out of the classroom, but they must demonstrate a clear commitment to and deep understanding of students' learning. System leaders must develop a capacity in their schools that focuses on improving learning based on well-researched and proven strategies built on the school's shared values. It is too easy to layer on the latest learning framework or system as another initiative. Leaders need to understand what will enhance learning in their own context. Only by being a confident pedagogue can a system leader make these judgements.

System leaders must be adaptable and pragmatic, especially when managing a range of very different learning sites. But that does not mean that they dilute core principles. Effective system leaders understand and deploy the power of moral purpose to motivate and mobilise others. They achieve a sense of security by doing 'the right thing' even if the way to achieve those values – such as inclusion and equity – require differing strategies and approaches in different schools/sites.

System leaders should be conscious of their own leadership practice and its effects on others. It enables them to articulate thinking and planning processes in a way that stimulates their own learning at the same time as inviting others to contribute. In this way, they can create opportunities for collaborative activity around them. System leaders need to be able to delegate, but in so doing need to know that what happens as a result should match the values and practices of the whole organisation. In other words, consistency and clarity are maintained. These aspects are important whether leaders operate in a formal or informal network.

Reflecting on my personal contexts of system leadership and the realities of learning my role on the job, I make the following key points that I have taken from my journey:

1. Hero leadership

Creating that community aspiration across 12 schools and a range of other town groups took a lot of personal energy and time and an infectious and compelling belief that this would happen. When this leads to an old English mining town feeling proud and eventually a visit from the Queen, inevitably people try to put you on a pedestal. Actually, they are only too happy for you to take the strain in order to make their job and use of resources easier. There has to be a point of transition from the inspiration and bidding to the implementation phase. So once funding is secured, finding the right person to take on the business management of projects is essential, as different skills are needed to implement, as opposed to develop, strategy.

I never fully made the transition from the project champion to the sustainer in those early days and as such some institutions became happy to remain overly dependent on the system rather than be active partners. Partnerships need to be sustained and people need to be reminded of the mission and of the cooperative advantages. Not everyone can benefit the same and at the same time.

Believing you are that hero leader is even worse and destroys the collaborative nature of the partnership. Jim Collins in *Good to Great* describes the sort of leadership required as 'building enduring greatness through a paradoxical blend of personal humility and professional will' (2001).

2. Creativity versus conformity

Moving towards a more formal partnership (e.g. a multi-academy trust) or business running a group of schools (e.g. Kunskapsskolan in Sweden) requires systems that work across each learning institution. Finding the balance of central as opposed to devolved services is tricky and different in every system.

If partnerships are formed through the underperformance of one or multiple institutions, the system leader has to be quite ruthless in driving forward new approaches often brought from more successful elements of existing or alternative partnerships. Institutions doing their own thing, even if there is a common set of values, makes this process of effective partnership even more challenging. Kunskapsskolan started their schools from scratch. They built them around a common pedagogical principle with centralised business functions. In so doing, they brought people together to develop practice, and more importantly benchmarked all elements of performance. If people all work in the same way but there are different outcomes, you can more easily explore what is happening.

Many systems try to build this structure from a starting point for a set of very disparate institutions. Head teachers in stand-alone schools have much authority to shape their school, so joining a system is a big deal and they are often concerned that they are giving away too much autonomy and the very culture of their school. This is a real risk, and leaders of systems need to take care that they do not believe that practices that have been successful in one school will automatically work in another with an entirely different context.

Questions to consider

- What assumptions about failure have you made when leading?
- What mechanisms could you use as a leader to check the vagrancy of such assumptions?

Even with schools that are in difficulty, it is better to do a critical analysis to identify successful practices that can be maintained, rather than assuming everything is failing. In fact, there is often practice in all schools that could inform the wider group. These decisions are fundamental to the feeling of ownership and self-worth that schools need to be able to succeed. The school we restarted had eight years of government scrutiny and termly visits from inspectors and suffered from institutional depression and a blame culture.[8] Creating an intrinsic motivation in such schools is vitally important.

So, creating conformity and synchronicity in a partnership is very important, but not at the expense of reducing talents. It is important to remember, though, that 'no-one should leave idle ideas about what works, for whom and in what circumstances' (Anderson, 2012, p. 328).

Kunskapsskolan clearly have real conformity of practice and their success draws on this and a constant review of practice and progress that drives further innovation and improvements. A lot of time is spent pulling school leaders and curriculum leads together and engaging them in the whole journey. But with such conformity there is always a risk that they do not encourage new practice in each of their schools, and as such teachers descend into just following the protocols and manuals and losing the rationale and reasons why!

Working with 20 schools in the UK inspired by Kunskapsskolan's educational philosophies is challenging because of the different practices and curriculum decisions they make. But it is also empowering because there is never a meeting where there isn't something new and innovating to share. Schools that learn are always willing to change practice to achieve even better outcomes. Balancing creativity and conformity is the biggest challenge in managing multiple institutions.

3. Fast failures

System leaders may have skills to motivate and set clear values and expectations, but they can also be ruthless in their decisions, for instance in excluding people or schools where values are clearly not shared. Schools that simply do not own or follow the principles of a partnership can become a real drain on the network. Within such systems/federations there comes a point when it's about changing the leader. But in voluntary networks it's about expelling them from the group. Coordinators are often reluctant to do this. They want to be optimistic and, having invested heavily up to that point, it feels like a sense of failure for them. But my experience of delaying it often gives succour to the discontent. Taking a tougher approach to expectations protects the heart of the network and creates a greater sense of discipline within the members. Inevitably, when a school joins a partnership or federation, it is wise to spend some time exploring what works well and who contributes to the school's successes – who shares the values and directions of the partnership. But this can go on too long and it is important to recognise those people and those strategies that are not going to get the school where it needs to be. Trying or recognising different approaches is great to give ownership and build an enterprising culture. But if it clearly isn't going to work, make it a fast failure and move on.

> **Question to consider**
> - What have been the implications within your institution of delayed fast failure recognition?

System leaders from around the world

It is important, now, not just to consider one perspective on system leadership, but a range of perspectives to test and debate practice for the betterment of leadership development. We asked three system leaders operating in the UK, South Africa, and globally to share their own experiences of leading complex organisations and systems, to reveal their biggest leadership challenges as well as the non-negotiables upon which their leadership practice was built.

Cecilia Carnefeldt – President and CEO of the Swedish education organization Kunskapsskolan, with more than 100 schools globally in their network
Glynn Hambling – CEO Unity Education Trust in the UK, a multi-academy trust operating a number of schools and units (i.e. resourced provision for children challenged by mainstream school provision)
Thana Peinaar – Executive Head at Prestige College School in South Africa

Building a network

When asked to consider what leadership strategies are important to her when building networked schools, Cecilia spoke of the need for consistency of purpose and practice, which required a clear vision for the network to be established from the beginning. This vision required a commitment from all stakeholders to achieve similar goals and an understanding of what those goals meant at both school and individual level. Seeing this vision *come alive* was paramount in order to benefit from the efficiencies of a network.

Glynn's emphasis as CEO was to spend enormous energy and time in each setting to understand the many issues, known and unknown to each school, to find aspects of practice and policy to support and challenge. He invested in developing authentic lines of communication across the trust by making it clear how line management would work and what meetings were required to support communication effectiveness. Time and resource were invested into developing learning and management teams across and within schools, with the development of an effective professional service team seen as a priority to provide first-class school management support.

Thana's experience of building a network of schools began with the building of one school. With one matriculation class, she and her colleagues invested in student learning. On the back of students achieving unprecedented high results, the school grew through the adding of additional year groups. Word got around. Thana was subsequently approached about franchising this highly successful education brand. 'If you have a winning recipe, it is selfish not to share it,' she was told. Thus, consideration was given to 'How can we make this work?' and 'How can we continue to lead and manage our school whilst at the same time make ourselves available to other schools?' With the vision and day-to-day operations now established at the first school, Thana envisaged her role in building a network of *Prestige* brand schools as being focused on training staff, mentoring principals, and assisting each school to find solutions to issues in line with *The Prestige Way*. Ultimately, she saw her role as one in the background, overseeing the network as a whole.

The biggest challenge in developing/leading a network

For Thana, prior to the challenge of establishing a network, the biggest challenge she faced at her first school was getting students to believe in themselves. It was only after out-performing more privileged schools at a regional sporting event that students started to 'believe they could do it'. To help further develop this belief, the school introduced chess as their first inter-mural activity and employed a high-profile chess coach. 'We focused on this and we made them believe they could do it. Since then, we are now feared!' However, after the success of the founding school, the challenges of network establishment quickly became apparent. Working with other principals who had ideas and ideals fundamentally different from Thana's meant consistent division. These divisions in vision and thinking were exacerbated by the franchising organisation's seemingly alternative agenda. For example, agreements were made in discussion, such as budgets, but when received on paper were markedly different. It was apparent to Thana that someone who was not an educator was making decisions on class size and layout of the new schools. She quickly lost respect for their systems and eventually pulled out of the franchise agreement.

Cecilia described a range of challenges. At the beginning, it was important to stay true to core values but still be able to adapt to local circumstances. Operating globally in such a variety of formats, in many different legal situations, with different partnerships and cultures, meant constant negotiation and compromise. When considering the question, 'Where do you draw the line regarding non-negotiables?' she responded with the view that 'determining what local adaptation is warranted as opposed to what is required is forever a challenge'.

One of the main challenges for Glynn related to stepping back from being the head teacher of one school to the CEO of many. Maintaining the balance between 'lighting wood piles across the schools and then withdrawing and expecting teams to take charge' and being 'measured and not running ahead of capacity' was of critical importance. Maintaining his value to each school within the system through the act of reviewing, reflecting, and challenging to facilitate the pursuit of higher ambitions was also considered a challenging responsibility.

Of significant importance

> **Question to consider**
> - Who are the on-site culture bearers in your institution?

Cecilia stated that having on-site culture bearers, who understand the values and intentions of the organisation, is vital for system success. 'To have the right staff who we can communicate with, who we understand and who are transparent is key.' When differences did appear within the system, it was important to 'take a slower pace to determine how we could continue to deliver what was expected, but at the same time what we believe in'. Making sure staff have an opportunity to evolve, innovate, and contribute – within organisation boundaries – was also important. 'Once the foundations were set, a confidence and maturity evolved which now means our people can self-evaluate and get involved in shaping students' learning in more creative ways.'

Understanding the business mentality of any business partner holds significant importance for Thana. 'Once we realised our main interests did not align, theirs being getting the schools started and using our brand pull, we decided to withdraw.'

Of importance to Glynn is that schools within the trust maintain their individual identities, are seen to be a key part of their local community, yet also part of something excitingly bigger. Glynn spent the first year of his appointment focusing on what the trust was about, what were its values, before focusing on the operational and organisational issues. This created what they call *The Unity Way*, which advocates the need for partnership and the expectation that along with the availability of support and advice each school is expected to 'give'. Important to Glynn is that schools are collaborative and build plans that include pledges as to what each school will provide each other and what they will commit to the whole trust.

Developing system leaders

From a leader development perspective, and reflecting on the views of our contributing system leaders, it was always Thana's intention to 'raise potential school leaders in our school, have *The Prestige Way* embedded before taking up a headship at another school'. Such leadership development structures have obvious merit and are reflected in Cecelia's views on having 'KED people who know *The KED Way*'. But what about training and continuing professional development (CPD) for system leaders?

Developing educational leaders into system leaders means consideration of when and how such development opportunities take place. At the time of writing, only few academic studies existed that comment on and/or explore the CPD requirements of system leaders in educational settings. In Kaz and Wilcox's (2017) study exploring the value of system leadership for leaders of children's centres in the UK, they stated that 'leadership development programmes need to be inquiry-based and developing a rich praxis' because 'working in the realm of the conceptual or practical alone may not achieve such powerful narratives of learning' (p. 484). The system leaders contributing to this chapter intimate experiences of a more practical 'on-the-job' approach to system leader development, although conceptual frameworks continue to develop. For example, as Close (2016) explains, the notion of leaders habitually working beyond their own schools means that 'system leadership is essentially a consultancy task' (p. 115). Accordingly, he developed a framework for system leader development based on consultancy research with six interrelated areas of enquiry: three *contextual dimensions* described as *values, analysis,* and *change,* and three *operating levels* known as *political coaching, organisational contracting,* and *knowledge production* (Close, 2016; Close, Kendrick, and Outhwaite, 2018). Utilising this, or a similar CPD framework such as David Hopkins' Curiosity and Powerful Learning programme, could also help focus the development of future multi-site and multi-institution system leaders through planned consideration of the following questions:

- How are system goals and strategies established, lived, and verified?
- Is there clarity around the identities of campuses and the central office?
- Are system committees or councils effective in recognising and considering the views of stakeholders within decision-making processes?
- What communication processes are in place to share system decisions?
- Is the application of system policies consistent?
- How do I ensure that the people affected by decisions made adhere to those decisions (Groenwald, 2017)?
- Are technologies adequate to facilitate shared knowledge management and quality assurance practices (Groenwald, 2017)?

Ultimately, as a multi-site or multi-institution system leader in HE, a balancing act is necessary that requires an understanding of the tensions that exist and knowledge of which lever to pull (or not to pull) to respond.

Notes

1. Moody's Investor Service is a financial market research and risk analysis firm.
2. Times Higher Education is an HE data provider for the sector.
3. EvoLLLution is an online newspaper providing analysis and insights into the HE sector.
4. Executive headships are commonly defined as leadership of two or more primary and/or secondary schools.
5. A multi-academy trust (MAT) is a group of state-funded schools operating in formal partnership.
6. My use of 'we' within this narrative is in recognition of the fact that these developments would only happen with the building of a collaborative partnership in the school and community around a shared vision. My use of 'I' signifies individual leadership responsibility.
7. The number of independent schools with public funding, so-called free schools, is growing in Sweden. Following a law change in the 1990s, parents and their children can choose among tuition-free schools, whether managed by the municipality or independently. They must be approved by the Schools Inspectorate and follow the national curricula and syllabuses, just like regular municipal schools.

8 This can often lead to the departure of some (often senior) individuals in order to enable the (re)building of a more positive culture.

References

Anderson, M. (2012). The struggle for collective leadership: Thinking and practice in a multi-campus school setting. *Educational Management Administration and Leadership*, 40(3), pp. 328–342.

Armstrong, P. (2015). Effective school partnerships and collaboration for school improvement: A review of the evidence: Research report. Department for Education. Available at: https://assets.publishing.service.gov.uk/government/uploads/system/uploads/attachment_data/file/467855/DFE-RR466_-_School_improvement_effective_school_partnerships.pdf [Accessed 7 June 2020].

Close, P. (2016). 'System leader' consultancy development in English schools: A long-term agenda for a democratic future? *School Leadership and Management*, 36(1), pp. 113–132. DOI: 10.1080/13632434.2016.1160214

Close, P., Kendrick, A. and Outhwaite, D. (2018). Developing system leaders: A research engagement approach. *Management in Education*, 32(2), pp. 79–84. DOI: 10.1177/0892020618762712

Collins, J. (2001). *Good to great: Why some companies make the leap and others don't*. New York: Harper Collins.

Fraser, D. and Stott, K. (2015). University satellite campus management models. *Australian Universities Review*, 57(2), pp. 79–83.

Fullan, M. (2004). *System thinkers in action: Moving beyond the standards plateau*. London: DfES Innovation Unit/NCSL.

Gerald, G. (2014). *Perspectives of leadership competencies by multi-campus community college leaders*. Ph.D. Thesis. San Diego State University. Available at ProQuest. (3633144). [Accessed 17th January 2020].

Groenwald, S. L. (2017). The challenges and opportunities in leading a multi-campus university. *The Journal of Professional Nursing*, 34, pp. 134–141.

Grove, J. (2015). Has the multi-campus university had its day? [Times Higher Education blog] 19 November. Available at: www.timeshighereducation.com/blog/has-multi-campus-university-had-its-day#survey-answer [Accessed 20th February 2020].

Hopkins, D. and Higham, R. (2007). System leadership: Mapping the landscape. *School Leadership and Management*, 27(2), pp. 147–166. DOI: 10.1080/13632430701237289

Hopkins, D., Stringfield, S., Harris, A., Stoll, L. and Mackay, T. (2014). School and system improvement: A narrative state-of-the-art review. *School Effectiveness and School Improvement*, 25(2), pp. 257–281. DOI: 10.1080/09243453.2014.885452

Kaz, S. and Wilcox, M. (2017). System leadership development in Children's Centres in the UK. *Sustainability Accounting, Management and Policy Journal*, 8(4), pp. 470–488.

Lee, E. and Bowen, F. (1971). *The multicampus university: A study of academic governance*. New York: McGraw-Hill.

Miller, C. (2013). *The future of multi-campus institutions*. Available at: https://evolllution.com/opinions/the-future-of-multi-campus-institutions/ [Accessed 7 June 2020].

Moodys.com. (2011). *Moody's: Emerging expansion trend creates risks, opportunities for US universities*. Available at: www.moodys.com/research/Moodys-Emerging-expansion-trend-creates-risks-opportunities-for-US-universities–PR_231969 [Accessed 17 January 2020].

Morrison, N. (2013). *The rise of the executive headteacher*. The Guardian [blog] 9 July. Available at: www.theguardian.com/teacher-network/teacher-blog/2013/jul/09/executive-headteacher-schools-leadership [Accessed 7 June 2020].

Pinheiro, R. and Nordstrand Berg, L. (2017). Categorizing and assessing multi-campus universities in contemporary higher education. *Tertiary Education and Management*, 23(1). 5–22, doi:10.1080/13583883.2016.1205124

Stringer, B. and Hudson, P. (2008). Sustaining educational futures for multi-campus TAFE environments: Change requirements for leadership roles and practices. In: *Proceedings of the AARE Conference*. 6-9 July, Brisbane, Australia.

Timberlake, G. (2004). Decision-making in multi-campus higher education institutions. *Community College Enterprise*, 10(2). 91–110.

CHAPTER 7

Academics in exile
A ghost chapter
Kendall Jarrett and Stephen Newton

In developing an overview of this book, Stephen and I wanted to include a chapter on leadership as experienced by academics in exile; specifically, in or from Syria. Authors were found and a focus of the chapter, in particular the identification of support and processes required to 're-become a leader' in HE, was agreed. Yet, the chapter, in its proposed form, was never written. The realities of the conflict in Syria, and explicitly in Idlib, meant a total refocus of attention to saving family members.

Rather than replace or substitute this chapter with another, we decided to include this ghost chapter (a pale reflection of the chapter we had planned) to highlight that, for some colleagues, the idea of leadership in HE is a luxury when viewed against the backdrop of conflict and its direct impact on the lives and livelihoods of self, family, and friends.

In late 2019 I was asked by a colleague from the Council of At-Risk Academics (CARA) to deliver an online session as part of the E-Learn Syria Soiree series. CARA are an organisation who support higher education colleagues in crisis with help offered to academics around the world in immediate danger who have been forced into exile or who choose to remain and work in their home countries (CARA 2020). CARA have been running support programmes for at-risk academics for nearly 90 years. Programmes such as the E-Learn Syria Soiree series provide an opportunity for colleagues to remain connected to their identities as academics and to have access to professional development opportunities. Most importantly, the role of CARA is to help at-risk academics feel supported and valued as academics.

The presentation, titled 'Preparing small-scale scholarship of teaching projects for publication', was prepared for Syrian academics currently residing in Turkey, all of whom had been displaced from their lives, careers, and livelihoods in Syria as a result of the ongoing conflict.

In preparing for the session I wanted to find out more about my audience. Articles by Tom Parkinson and colleagues (2018, 2019) provided me with an insight into the Syrian programme being facilitated by CARA, but what touched me the most were extracts from an anonymous article published in *The Guardian* (2016) titled 'I fled Syria for Kent – and regained my life as an academic':

> A great number of Syrian academics have been killed, tortured, abducted or forced to leave the country to save their lives and their families. My supervising professor had to flee the country without prior notice after her husband, also a respected professor at the same university, was abducted. She feared she would be next.
>
> Achieving academic excellence was always my ambition, but once the war started it also felt like an obligation. I wanted to learn the skills that I could later use to help rebuild my country.
>
> As the war went on, with no foreseeable ending, I knew that those dreams were on the verge of being lost.
>
> CARA saved my dreams from dying.

Throughout this book, we have commented upon the rapid pace of change in the field of HE, as well as the degree of change. Nowhere are these factors more acute than in conflict zones, especially where the conflict is underpinned by apparently unresolvable differences of religious belief and/or political persuasion, let alone ethnicity. Syria today is simply one case in point.

This of course begs numerous questions regarding the mechanics of leadership and the approach of individual leaders. Their need for resilience and adaptability is self-evident. We suggest that the need for strong self-leadership (as outlined in Chapter 1) is also clear. Some of the other issues that academics in exile need to consider include:

- how to bring together (or at least maintain contact with) students and colleagues when their former HE institution is either destroyed or no longer accessible;
- how to establish some kind of routine in terms of research, teaching, and administration as well as ongoing funding;
- how to retain (or regain) freedom of speech and of academic research in what may have become a totalitarian regime;
- how to publish research, etc., under such a regime, especially internationally;
- how to balance the imperative of personal survival and ensuring the safety of family members with the continuation of academic work, research, and teaching,
- how to enable the assessment and delivery of academic qualifications for students;

- how to build the resilience to sustain academic effort in the context of a conflict zone and do so indefinitely, rather than merely for a matter of weeks;
- how to define, locate, and access necessary external support;
- how to regain – or retain – one's identity as an academic: to what extent might it matter to you?

We feel that the overwhelming issue for academics in such situations is simply keeping going without necessarily having an end to the situation in sight. We have nothing but admiration for their efforts in doing so.

References

CARA. (2020). What we do. Available at: www.cara.ngo/what-we-do/srisks. [Accessed 20 January 2020]Cara also supports higher education institutions whose work is a.

Parkinson, T., S. Brewer, C. Camps, J. Turner, K. Robertson, K. Whiteside, and T. Zoubir (2018). Supporting Syrian academics to be agents for change: The role of UK universities. *Educational Developments*, 19(3), pp. 1–6.

Parkinson, T., K. McDonald, and K. Quinlan (2019). Reconceptualising academic development as community development: Lessons from working with Syrian academics in exile. *Higher Education*, 79, pp. 183–201.

The Guardian. (2016). Anonymous academic. I fled Syria for Kent - and regained my life as an academic. Availableat: www.theguardian.com/higher-education-network/2016/jul/15/i-fled-syria-for-kent-and-regained-my-life-as-an-academic [Accessed 1st March 2020].

CHAPTER 8

Leadership legacy in higher education
Sally Brown and Pauline Kneale

Creating a legacy through leadership is a challenge, since every action is interpreted differently by the viewer. This chapter reflects on opportunities to think through the later part of a senior manager role, and to develop a strategy to continue in leadership in HE or other roles.

Building a leadership legacy

A legacy is, in essence, the story of what an individual achieved over time, warts and all, capturing how they are remembered and the impact of their actions. Interestingly everyone has different memories and perspectives on any episode in anyone's career, so creating and managing a legacy is a challenge. Life stories will be recalled and discussed by others when considering their own pathways, influencing their decisions. Colleagues are always watching.

An academic's legacy is usually primarily embodied in their research papers and outputs, including books, reusable learning objects and other artefacts, and evidence of the influence they have had, for good and ill, on decades of students. An individual's leadership legacy at university, national, or international level will be built on in future years by others in ways that cannot be controlled, as ideas, strategies, policies, and practices are disseminated, adapted, and changed by those who follow.

Earlier chapters have discussed the processes and skills involved in becoming and being leaders: in this chapter aspects of leadership that create a legacy in the context of this and future roles are explored. For most academics, any 'leadership years' are highly challenging, satisfying, and complicated, and legacies tend to be created without the originator particularly noticing. Enthusiasm, appreciation, passion, tact, common sense, emotional intelligence, tolerance for ambiguity, and exasperation are just some of the daily mix of skills required and emotions experienced. Arguably these complex facets of leadership, and the associated diverse capabilities and experiences, provide a huge resource to build from in later life, whatever that might involve. Within and beyond higher education, life is hugely complex, volatility is normal, and uncertainty dominates. The fundamental advantage for leaders progressing through and beyond HE in the 2020s is that they have worked and lived Warren Buffet's 'uncertain times', all of which are excellent preparation for further leadership and for roles beyond higher education.

Continuing in higher education is not for everyone, and some people plan early for a change of scene. This chapter focuses on some of the transitional issues and opportunities which can help ensure that the next phase of life is as rewarding as the present. Some actions will fall naturally as part of delivering in senior positions; others may seem to be left-field but could provide an excellent base for moving forward. Most importantly, it is necessary to create the diary space and keep having fun throughout.

Leaving leadership: what next?

Most leaders would love to think that they leave a legacy of good works, but how legacies are framed or influenced is somewhat dependent on personal ambitions and plans for future employment, retirement, or semi-retirement. In addition, planned leaving dates may become more fluid. What comes next is largely a matter of individual choice and will benefit from early thinking and planning (Altman et al., 2019). There is no compulsory retirement age in some nations (e.g. the USA) and age discrimination is illegal in the European Union, so with life expectancy increasing, many academics are choosing to work beyond former 'normal' retirement ages of between 65 and 70. What choices are available when leaving a senior management position in a university? Possibly:

1. 'I want to build on my leadership experiences and move on to new positions in this university or to a different organisation as a leader for the foreseeable future.'
2. 'I am a keen, active researcher. I want to continue to research and write after retirement with my colleagues. However, in my university it is not possible, so I will find a position elsewhere.'
3. 'I am 100% a researcher, I am going to continue to research and write, paid or pro bono, with my colleagues for as long as I can, and certainly into my seventh and possibly eighth decade. Happily, in my department it will be possible. For me retiring means coming to the university each day, but no committees.'
4. 'Before I finally leave the university, I want to finish my research and writing projects, see my PhD students complete, and finish my national and international projects and organisational roles. Moving to part-time for the last couple of years could be ideal. I like the idea of a phased departure,

where I can continue to add value to the university, for example as a professor without leadership responsibilities.'
5. 'That's it, I have given everything to my role for many years, loved it – now it is time for a complete change. The clean break option suits me best so I can pursue other interests and look after my health and well-being.'

The approaches described in this chapter apply to all leaders to some extent, depending on context and ambition. The first option, above, can lead towards closer work with relevant national and international organisations. Working with head-hunters to find new roles, on a permanent or an interim basis, can be an attractive option. Professors who can imagine themselves as part of an active research group well into their 80s may prioritise their collaborative research work and mentoring in their leadership years. Those wanting to move to a new institution to continue working in retirement will find building links with other HEIs and research teams well in advance is crucial to ensure continuity.

> **Question to consider**
>
> - Think about how you would like to enjoy the next five to ten years. Which of these options, variations on these, or other approaches will give you most pleasure?

Choosing when to move from fully paid to retired status is a major life-changing decision, which can benefit from a variety of forms of professional guidance, particularly financial advice. A crucial step is to check regularly on pension entitlements, certainly every couple of years. This can be a complex matter where emoluments for senior roles are 'unconsolidated' (i.e. additional payments that do not count towards pension entitlement), where people have moved between institutions with different pension schemes or worked in different countries. Determining the precise date on which to start to draw down a pension can have considerable financial implications. This is such an important area that relying on informal advice from colleagues or friends is a bad idea, and consulting an independent financial advisor an excellent one. If possible, avoid being bounced into taking decisions at very short notice and prepare well before the end of employment.

At a time when universities are in a process of continuous change in relation to priorities and strategic imperatives, retiring senior managers are often very well placed to undertake short- or longer-term consultancy work, since other HEIs can benefit from highly experienced external perspectives.

Researchers in later life clearly hugely enjoy being able to focus on projects and writing, without the interference of university administration and academic citizenship duties. Research students, the next generation of academics and managers, really appreciate mentoring and advising from senior colleagues, a role frequently pushed aside by the other demands on senior leaders.

Whatever longer-term choices are made, it is likely that moving from senior roles to situations away from the front line of managing universities will require substantial changes of mindset as well as day-to-day activities. The next section provides advice on how to manage the sometimes-challenging process positively.

Leadership actions to enhance a legacy

Time out to plan

All leaders plan and implement usually in short to ten-year envelopes. Taking time to consider personal goals on a longer scale is advocated here. Kubicek's (2012) intentional leadership speaks of the advantages of reaching beyond the weekly list of priorities and days dominated by firefighting to developing a holistic perspective, purposeful leadership approach. Developing this capacity

> requires a mind-set change ... that occurs around time, and time is hard to give up or to plan effectively – but it can be done. Those who figure this out develop cultures of leaders, which in turn lead to long-term results and fulfilment.
>
> (Kubicek, 2012, p. 39)

Take the time to consider the mindset evolution that a change in circumstances will bring.

Making private time to think and update plans is a crucial essential part of leadership. Be more specific, think through dreams for future leadership and other roles in HE and post-retirement ambitions and plans. Take an 'intentional approach', rather than letting the current overwhelming workload dictate a rudderless drift towards departure that feels out of control. Create an exit strategy. Colleagues' strategies to manage the transition vary. Some might choose to:

- organise a personal away day every year after retirement in place of the institutional annual review process;
- implement a planning journal, enabling a longer perspective and preventing the retiree from inadvertently filling their life with commitments as demanding as those in the management role;

- designate a couple of commitment- and family-free days every six months, to review commitments and contemplate next steps;
- use regular rail travel, walking, gym, or swimming time as thinking space to ensure a sensible balance is being maintained;
- maintain conference attendance to ensure currency and keep up with key networks.

It is important to recognise that careful planning and reflection may not result in the anticipated or desired outcome, but it is an improvement on trusting to fate to shape life post-retirement.

A leader's mega skill set

There is a potential trap for academics who feel that their leadership skills do not parallel those acquired in other occupations. University leaders are often selected because of their scholarship and professional standing in their research or teaching discipline. However, faculty and senior leaders participate in many discussions and much decision-making, and potentially lead or are involved in multiple projects. This gives leaders extensive experience of working with and supporting students and colleagues, discussing estates matters, hiring and probably disciplining and dismissing employees, encountering and delivering impossible budgets, working with governmental agencies on regional, national, and international agendas, resulting in an extensive and valuable skill set which other organisations seek.

Managing in universities, and particularly bringing about meaningful change, is not a matter of simple instruction or direction: instead, it requires high levels of persuasive powers and the ability to convince sometimes reluctant colleagues using research and evidence-based practice, a Sisyphean task indeed (Brown, 2011, 2012). Highly intelligent colleagues can be very effective in blocking changes if they are not convinced of their value. However, the skills developed in managing difficult situations are sought after in many contexts, including voluntary work, governorship of schools and colleges, trusteeships for charities and other organisations, and many other contexts.

> Question to consider
> - Consider your current skill set and how this might qualify you for future roles. How can you use your capabilities in fulfilling and satisfying ways that are useful to the communities in which you still serve?

Take this skills legacy into new settings where flexibility, independence of thought, ability to see different solutions, strategic planning skills, project management, evidence-led decision-making, and extensive committee experience combined with high levels of stamina and resilience are welcome. If possible, investigate and take advantage of the CPD opportunities, face-to-face or online, to update skills that will have relevance in future roles. For example, aspects of finance or law might be invaluable in the charity sector.

Mentoring

Senior leaders experience mentoring in a variety of contexts and are often critical of the process, which can be regarded as under-researched and sometimes dysfunctional (Baker, 2015; Heewon, Longman and Franco, 2014; Lunsford et al., 2013). Consider examples of positive instances of mentoring, where it has been personally beneficial, and what else might have happened (Rudick and Dannels, 2019). Chandler and Kram (2005) outline the diversity of mentoring styles, but generally good mentors have excellent people skills and a real desire to nurture the next generation. Typically, this involves being available to have regular, meaningful, confidential conversations every month, term, or semester. There is considerable skill in listening without immediately offering guidance or solutions, avoiding giving people immediate answers, and encouraging people to find different perspectives and to create their own solutions. Generally, it is about helping colleagues to see above the immediate horizons and develop wider perspectives.

Mentoring is a positive, legacy development skill likely to offer huge personal satisfaction, and one which has plenty of applications beyond HE. Mentoring younger colleagues can help to build a research team, encourage younger colleagues to request contributions to funding applications, and help to maintain currency with wider university agendas. Supporting less experienced colleagues to publish or present at conferences can also be hugely beneficial. Reverse mentoring, where younger staff are attached to more experienced colleagues to gain insights into senior roles and explain about processes and give insights into the organisation at different levels, is effective for some (Chaudhuri, 2019; Lytle, 2017). For those anticipating moving elsewhere, developing relationships with staff in relevant departments, being available and effective, could be vitally useful in the longer term. Additionally, externally, many organisations need volunteers, for example on their governing bodies, where opportunities to mentor the next generation can be very rewarding.

Keeping in touch

In some universities there is a timetabled period each week with no university meetings, enabling senior colleagues to work with their research groups, externally teach, advise, and write. Departmental and research legacy continues. Where this is not normal practice, there are likely to be other occasions for keeping in touch with colleagues informally, for example in social events like barbecues and parties, or at graduation ceremonies, where willingness to take part might be hugely appreciated, or at inaugural professorial lectures.

Researching and writing about higher education practice

For those whose academic practice has largely involved research and writing in their discipline, this later career phase might be the time to start disseminating leadership experience through carefully researched, well-evidenced papers or 'think pieces'. There is no shortage of journals (e.g. *Higher Education Quarterly, Journal of Higher Education Policy and Management, Higher Education, Higher Education Review, Quality in Higher Education*) which address the rapidly evolving processes and practices in higher education. Opportunities might also arise to build research collaborations with colleagues in schools of education, business, management, human resources, and psychology to generate the research evidence and share aspects of change in the university.

Journal or book series editing

The time pressures of leadership often squeeze out journal and book editing, but previous relationships can be reactivated, and new roles developed with a view to editing when retired. Encouraging new authors, commissioning articles, working with conference organisers to create new publications as well as traditional reviewing is time-consuming but hugely rewarding. The process of editing a collective volume maintains contacts with colleagues and currency within the discipline.

Wellbeing

The importance of fitness and stress minimisation is commonly emphasised in leadership training. Those leaving leadership roles may need to remember that, in managing 'free' time, it is important to maintain a healthy balance between engaging with satisfying and fulfilling academic work, and making the most of the later stages of working lives to live well and enjoy life. The support mechanisms may have involved mindfulness (King and Badham, 2018), therapeutic massage, or other forms of self-care, physical activities including sport, engagement in the arts, and backup from (sometimes long-suffering) friends and family. These need to be continued and built upon in this next life phase.

Career break or sabbatical

In some institutions, leaders have the opportunity of a sabbatical semester or year at the end of their terms of office and this makes a wonderful opportunity to review options and make decisions. This is usually an administration- and teaching-free period, used to prioritise research, write papers, catch up with the literature, attend conferences, and focus on new funding applications. Here also is time to re-establish relationships and do detailed planning for the next few years, building the legacy.

Following a very intense leadership role, a career break or 'career gap' year might be a possibility. This option involves stepping off the academic track for a period negotiated with the employer, to do something completely different, which might include a salary break too if this is seen to have personal rather than professional advantage to the university. But, for example, a break to learn a new language through immersion in another country for six months, as a prelude to developing new research with academics in that language, might be funded. Note that career breaks are normally at an employer's discretion, so it is a good idea to sound out precedents and to chat informally in advance with line managers.

For those for whom the end of the term of office means leaving an institution as well, particularly if a lump sum is paid on termination, a complete break before taking up further roles can be hugely attractive. It gives time to decide to stop working altogether or to discover whether the absence of companionship, stimulation, and financial remuneration encourages the search for another role.

Making the break from leadership

Losing practical support

Senior leaders in role normally have excellent support from administrators, finance officers, and IT support, and leaving all this behind can be a horrible shock (particularly areas like IT support and diary management). Retirees need to be ready for the loss of support in multiple areas and to put in place contingency plans such as buying in specialist support and learning to use, for example, unfamiliar systems and tasks through paid-for training. Again, good advance planning would suggest using internal CPD opportunities.

Transition identity in HE leadership

An academic's identity typically evolves from managing the tensions between researcher and teacher roles, expanding to national and international teaching and research roles, and adding in professional managerial roles. Senior management leadership takes one into the liminal 'third space' (Whitchurch, 2008, 2009) between disciplines, where one is neither 'belonging' nor 'not belonging' entirely to either the professional or academic domains (Mathany, Clow and Aspenlieder, 2017). Leaving these senior roles, with high levels of responsibility but also associated esteem and even deference, can be a shock to the system that has been likened to bereavement. In addition, if one remains within or close to the university, it can be frustrating to watch successors making their mark by changing or dismantling many of the processes or teams once regarded as considerable achievements. For those unable to maintain a Zen-like calm, it may be necessary to keep a (literal or metaphoric) distance.

Remaining within learning communities

Maintaining involvement with the professional bodies, learned societies, and conferences that stimulated academic life is important to many retired academics. Check out the annual fees for retired staff: the lifetime fellowship fee may be very good value and provide access to some disciplines' journals. Now may be the time to contribute to the organisation's committees.

Continuing to work will need some thought about paying for conferences and associated travel expenses. Consider taking a holiday around conferences to get the benefit from the travel. Attendance at such events helps to maintain currency and professional networks. Invitations to keynote at institutional and other conferences are a bonus. It is worth letting colleagues know that offers of this kind are welcome. Leaders are frequently frustrated by limited conference time, leaving immediately after personal inputs to deal with other pressing matters. After retirement, enjoy the whole event, see what the next generation are developing, and explore more of the surroundings than was possible when work demands took precedence.

Lifelong learning

Taking higher education courses in retirement, especially in new disciplines, can be an attractive leisure activity, provide new friendships, and retain links within HE (Jamieson, 2016). Opportunities depend on the availability of extramural studies in the vicinity: consider learning with or contributing to U3A (University of the Third Age) in France, Australia, the UK, and New Zealand, and the Third Age Network in Ontario. Look beyond local options. A one- or two-week course in an attractive holiday location can be a great way of exploring yoga, bridge, renaissance music, vegan gastronomy, and many other topics. From home, MOOCs (Massive Open Online Courses) and many other online courses are available.

Pre-departure thoughts

In the weeks before leaving a role, make decisions about possessions and practicalities. Start early rather than leaving the drudgery to the last day or two, and please don't ask support staff to do it. In relation to office contents:

1. *Data on computers*: Save crucial information to personal external storage, and delete the rest, being especially careful with confidential information. Many institutions delete staff from email and other systems the day after departure. Be certain to keep the contact information for people to stay in touch with.
2. *Paperwork*: Ensure the only papers taken home are valuable (for example, all retirement/pensions papers). Don't take home unsorted piles of paper and old files. Pass to colleagues the papers necessary for their work (for example, documents unavailable electronically), select a few items of personal or sentimental value to keep, and shred everything else.
3. *Books*: Work out which are likely to be useful and take them home. Sort the rest into what others (including charities) might find useful and dispose of old and outdated volumes.
4. *Gifts*: Many senior managers are gifted items by international delegations. Be tactful in deciding whether to leave for the next incumbent or pass to relevant colleagues.
5. *Office equipment*: Talk to the IT department about what needs to happen to devices, phones, and laptops.
6. *Personal possessions*: It is unfair to leave them for someone else to dispose of: gift, give to charity, or throw away mugs, coffee machines, tea pots, and similar items.

> **Question to consider**
> - In the weeks or months before you leave your leadership role, what pre-planning is required to make your transition easier?

Clearing out can be surprisingly satisfying, although it may take more time than expected. A surprising amount of stationery will go back to the storeroom.

Emeritus professorships

Some universities recognise the contribution made by senior colleagues by awarding them emeritus status, which carries with it positive advantages, including the ability to keep using the title 'professor' and usually access to university email, the university library, and invitations to university events. Emeritus status is not an automatic right and it is up to the university whether to offer this, and whether to do so for a fixed period or indefinitely.

Departure date

Final days in office filled with a flurry of meetings and manic clearing will not be enjoyable: try to control the pace and timing of leaving. Negotiate an earlier departure if that suits everyone. Aim to provide comprehensive handover files and information, but do not worry about 'missing' links. The best new job training involves coping with the gaps left by predecessors.

After departure

Retirees who haunt their old universities without good reason can be a nuisance to themselves and others. But while it is wise to keep a healthy distance from the old workplace to acclimatise to the transition, do meet very good friends and colleagues for lunch, coffee, or a walk. Work at keeping these personal links. Arranging to meet colleagues off the premises may provide a much-appreciated break for them. Recognise that some colleagues will never be lifelong friends. For those sending Christmas cards, the list should be significantly reduced.

In conclusion: a legacy of support to the next generation

Worrying excessively about how you are remembered, the legacy, is pointless. Every project is someone else's after departure. Some measures in place in advance will ensure key tasks get completed, but what happens next is another's responsibility. Excellent projects will disappear, teams be disbanded, and new strategies and policies emerge. The new leaders have their own mark to make, and their own vision for projects to take the institution forward. Consider researching and writing about projects to create a more lasting and widely available legacy.

At some point health and personal circumstances will mean it is necessary to stop working altogether. Take time each year to reflect on the life plan, current roles, and contributions. There is a neat trick to leaving while colleagues still welcome and value effective inputs. Judging this moment is crucial and not always easy. Take soundings from impartial colleagues, and act on the advice.

Leaders work with strategies and action plans all the time. Use these strategic approaches at each stage of working life, so connections are maintained across generations with interesting people and organisations in mutually beneficial relationships. As time progresses, expect that life is going to be very different indeed, but with luck and good preparation, could be better than before.

References

Altman, Y., Baruch, Y., Manrique-de-Lara, P.Z., and Armas, M.M.V. (2019). Baby boomers at the cusp of their academic career: Storming ahead, hanging on, or calling it a day. *Studies in Higher Education*, 44, pp. 1–16. DOI: 10.1080/03075079.2019.1610864.

Baker, V.L. (2015). People strategy in human resources: Lessons for mentoring in higher education. *Mentoring & Tutoring: Partnership in Learning*, 23(1), pp. 6–18. DOI: 10.1080/13611267.2015.1011034.

Brown, S. (2011). Bringing about positive change in higher education; a case study. *Quality Assurance in Education*, 19(3), pp. 195–207. ISSN 0968-4883.

Brown, S. (2012). Managing change in universities: A Sisyphean task? *Quality in Higher Education*, 18(1), pp. 139–146. DOI: 10.1080/13538322.2012.663547.

Chandler, D.E. and Kram, K.E. (2005). Applying an adult development perspective to developmental networks. *Career Development International*, 10, pp. 548–567. ISSN 1362-0436.

Chaudhuri, S. (2019). Perspectives in HRD—Reverse mentoring: Hallmarks for implementing an intergenerational intervention. *New Horizons in Adult Education and Human Resource Development*, 31(3), pp. 65–71. DOI: 10.1002/nha3.20256.

Heewon, C., Longman, K.A., and Franco, M.A. (2014). Leadership development through mentoring in higher education: A collaborative autoethnography of leaders of color. *Mentoring and Tutoring: Partnership in Learning*, 22(4), pp. 373–389. DOI: 10.1080/13611267.2014.945734.

Jamieson, A. (2016). Retirement, learning and the role of higher education. *International Journal of Lifelong Education*, 35(5), pp. 477–489. DOI: 10.1080/02601370.2016.1224036.

King, E. and Badham, R. (2018). The wheel of mindfulness: A generative framework for second-generation mindful leadership. In: King, E. and Badham, R.,eds. *Mindfulness*, 4(3), pp. 1–11. DOI: 10.1007/s12671-018-0890-7.

Kubicek, J. (2012). Intentional leadership. *Leader to Leader*, 64, pp. 38–43. DOI: 10.1002/ltl.20021.

Lunsford, L.G., Baker, V., Griffin, K.A., and Johnson, W.B. (2013). Mentoring: A typology of costs for higher education faculty. *Mentoring and Tutoring: Partnership in Learning*, 21, pp. 126–149. DOI: 10.1080/13611267.2013.813725.

Lytle, T. (2017). Putting mentoring in reverse. *HR Magazine*, 62(4), pp. 46–51. ISSN: 1047-3149.

Mathany, C., Clow, K.M., and Aspenlieder, E.D. (2017). Exploring the role of the scholarship of teaching and learning in the context of the professional identities of faculty, graduate students, and staff in higher education. *The Canadian Journal for the Scholarship of Teaching and Learning*, 8(3), p. 10. DOI: 10.5206/cjsotl-rcacea.2017.3.10.

Rudick, C.K. and Dannels, D.P. (2019). "Yes, and …": Continuing the scholarly conversation about mentoring in higher education. *Communication Education*, 68(1), pp. 128–131. DOI: 10.1080/03634523.2017.1392584.

Whitchurch, C. (2008). Shifting identities and blurring boundaries: The emergence of third space professionals in UK higher education. *Higher Education Quarterly*, 62(4), pp. 377–396. DOI: 10.1111/j.1468-2273.2008.00387.

Whitchurch, C. (2009). The rise of the blended professional in higher education: A comparison between the United Kingdom, Australia and the United States. *Higher Education*, 58(3), pp. 407–418. DOI: 10.1007/s10734-009-9202-4.

PART 2B
Leadership insights
From outside the sector

CHAPTER 9

Lessons from corporate leadership
Stephen Newton

In previous chapters we have explored various aspects of good leadership including leadership character and some aspects of good leadership practice. In this chapter, I look at what can happen when these are absent in some way, wholly or in part, based on real-world examples of corporate failures of various kinds. I have deliberately chosen quite historic examples because immediacy can give rise to a loss of perspective. As a Chinese lecturer in history at an Oxford college dinner in the early 2000s once replied when asked to comment on the results of the Cultural Revolution, 'It is far too early to tell, as it requires at least a further generation to gain adequate perspective.'

It is clearly too simplistic to say that 'bad leadership' is simply the reverse of good or effective leadership: the position is far more nuanced. In some cases, what may be perceived as the strengths of a good leader, when taken to excess, can become weaknesses, leading to negative results. Those negative results may impact the organisation as a whole, individuals or groups within it, and/or the leader in question. The issues we explore below impact HE in much the same way as would be the case in corporates or the professions. Context and organisational culture are different, but the results will tend to be similar.

'Good' and 'bad' corporate leadership

To reprise what 'good' leadership looks like, it may be useful to summarise (and paraphrase) the key leadership competencies identified by Dr Sunnie Giles[1] in her article of 15 March 2016, published in *Harvard Business Review*. She identifies five themes and ten competencies within those themes:

1. Shows strong ethics and safety
   - High ethical and moral standards
   - Clearly communicates expectations

2. Is self-organising
   - Sets clear goals and objectives with loose guidelines for delivery processes
3. Exhibits efficient learning
   - Has flexibility to change opinions
   - Open to new ideas and approaches
   - Provides safety for trial and error
4. Nurtures growth
   - Is committed to ongoing training and development
   - Helps individuals to grow into next-generation leaders
5. Creates a shared sense of connection and belonging
   - Communicates often and openly
   - Creates the feeling of both succeeding and failing together

In a recent *Harvard Business Review* article (24 October 2018), Ron Ashkenas and Brook Manville[2] examine six core leadership skills every leader should practise. These can be summarised as:

1. Shape a vision that is exciting to your team.
2. Translate that vision into a clear strategy – so that team members know what actions to take (and what actions not to take).
3. Recruit, develop, and reward a team of great people to implement the clear strategy.
4. Focus on measurable results.
5. Foster innovation and learning.
6. Lead yourself: know yourself, improve yourself, and manage the appropriate degree of balance in your own life.

There is considerable overlap between these lists and the skills, traits, and characteristics explored in previous chapters. If we now know what 'good' looks like, what occurs when things go wrong or leaders fail to exhibit or espouse such characteristics?

Signs of problems ahead for an organisation may include:

- Stasis – the organisation rests on its laurels rather than focusing on developing new ideas and products. Leaders fail to scan the horizon and to spot new opportunities. This leads to failure to adapt to changing circumstances and potentially to underestimating competitors.
- A change of culture, from one of innovation to one of process and control – this tends to give rise to fear among junior employees – both of making mistakes and of highlighting potential problems. This can manifest as leaders setting unrealistic targets and employees massaging metrics to

allow them to report that these targets have been achieved: failure is not perceived to be tolerated.
- Lack of optimism and passion among staff – this tends to manifest in the way in which employees talk to each other and to others outside the organisation.
- High levels of staff turnover, especially at middle management levels and among younger staff members – this can betray a lack of investment in the growth of individuals as well as a more general toxicity of culture.
- Risk-aversion or the reverse, 'fool's courage' –both can be by-products of all of the above points.
- A mismatch between the stated cultural aspirations of the organisation and the ways in which staff are encouraged (or forced) to act – for example, by way of rigid and unrealistic evaluation metrics.

In the following sections, I look at various examples of corporate leadership failure from a number of different industry sectors. Each case is complex, so I have attempted to summarise the bare bones of the facts with a view only to highlighting issues of leadership and not to suggesting or apportioning blame. I do not suggest that these summaries are comprehensive, and although the failings highlighted may appear to be specific to one particular industry, I suggest that similar issues can equally occur in any industry although the results may not be similar.

Oil and gas

This is an industry in which the stakes are high, not only in financial terms, but in terms of risk and complexity. Most of the locations in which oil and gas exploration take place are inhospitable, whether due to harsh weather conditions (such as those on Alaska's North Slope) or to deep water, such as the Gulf of Mexico, where weather conditions may also contribute to the technical difficulty of the work.

We explore in outline two examples where leadership failures resulted in environmental damage and/or loss of human lives:

- *Exxon Valdez*
- *Deepwater Horizon*

Whilst there were undoubtedly failings in leadership by individuals, one of the overriding factors in both cases appears to be a failure of corporate culture – itself a result of multiple individual leadership failures over an extended period. In both cases the bare facts are well known.

124 Stephen Newton

Exxon Valdez

> **Questions to consider**
> - What could go wrong, and what might be the consequences?
> - Are we taking good care of our people?
> - What could 'reasonable' risk mitigation look like?
> - Where we have given commitments, internally or externally, have we kept our promises?

The *Exxon Valdez* was an oil tanker carrying approximately 53 million US gallons of crude oil, bound for Long Beach, California. The ship struck the Bligh Reef in Prince William Sound, Alaska, on 24 March 1989, rupturing the hull and resulting in the spillage of c. 10.8 million US gallons of crude oil into the sea. Prince William Sound was home to numerous sea otters, seals, orcas, various varieties of salmon, herring, and many sea birds, as well as large volumes of shellfish. All suffered from the spilled oil.[3]

What caused the disaster? Early reports indicated that the captain, Joseph Hazelwood, had been drinking prior to the collision. However, he was later exonerated. Captain Hazelwood had handed over control of the ship to the third mate prior to the collision, the ship having moved out of the normal shipping lane to avoid possible small icebergs.

The third mate plotted the position of the ship incorrectly. No check was made on the plot. The state pilot had disembarked before the ship had reached open water. The ship had been lost to monitoring by radar at the Coast Guard's Vessel Traffic Centre at Valdez, where the equipment had been replaced with items of lower power. The practice of tracking vessels as far as Bligh Reef had been discontinued, but this had not been notified to crews who relied on Coast Guard guidance – something required by the Coast Guard Operating Manual. The average size of crews on tankers operating from Valdez had been reduced by around half over the preceding dozen years in order to cut operating costs, resulting in a need for crew members to work 12–14-hour shifts, sometimes with added overtime.[4] The obvious result was a likelihood of crew fatigue.

Had the ship's Raytheon Collision Avoidance System (RAYCAS) radar been working, it seems likely that the collision with Bligh Reef could have been avoided. The RAYCAS was not working and had not been for almost a year prior to the incident – something that Exxon management knew, according to investigative journalist Greg Palast.[5] The equipment was apparently too costly to maintain or to fix. In gaining congressional approval for the Alaska oil pipeline and tanker transportation network, oil companies had agreed to construct and use tankers with double hulls – something Exxon Valdez lacked.

What about the aftermath? Despite extensive clean-up operations, only around 10% of the spilled oil was recovered. Exxon was criticised for a slow response in cleaning up the spill. It was suggested that the company was awaiting permission from the Alaskan authorities to use certain dispersant chemicals at the time of the incident. However, the State pointed out that there was a pre-existing agreement to use dispersants to clean up spills, so no such permission was required.

Leaving aside the environmental damage, the economic and personal costs to Alaskan residents and businesses were significant. Tourism and commercial and recreational fishing all suffered. A 2010 CNN report[6] alleged that many oil spill clean-up workers had subsequently become sick – something Exxon contested.

Litigation over the incident continued over several years. A jury in Anchorage initially awarded actual damages of $287 million against Exxon and $5 billion of punitive damages. By 2006, following appeals, damages had been reduced to $2.5 billion. These were eventually reduced further to $507.5 million after the case was remanded back to the lower court in June 2008. Exxon's actions were deemed 'worse than negligent but less than malicious' according to a 2008 LA Times article by David G. Savage,[7] and it was argued that the previously awarded damages were too high when considered in the context of the common law of the sea.

Deepwater Horizon

What of *Deepwater Horizon*? The events of the incident are of course very different from those of *Exxon Valdez*. *Deepwater Horizon* was a mobile oil-drilling rig owned by Transocean and contracted to BP, with Halliburton contracted for various operations. At the time of the incident, the rig was operating in some 5,000 feet of water in the Gulf of Mexico and had finished the drilling of a new well some 18,000 feet deep below the seabed. That well was about to be sealed so that a so-called 'completion crew' could take up the work of bringing the well on stream.

A series of unfortunate events occurred on 20 April 2010 that allowed methane gas under high pressure to erupt from the riser pipe leading up from the well, through some 5,000 feet of seawater, to the drilling platform. The gas ignited, causing an explosion, which killed 11 people immediately and injured 17 others. Ninety-four crew members were rescued by lifeboat or helicopter. *Deepwater Horizon* sank on 22 April.[8]

According to the US Congress investigation, the blowout preventer on the rig had a hydraulic leak. It also had a failed battery and thus failed to act as it should.[9] As is often the case with serious incidents, with the benefit of hindsight, one can see a domino effect occurring, leading to an eventual catastrophe. A report by the Oil Spill Commission in November 2010 found that 'There was not a culture of safety on that rig.'[10]

Oil began to leak from the ruptured piping and from the well head, with oil continuing to flow, despite containment efforts, for 87 days. An estimated 210 million US gallons escaped into the Gulf of Mexico. Satellite images indicated that the oil affected c. 68,000 square miles of ocean and, ultimately, over 1,000 miles of coastline.

Leaving aside the environmental impact, which was considerable, the economic consequences for coastal residents affected by the spill were significant. As of 2013, it was estimated that the overall cost to Gulf Coast tourism was some $22 billon.[11] The costs in terms of commercial and other fishing activities were estimated to be up to $8.7 billion by 2020.

The direct costs to BP were also significant, including fines and other costs totalling an estimated $65 billion by 2018. In a judgment by US District Judge Carl Barbier on 4 September 2014, BP was found to be primarily responsible for the spill because of its 'gross negligence and reckless conduct',[12] with BP and its partners blamed for cost-cutting decisions and inadequate safety systems – claims BP contested. In 2015, BP agreed to pay $18.7 billion in fines. However, it was recognised that there were some systemic root causes of the incident and in the event of 'absent significant reform of industry practices and government policy',[13] such incidents might recur.

Setting aside the leadership aspects of alleged cost-cutting and inadequacy of safety systems, perhaps the most significant immediate impact for BP was reputational and driven by mis-steps in communication. Senior leaders in BP were perceived to have metaphorically shot themselves in the foot in that:

- They initially estimated the size of the spill at 1,000 to 5,000 barrels per day versus an estimate from the Flow Rate Technical Group (FRTG) of 62,000 barrels per day. They continued to do so despite internal BP emails showing higher estimates (in line with those of FRTG) released in 2012.[14]
- BP denied media access to oil clean-up sites.[15] This led to perceptions of some form of cover-up.
- CEO Tony Hayward was castigated in the media for remarking that he 'wanted to get his life back' at the height of the incident.[16]
- The negative perception produced by that statement was exceeded by the comment from then Chairman Carl-Henric Svansberg referring to residents on the Gulf Coast affected by the spill as 'small people'.[17]

> **Questions to consider**
> - Have we looked after our people and the communities where we operate?
> - When something goes wrong, how do we best avoid perceptions of a cover-up?
> - How might others see us as an organisation when something goes amiss?
> - Who will lead communication for us when a problem occurs? What values must they evidence?

By the same token, the Obama administration was criticised for what some felt was an unduly aggressive approach in its dealings with BP: such as the infamous 'boot on the neck' comment by Interior Secretary Ken Salazar.[18] Whilst leadership failures may result in cost-cutting that impacts safety and costs or affects lives, failures of leadership communication can have equal or greater impact on the reputation of the organisation.

Energy trading and the audit profession

We now turn to two linked examples from the field of energy trading and the audit profession:

- Enron
- Arthur Andersen

Enron was formed in 1985 through a merger between two gas companies, InterNorth and Houston Natural Gas. It began aggressively to expand into the newly deregulated energy markets across the US and elsewhere. In 1990, company founder Ken Lay hired Jeffrey Skilling to run a newly established firm, Enron Finance Corporation, an energy trader and supplier.

Skilling introduced the use of 'mark to market' (MTM) accounting to Enron, as opposed to traditional 'historic cost' based accounting. MTM aims to provide a reasonable estimate of a company's actual 'fair value' financial position and is both legitimate and widely used. In this case, it was used to account for expected future profit as actual profit.[19] Combined with the use of complex, off-balance-sheet structures known as special purpose vehicles (SPVs), which served to mask debt and were capitalised by Enron stock, this had the effect of inflating Enron's reported profits and hence its share price, to the benefit of shareholders including senior management. Enron employees were encouraged to buy Enron stock in their personal pension funds, which had the effect of supporting the share price.

In August 2001, an Enron employee, Sherron Watkins, sent a letter to Ken Lay expressing concern that 'we will implode in a wave of accounting scandals'. Lay promised to have the company's lawyers review her concerns. They responded that Enron had done nothing wrong in its accounting practices, as Arthur Andersen had approved each issue.

The Enron share price had achieved a high point of almost $91 per share in mid-2000. By the following November, it had dropped to under $1. Following questions from Wall Street analysts and others, Enron announced, in mid-October 2001, that it would be necessary to restate its financial statements for the period 1997–2000. These restatements reduced earnings by $613 million, increased liabilities by $628 million to the end of 2000, and reduced equity at that time by $1.2 billion.

A competitor, Dynergy, offered to buy Enron at a very low valuation. However, that offer fell through. In November 2001, credit rating agencies downgraded Enron to junk status. Dynergy withdrew its offer to buy Enron, and in December 2001, Enron filed for bankruptcy.

Sixteen people pleaded guilty to crimes committed at the company and five others were found guilty. CFO Andrew Fastow pleaded guilty to two charges of conspiracy in a plea bargain to testify against company founder Ken Lay and CEO Jeffrey Skilling. He had initially been charged with 98 counts of fraud, money laundering, and insider trading. Lay and Skilling went on trial in 2006. Lay was convicted of securities and wire fraud and was subject to a maximum of 45 years in prison. He died before sentencing. Skilling was convicted on 19 out of 28 charges and sentenced to 24 years and four months in prison. This was subsequently reduced by ten years.

Arthur Andersen, Enron's auditor in the period leading up to its collapse, was one of the most respected names in the accounting/audit profession at the time, with a reputation for high standards. However, in their book, *The Smartest Guys in the Room*,[20] Bethany McLean and Peter Elkind took a less positive view of their work for Enron.

Arthur Andersen had grown rapidly since it was founded in 1913. At its peak Andersen had almost 100,000 staff and was known as one of the 'Big Five' accounting firms (alongside what are now the Big Four: EY, PwC, KPMG, and Deloitte). Andersen had not only signed off on the Enron audits for a number of years but had also approved the structuring of the SPVs created by Enron. Andersen was accused of applying a reckless approach to its Enron audits due to the significant consulting fees generated by Enron – a conflict of interest.

The Securities Exchange Commission (SEC) had announced in November 2001 that it was pursuing an investigation into Enron. On 10 January 2002, in the immediate aftermath of the collapse of Enron, which was one of the firm's largest audit clients, Arthur Andersen disclosed that employees had shredded documents and destroyed emails relating to Enron.

> **Questions to consider**
> - As a senior leader, do I see things in my organisation that seem too good to be true?
> - With whom can I raise my concerns? Who can I trust?
> - To what extent do I truly understand the information I am given?
> - Do I understand what I am not being told – and why?
> - Am I convinced that our governance processes are robust and appropriate?

Although only a few Andersen employees were involved, and the partner in charge of the relationship with Enron was fired,[21] the firm was found guilty of obstruction of justice (a felony). As the SEC is not able to accept audits from convicted felons, this in effect put Andersen out of business and the firm surrendered its CPA licence in August 2001. The conviction was subsequently overturned by the US Supreme Court on the grounds that the jury in the initial trial had not been properly instructed on the charge against the firm.

What might be the key takeaways regarding leadership failings for these two firms leading to their demise? One might suggest these include:

- Failings of self-leadership for some key individuals in both firms;
- (In the case of Enron) allowing (or even encouraging) the development of a dysfunctional culture focused on short-term profit, leading to an inflated stock price that supported individual bonuses: 'What gets measured gets done; what gets rewarded gets done better…,' as Peter Drucker remarked in another context;
- Failings of internal oversight processes for both firms. For example, it should, arguably, not have been possible for anyone at Andersen to order the destruction of documents without alarm bells sounding immediately across the firm. The Enron Audit Committee arguably did not delve deeply enough into the accounting practices adopted by the firm nor into the complexities of the SPVs.

In the case of Enron, senior leaders were found to be running the firm in a way that amounted to fraud. One could say that this was a failure of self-leadership. Those leaders created a culture where it was hard to ask 'awkward' questions. When Sherron Watkins raised her concerns to Kenneth Lay over the possibility of accounting scandals, it was an act of courage (Jeffrey Skilling had a reputation for dealing abrasively with Wall Street analysts who asked awkward questions).

One might suggest that leaders among the regulators should have been alerted to potential problems due to the meteoric rise in the Enron share price. However, this was the time of the 'dot com' bubble, when spiking share prices were all too common.

Should other senior leaders within Enron have been more aware of possible issues and taken action? In its review of best corporate boards for 2000, *Chief Executive* magazine rated Enron's board as among its top five.[22]

Many board members were outsiders with significant ownership stakes in the company. There was a talented audit committee: however, its meetings were kept short to reduce detailed discussions – something for which the committee was criticised. The firm was praised for its innovative financial risk management tools. Nonetheless, the firm's performance management system and compensation arrangements contributed to a dysfunctional culture that focused on short-term earnings to maximise bonuses.

The board was notified of the company's accounting practices and, in a sense, could be said to have seen what it wanted to see. However, it seems unlikely that the consequences of the widespread use of derivatives was fully understood. In other words, the board did not have a sufficiently detailed understanding of what they were told by senior employees. A by-product of the Enron collapse was the Sarbanes-Oxley Act, which, among other things, imposed regulations on the composition of audit committees and established the Public Company Accounting Oversight Board.

Technology

Next, some examples from the world of technology:

- Blackberry
- Nokia
- Kodak

All three were titans in their respective industries. All three can be said to have suffered from complacency among senior leaders who failed to spot or to capitalise on game-changing developments of which competitors took advantage. All appear to have suffered from a failure to reinvent themselves over time and lacked agility. All three survive, but in greatly altered form.

Kodak was an innovator. The company could be said to have invented consumer photography. It offered simple but effective cameras at affordable prices. The operation of those cameras was summarised in advertising as, 'You push the button; we do the rest.' Initially, Kodak sold cameras, pre-loaded with film. Once the user had used up the film, the camera went back to Kodak for film processing and printing. The core product was not the camera but the film and photo printing.

The combination of a cheap camera and relatively expensive film and processing was highly profitable and remained so for a number of decades. By the late 1970s, Kodak had a 90% share of the film market and 85% of cameras. Kodak actually invented the digital camera in 1991. However, it failed to capitalise on that and continued to sell analogue cameras and film. It also branched out into printers, reversing the approach of competitors by selling relatively costly printers but cheap inks.

Kodak failed to spot the importance of two linked developments: smartphones incorporating cameras and the advance of social media sites allowing (indeed encouraging) images to be posted. Kodak filed for bankruptcy in 2012 – roughly at the same time as Facebook acquired Instagram in a $1 billion deal.

In 1998, Nokia was the best-selling mobile phone brand worldwide, achieving c. $4 billion of operating profit the following year. Nokia launched the 1100 phone in 2003 – becoming the best-selling mobile phone of all time. In 2007, Apple launched the iPhone, combining phone, camera, and MP3 player in one handset and gaining 5% market share versus Nokia's 50%. In 2013, Nokia's mobile phone business was acquired by Microsoft. How and why did that occur?

Conventional wisdom is that Nokia failed to evolve its technology, to innovate and to maintain product quality due to lack of vision among senior leaders. A 2015 study by Tim Vuori and Qui Huy[23] found that Nokia suffered from a culture of fear as an organisation.

Yves Doz[24] notes that Nokia's early success sowed the seeds of its downfall in the mobile communications field, with a decline in strategy processes leading to poor strategic decisions. Despite the launch of the Nokia Ventures Organisation aiming to find and exploit new growth areas, and a restructuring into a matrix organisation in 2004, which aimed to achieve greater agility, Nokia struggled to maintain its growth. In part the 2004 reorganisation generated internal tensions because mid-level executives lacked the skills necessary to navigate what became a fundamentally different organisational culture as well as structure. New product launches were impacted by the shortcomings of the Nokia operating system, Symbian, of which, by 2009, Nokia was running 57 different and incompatible versions. It would have taken years to develop something that could compete with iOS.

Senior executives were afraid of losing investors, and relationships with suppliers and customers if they acknowledged the superiority of the Apple product. Middle managers felt intimidated over failures to achieve targets and arguably told superiors what they wanted to hear. Some executives and top managers lacked technical competence to understand the reality of their company's competitive position in terms of its operating system software. They focused resources on developing new phones rather than on resolving operating system shortfalls.

Blackberry's case is not unlike that of Nokia in that its fall from grace was rapid and severe. In 2008, Blackberry's share price was $144. By 2013, it had fallen to $6.50. In 2011 Blackberry had 50 million active users and sold 14.6 million handsets worldwide, bringing in revenue of $19.9 billion. In 2016, Blackberry stepped back from the smartphone field to focus on software development, although it now offers a range of phones using the Android OS.

The issue for Blackberry was less to do with organisational fear and more to do with adaptability. It was, however, not that Blackberry's executive team did not adapt; just that they made what proved to be the wrong choices in adapting.

Blackberry made its name as the communication tool of choice in the corporate world. Blackberry assumed that corporates would remain its primary sales driver. Business users loved the physical QWERTY keyboard, the secure connectivity, and enterprise-grade email. Blackberry largely ignored the rest of the population, which ultimately proved to be a more lucrative segment.

Blackberry failed to acknowledge the changes in user demand that followed the introduction of Apple's iPhone or subsequent Android offerings. These combined both business capability, good in-built cameras, and a rich entertainment environment as well as the possibility for devices including tablet and laptop to synchronise automatically. Touch screens offered better navigation than keypads. The Apple App Store® offered innumerable apps. Blackberry handsets eventually gained a reputation for relatively poor design, relatively poor user experience, relatively poor value for money, and mediocre performance.

Blackberry assumed that competitors such as Apple were not a threat to its dominance of the corporate market. However, by offering a full internet browser combined with a slick user experience, among other things, Apple's initial iPhone offering stole considerable market share from Blackberry. The rise of third-party apps developed by independents for use with iOS or (later) Android operating systems and authorised for distribution via the App Store or what is now Google Play Store (originally Android Market) contrasted with the dearth of apps for the Blackberry OS. Its inefficiency imposed significant restrictions on developers, which, combined with a rapidly declining user base, made it non-viable for development.

What are the leadership takeaways here? First, perhaps, that assumption is the mother of all errors. Senior leaders were surprised by changes in their core corporate market and failed to keep up with the changing game, let alone stay ahead. This was a failure to adequately scan the horizon and to understand what was already visible in the market.

> **Questions to consider**
>
> - Do we truly understand what our core customers both want and need?
> - Are we equipped to delight our customers now and in the future (say one to two years)?
> - How could our competitors outpace us?
> - Where could we win through collaboration?

Second, it seems that Blackberry's executives had become content with their current marketplace but failed to keep up with its changing dynamics – a failure to focus on, and truly understand, their core customers. Blackberry had apparently failed as a learning organisation that was continually curious about what was happening outside its own eco-system and what could be learned from that.

Successful corporate leadership (to date)

Having focused on leadership issues based on failures, it may be useful to add a couple of examples from organisations that have been (at least to date) successful. Let's start with Apple. It is today one of the world's most successful companies. It was not always so: indeed, in August 1997 Bill Gates injected $150 million into Apple, which was at the time close to bankruptcy.

The rivalry between Gates and Steve Jobs was well known. The shift of mindset that enabled Jobs to seek help from Gates (and Gates to provide it) was the recognition that it was not necessary for Microsoft (MS) to lose in order for Apple to win (and vice versa) and that there was a huge opportunity for the two companies to develop a synergistic relationship to the benefit of both. Essentially, MS was then (and would remain for many years) a software company. Enabling MS software such as the Office suite to run on the Mac operating system opened up a whole new user base for MS. It arguably encouraged dyed in the wool corporate users who relied on MS Office to switch to Macs, opening new sales opportunities for Apple.

Separately, Jobs encouraged staff at Apple to be willing to take risks. Quoted in a *Business Insider* (BI) article,[25] he said: 'We're gambling on our vision and we'd rather do that than make "me too" products.' That vision revolved around innovative products that were simple to operate. As designer Jonathan Ives remarked (quoted in the same BI article): 'We are absolutely consumed by trying to develop a solution that is very simple, because as physical beings we understand clarity.'

Not only were those products innovative in their own right, but they were also designed to connect and synchronise seamlessly with other products in the same Apple ecosystem – initially, for example, iTunes, iPods, and the iTunes Music Store, but also automated synchronisation of devices such as iPhone, MacBook, and iPad. Under Jobs, Apple not only encouraged risk-taking in terms of product design; he extended that into his hiring approach, taking on individuals who were not only excellent computer scientists but who brought experience from many other fields – music, the arts, etc.

Another example of success is of course Amazon. A key takeaway here is not simply the willingness to take risk but also to learn from failures. Following the purchase by Amazon of Whole Foods in 2017, Jeff Bezos remarked:[26]

> If you're going to take bold bets, they're going to be experiments. And if they're experiments you don't know ahead of time if they're going to work. Experiments are by their very nature prone to failure. But a few successes compensate for dozens and dozens of things that didn't work.

Success does not occur without setbacks and missteps. Simply put, organisations cannot espouse creativity and innovation without accepting the likelihood of mistakes and disappointments. As a colleague put it to his young daughter after a difficult day for her at school: 'The word "fail" is an acronym – First Attempt In Learning.'

Notes

1 Dr Sunnie Giles is President of Quantum Leadership Group and a professionally certified executive coach, leadership development consultant, and organisational scientist.
2 Ron Ashkenas is a co-author of the *Harvard Business Review Leader's Handbook* and a Partner Emeritus at Schaffer Consulting. His previous books include *The Boundaryless Organization*, *The GE Work-Out*, and *Simply Effective*. Brook Manville is a co-author of the Harvard Business Review Leader's Handbook and Principal of Brook Manville LLC, a consultancy in strategy, organization, and leadership development. His previous Harvard Business Review Press books are *Judgment Calls* and *A Company of Citizens*. He also blogs about leadership at Forbes.com.
3 Mambra, S. (Oct 2nd 2019). The Complete Story of the Exxon Valdez Oil Spill. https://www.marineinsight.com/maritime-history/the-complete-story-of-the-exxon-valdez-oil-spill/ (Accessed 3 Feb 20)
4 Leveson, N. G. (2004). *Software System Safety*. Presentation from taught course at MIT. Available at: https://ocw.mit.edu/courses/aeronautics-and-astronautics/16-355j-software-engineering-concepts-fall-2005/lecture-notes/cnotes11.pdf (Accessed 7th June 2020)

5 Palast, G. (March 21, 1999). Ten years after but who was to blame? Available at: https://www.gregpalast.com/ten-years-after-but-who-was-to-blame/ (Accessed 3 Feb 20)
6 Griffin, D. (July 8th 2010). Critics call Valdez cleanup a warning for Gulf workers. Available at: https://edition.cnn.com/2010/US/07/07/oil.spill.valdez.workers/ (Accessed 2 Feb 20)
7 www.latimes.com/archives/la-xpm-2008-jun-26-na-valdez26-story.html (accessed 2 February 2020).
8 www.nytimes.com/2011/09/15/science/earth/15spill.html
9 http://news.bbc.co.uk/1/hi/world/americas/8679090.stm (accessed 2 February 2020).
10 www.bbc.co.uk/news/world-us-canada-11720907 (accessed 2 February 2020).
11 "Potential Impact of the Gulf Oil Spill on Tourism". *Oxford Economics.* 21 July 2010.
12 www.nytimes.com/2014/09/05/business/bp-negligent-in-2010-oil-spill-us-judge-rules.html (accessed 2 February 2020).
13 www.telegraph.co.uk/news/earth/energy/oil/8242717/Systemic-failures-to-blame-for-BP-Deepwater-Horizon-spill-US-commission-finds.html (accessed 3 February 2020).
14 https://oilprice.com/Latest-Energy-News/World-News/The-Cover-Up-E-mails-Show-BP-Lied-to-Authorities-on-The-Deepwater-Horizon-Spill.html
15 www.washingtonpost.com/wp-dyn/content/article/2010/06/03/AR2010060300848.html (accessed 3 February 2020).
16 www.businessinsider.com/bp-ceo-tony-hayward-apologizes-for-saying-id-like-my-life-back-2010-6?r=US&IR=T (accessed 3 February 2020).
17 www.nbcnews.com/id/37739658/ns/disaster_in_the_gulf/t/bp-boss-sorry-about-small-people-remark/#.Xjgt9y2cb1s
18 www.nbcnews.com/id/37273085/ns/politics-decision_2010/t/rand-paul-obama-bp-criticism-un-american/#.XjgVxC2cb1s (accessed 2 February 2020).
19 www.webcitation.org/5tZ0yCA9i (accessed 2 February 2020).
20 Published by Penguin, Copyright Fortune, a Division of Time Inc. 2003.
21 www.nytimes.com/2002/01/16/business/enron-s-collapse-overview-arthur-andersen-fires-executive-for-enron-orders.html (accessed 3 February 2020).
22 *Corporate Governance: Promises Kept, Promises Broken* – Jonathan R. Macey (p. 79) – Princeton University Press 2008.
23 knowledge.insead.edu/sites/www.insead.edu/files/images/asq_2015_print_vuori_huy_distributed_attention_and_shared_emotions_in_innovation_process.pdf (accessed 2 February 2020).
24 https://knowledge.insead.edu/strategy/the-strategic-decisions-that-caused-nokias-failure-7766 (accessed 3 February 2020).
25 www.businessinsider.com/how-steve-jobs-took-apple-from-near-bankruptcy-to-billions-in-13-years-2011-1?r=US&IR=T#2004-itunes-leads-to-70-market-share-ipod-mini-released-8
26 www.nytimes.com/2017/06/17/technology/whole-foods-amazon.html

CHAPTER 10

Military leadership
Stephen Newton

Leadership in the professions, the corporate world, and HE is often seen in terms of the ability to influence peers whilst being respected as technically excellent in one's own field. In such environments leadership capability may be desirable, but may not be seen as essential to professional success or to gaining promotion. Indeed, effective management capability may well be seen as sufficient. In the military context, however, leadership is considered a core competence; it is what officers and non-commissioned officers (NCOs) 'do'. As such, selection and training for leadership capability starts at a very early stage in any military career.

What is military leadership?

Military leadership encompasses a number of characteristics that are mutually understood between officers, NCOs, and those under their command. Those include, but are not limited to, honesty, loyalty, respect, and professional and personal trust. All are gained over time rather than being given automatically as of right. The word 'comradeship' is sometimes used to describe that combination of attributes. All are elements of a shared culture which runs through the military, even if the emphasis may vary by service (i.e. Navy, Army, Air Force) or even by branch (Infantry, Artillery) or unit (e.g. Regiment, Battery).

Honesty is seen as a given for the vast majority of the military; it is expected that service personnel will tell the truth as they see it. At senior levels, politics may come into play, but the rule of thumb holds good. Loyalty can extend to putting one's own personal safety at risk in order to protect a comrade when on operations. Loyalty works regardless of hierarchy – upwards and downwards. Respect derives in part from the knowledge that those around you will exercise that degree of loyalty and have both the capability and the willingness to provide mutual support even in such challenging circumstances.

By tradition in the British military, senior officers do not normally discipline a junior in another sub-unit directly; they do so via that person's immediate superiors. That in turn engenders a style of leadership that operates through and respects the chain of command rather than by direct action. One by-product of this approach is to free senior leaders from the felt need to micromanage, allowing them to focus instead on defining and achieving strategic aims. During operations, commanders will set objectives to be attained and outline any additional support resources available. It is left to commanders at the next level down to decide how to use the resources at their disposal to achieve the objective set. In other words, senior leaders set the context and parameters and a clear, unambiguous aim: tactical execution is left to subordinates.

Many of these concepts are to be found routinely in leadership and management literature. They are not so frequently apparent in practice outside the military; largely it appears due to differences of organisational culture. In the field of HE, the fact that an increasing proportion of academics are now employed on short-term contracts and in some cases across several organisations is likely to cause friction in building the kind of mutual trust, loyalty, etc., that are considered commonplace in the military.

> Questions to consider
>
> - To what extent does your organisation have a strong, well-defined culture that is commonly understood?
> - To what extent are traits such as loyalty, respect, etc., relevant in the culture of your organisation?
> - What would be different if they were?

The military, too, operates on short-term deployments. Indeed, a normal tour of duty may be only two or three years at the end of which an individual may move to a new role in a new unit, whether at the same or a more senior level. Additionally, units themselves may relocate periodically. However, the military tends to develop a common, shared culture that can transcend unit, branch, or service. Broadly, individuals can be expected to share a common set of values and behaviours, which will have been fostered from the beginning of their careers. That culture includes an accepted need to get on, professionally, with one's colleagues, which helps with rapid assimilation of individuals into new units and roles.

Approaches to leadership

The military has long recognised the power of high-performing teams (as opposed to effective working groups). Operational training is designed in part to develop technical skills, but more importantly to foster team working that takes those basic technical skills to a higher level.

There is a perception among many civilians that effective military leadership relies on strict hierarchy and obedience to orders. If that were ever the case, it is no longer. Modern military action requires a degree of (mental) agility and adaptability that cannot thrive under pure autocracy. That in turn requires juniors to be able to think for themselves – to understand what the Americans call 'the Commander's intent' and act accordingly when things go awry, as they inevitably do in what Carl von Clausewitz referred to as 'the fog of war' in his posthumously published book *On War* ([1]).

Interestingly, the Soviet military, which one might expect to have been driven by blind obedience to orders more than most, adopted a similar approach. Operational orders focused on the 'Commander's intent' with even the most junior soldiers permitted – indeed expected – to adjust their actions as necessary in light of events in order to achieve that intent. This was encapsulated in the concept of 'Operational Art' – a term coined by military theorist Svechin in 1928 and which persisted into the 1980s (Svechin, [2]).

If effective military leadership is not about hierarchy, autocracy, or micromanagement, how else might it be characterized? *Serve to Lead* is not only the cap badge motto of cadets at the Royal Military Academy Sandhurst in the UK, it is also the title of a privately published book issued to cadets in the first few days of their time at the Academy. It contains practical examples of military leadership drawn from a range of conflicts, mostly over the last hundred years or so. It is updated periodically to keep the book current. It also contains extracts from speeches and books on leadership by well-known military leaders such as Field Marshalls Slim and Montgomery.

One of the better-known of these extracts is from Field Marshall Sir Bill Slim speaking to young officers in a series entitled *Courage and Other Broadcasts* ([3]):

> Unselfishness as far as you are concerned means simply this – you will put first the honour and interests of your country and your regiment. Next you will put the safety, well-being and comfort of your men; and last – and last all the time – you will put your own interest, your own safety, your own comfort.

This sentiment holds good today. It speaks to a kind of social contract under which officers are expected not simply to lead their soldiers (or sailors or airmen) in combat operations but to pay attention to their welfare and that of their families. That may include counselling on the management of their finances or of their marital relationships. Officers (and their spouses) have long been expected to act as unpaid social workers in 'looking after their men' as it used to be termed. In the UK, cutbacks to defence budgets resulting in what is known as 'overstretch' have raised concerns that this informal social contract is under threat.

Such issues do not typically impact on leaders in HE, the professions, or in the corporate world – at least not to the same extent, although there is a growing recognition that organisations across all sectors can face significant additional human and financial cost by failing to recognise and address stress and other mental health issues. However, HE leaders may well find value in other concepts that are commonplace in the military:

- *Standards need to be set and enforced.* One can look at this in, broadly, two different ways. One approach is to establish an organisational culture that fosters personal pride in (for example) high standards of appearance and achievement. Obvious examples from the British military could include the Guards Regiments and Household Cavalry. In such cases, standards tend to be self-enforcing. Another approach is to establish detailed processes and procedures that seek to create a zero-error environment. An example could be the deployment of tactical nuclear weapons. Experience indicates that it is very hard to achieve a zero-error environment and that to do so can stifle initiative (which, in the case of nuclear deployment, may be seen as a good thing).
- *Constructive scepticism.* This means recognising as problematic and hence avoiding seductive 'good ideas' put forward by less experienced colleagues. This can be tricky in an HE research environment, where what might appear to be surprising ideas may prove to open new opportunities (the discovery of penicillin, the Higgs Boson…). A key filter is whether or not the initiator of the idea can articulate clearly what benefits are expected or what problem will be addressed and has a viable implementation plan.
- *Support functions* (such as IT) are vital. It is easy to focus on the front end of any business (typically winning new sales or new clients, delivering products, or doing technical work). Few businesses, including HE, can function without effective support functions and especially, nowadays, IT.
- *The process of planning is essential* (although plans rarely survive contact with reality). This is a well-rehearsed idea. In many cases, the military will develop not one plan to achieve a given objective, but several – each using a different approach and different assumptions. The approach ultimately adopted may be a combination of elements from a number of different plans, recognising new information or developing circumstances. Being flexible in attitude and comfortable with uncertainty are helpful attributes of leaders.
- *Promote your best people; support the less effective.* Promotion in this context does not mean simply a jump in rank. In the military, effective

leaders seek to raise the profile of their best people and to ensure they have opportunities to both develop their skills and deploy them to best advantage so that they gain cumulative experience. Similarly, they will identify the apparent capability gaps in those under their command who perform less well, and do their best to support those individuals to address those shortfalls. Alternatively, different career paths will be identified that allow those individuals to play to their strengths.

For example, the best individuals (who are perceived to have the necessary capabilities including mindset) in any unit may be offered the opportunity to go forward for Special Forces selection. That is in itself an accolade. Unit commanders might be expected to fret at the possible loss of talent to their unit. In the vast majority of cases, they are in fact very willing to release these individuals, recognising that they will likely return after their time in Special Forces, should they succeed in selection, bringing with them a range of new or more highly developed skills that can be fed into the unit as a whole, raising the game for all.

This has not been my experience in working with professional firms, where there is often a marked reluctance on the part of partners to release high-potential team members to move to other parts of the firm or to other locations due to the difficulty of finding replacements of similar calibre. That in turn usually indicates a failure of talent/pipeline management. HE leaders will need to consider this carefully and take steps to develop what is known in American football as 'bench strength' in their teams.

- *Establish a 'rhythm of work' that is sustainable indefinitely.* Military commanders need to be able to sustain readiness over long periods. The same applies to work in most parts of HE, especially during academic terms. It applies both to individuals and to groups and can serve to promote the overall wellbeing of both by reducing stress.

One way of doing this is to ensure that leaders delegate as much as possible whilst at the same time training subordinates to do the job of their immediate superior and perhaps even one level above that. In the military, that is typically done during field exercises by 'taking out' sub-unit commanders for a period of time and making their subordinates step up into their roles. Budget constraints may militate against this.

- *Leaders must be willing and able to use upwards and peer influence to achieve their aims.* Simply giving orders will not work. The key is to identify what is most important to each individual or group of stakeholders and seek to balance those interests. Communication skills of a high order are needed

in order to do this effectively – including the ability to say 'no' on occasion and the willingness to stand firm when necessary. Part of this influencing approach typically involves actively asking for ideas and support and engaging both peers and subordinates in developing plans. In the literature of management this is often described as 'leadership vulnerability'.
- *When communicating as a leader, avoid the trap of 'too much information'.* Too much information confuses and decision-making becomes harder. There have been several pieces of research in the field of psychology over the last 60 years or so into the amount of information that a human being can hold in short-term memory or can process simultaneously. The first was a hypothesis produced by George Miller at Harvard in 1956.[4] This stated that humans can hold seven items of random data in short-term memory ± 2 – i.e. between five and nine items.

Halford and colleagues (2005) at the University of Queensland found that most humans can only hold around four items in working memory and process them at the same time.[5] It is clearly easy to overwhelm the capacity of even the most intelligent individuals to keep up with a flow of complex ideas that is simply too long.

- *Simply be yourself.* You cannot be anyone else and lead successfully. This speaks to an idea that has gained particular currency over recent years – authenticity. In order to be credible and hence able to bring teams together to coalesce around a particular purpose, a leader must be authentic. Humans appear to be gifted with the ability to detect a perceived lack of authenticity very rapidly. That lack of authenticity in turn throws up a lack of trust and maybe even a sense of dislike, which damages the capacity of the individual to lead effectively or even to be accepted as a member of the team.

Whilst the words of Field Marshall Slim (see previous quote) were addressed to young commissioned officers, a similar leadership ethos is commonly expected of NCOs and warrant officers. Indeed, in many instances, these experienced people will support young, newly commissioned officers during their initial tour of duty and help to hone basic skills gained during training prior to being commissioned. These NCOs and warrant officers will likely have less in the way of formal academic education than their nominal 'boss' but considerably more practical experience. A young officer willing to ask for, and to accept, their advice reaps great benefit. This kind of 'upwards (or reverse) mentoring' is rare, in my experience, outside the military, except, for example, young professionals providing expertise to older colleagues on topics such as the use of social media.

> **Questions to consider**
> - Which of the headline concepts outlined above do you feel are relevant in your organisation?
> - Why are the remainder not relevant?
> - How would you make each of these real in your organisation?

Developing leadership capability

In some civilian organisations, such as larger investment management firms, graduate trainees used to spend time working in various operations functions in order to better understand, for example, how investment transactions are processed and reports for clients produced. Nowadays, however, many such organisations focus on pushing trainees through the relevant qualification process, including passing any mandatory exams, so that they can begin to generate fees in their own right.

Similar approaches can be seen in the professions, with trainees encouraged to gain necessary qualifications at speed and then to maximise the amount of paid work they undertake. Development beyond the required qualifications tends increasingly to be technical in nature, with so-called 'soft skills' taking a sometimes distant second place. In some firms, such non-technical training must be paid for by those who seek it, although there may be training, mentoring, and some coaching to build business development and client relationship management skills in the lead-up to promotion to partner level.

> **Questions to consider**
> - How does your organisation seek to develop leadership capability in its staff (regardless of employment status) today?
> - How could it be done differently or better?
> - What could be the result?

By contrast, military 'basic training' is simply the start of career-long development, focused on both the technical knowledge and leadership skills appropriate for the next levels of promotion. Senior leaders are expected to support juniors under their command in building these skill sets. They are also expected to help in managing their career trajectories so that they not only achieve their maximum potential but also deliver optimal value to the service, recognising that this may not always match the aspirations of the individual. For several decades, the British armed services have sought to identify those with senior leadership potential at an early stage and then both to test and to groom them for promotion by way of relevant training and experience, the latter where possible involving active service.

Increasingly, officer candidates on both sides of the Atlantic will have a first degree before starting their service. At post-graduate level, the military now recognises the value of development opportunities such as MBA degrees in addition to extended internal courses such as the staff college, which are now mandatory to enable promotion to and beyond the rank of major in the UK. Annual performance evaluation reports will include a recommendation (or otherwise) that an individual be selected to attend staff college and/or for promotion.

Extremes of leadership characteristics

For the most part, military leaders seek to ensure the success of their subordinates. That will also serve to ensure success of the team as a whole and, put simply, team success makes the leader look good. However, leadership literature tends to focus on the actions and approaches of individuals who are seen to have achieved notable success in their own right.

Such leaders may in fact be so-called 'productive narcissists'. They embody the positive aspects of what is commonly thought of as a negative trait. They typically have the capability to deliver excellent performance, including a clear and impressive vision. Combined with a charismatic personality, they are able to energise others around that vision. They may also be effective at mobilising groups to deliver it, especially if it is somewhat revolutionary. As Napoleon put it, 'Revolutions are the ideal times for soldiers with a lot of wit, and the courage to act.'

Narcissists may be able to use their command of language (combined with magnetic personality) to generate energy among others around the delivery of projects. However, they may lack the empathy to keep them engaged over the long term. They may also lack the desire to mentor subordinates in order to enable them to become more effective. In part that is likely to be due to the highly competitive nature of the narcissist and their unwillingness to acknowledge the contributions of others due to an over-inflated sense of self-worth.

The reverse of the narcissist is the obsessive personality. Such people tend to excel in roles where attention to detail and high levels of control are valued – for example, operations, logistics, and engineering. The two personalities can co-exist productively, and it is arguable that the narcissist benefits from having obsessives around them to ensure delivery. Obsessives can also act as effective counsellors or mentors to narcissists, especially if each recognises the other as a peer, albeit operating in different fields, and is open to constructive challenge.

> **Questions to consider**
> - To what extent can you identify narcissists in your organisation?
> - What is their impact?
> - If it is negative, how do you neutralise it?

Whilst there are undoubtedly examples of productive narcissism among military leaders, they tend to come to prominence during periods of uncertainty (of which war is an obvious and extreme example). Such individuals tend to be mistrusted as they may be seen to be too willing to exercise the courage of others and to be careless of their safety. Otherwise, as in the corporate world, they tend to be kept in check by their senior colleagues or directed to roles where their strengths can be given free rein for a time. Perhaps counterintuitively, they tend not (in my experience) to end up in a Special Forces environment.

A useful discussion of narcissism among leaders can be found in an article entitled 'Narcisstic Leaders: the Incredible Pros, the Inevitable Cons', by Michael Maccoby ([6]). A further interesting article is 'The Type of Narcissist That Can Make a Good Leader', by Randall S. Peterson and S. Wiley Wakeman ([7]).

Leadership within Special Forces

Despite their reputation, whilst Special Forces soldiers are usually willing to accepts high levels of risk, they seek to avoid unnecessary risk, not least because stakes are so high for them when they are called upon to go on operations. They do exhibit high levels of resilience and retain a highly flexible mindset, allowing them to adapt and respond to rapidly changing circumstances whilst retaining a high degree of focus. They also operate as true teams in which the dominant traits of the narcissist outlined above have little place and in which leadership is flexible, allowing the person with the greatest expertise in a given situation to take charge regardless of hierarchy. In part this reflects the fact that Special Forces personnel are both experienced and highly trained: hence they require little direction as such. This different context inevitably demands a different approach to leadership.

Leadership is ultimately about people

The actions and impact of the individual (regardless of their personality type) in any given organisation may be lauded or derided depending on one's point of view. Ultimately, however, the gravity of leadership applies itself and it becomes clear that leadership is about bringing together individuals to act in concert. It revolves around 'getting the right people on your bus', as Jim Collins put it[8] – getting others to coalesce around a common purpose, to believe that the purpose is both worthwhile and achievable, and to believe that each team member can fulfil their part in achieving it.

It takes time to establish a team and time seems increasingly to be short in HE – as it is elsewhere. It also appears that the culture of team working in HE may be less pervasive than in the military, where the mutual support provided by a true team is seen as a necessary survival factor during combat operations. Within HE, it seems that although groups may think of themselves as a team, they may more often be, in fact, a working group that coalesces around a specific project and then disperses. That could be driven by the increasingly short-term nature of employment contracts, the fact that many academics now have roles across a number of HEIs, and by the discontinuity of funding for research (and even in some cases for teaching).

As Jon Katzenbach (co-author of *The Wisdom of Teams*[9]) observes, there is nothing wrong with creating an effective working group as opposed to a team – and indeed results can be similar at least in the short term. In many professional firms, and especially the larger ones, the normal modus operandi is to bring together working groups to deliver a project or to address a range of diverse needs for a client in a coordinated fashion. Establishing a true team takes time and the need for ongoing team working may not exist once a given project is completed. The larger accounting firms and especially the so-called 'Big Four' – EY, PwC, Deloitte, and KPMG – have become adept at bringing together at short notice such effective working groups to serve clients. The same can be said of larger consulting firms such as McKinsey.

Questions to consider

- Do you observe true teams operating in your organisation?
- What could be the value of developing greater 'teamness'?

Can HE learn from the military in establishing and maintaining teams? What might be the benefit? In short, it is not immediately clear that team creation (as opposed to the working group approach) is always necessary within HE.

Whilst it may be seen as a desirable aspiration over time, it may not be something to strive for from the outset. Much will depend on the culture of the organisation and the stability of its staffing.

Establishing a learning organisation and how to keep learning

It used to be said that the term 'military intelligence' was an oxymoron and also that the most difficult thing about introducing a new idea to the military mind was extracting the old one to make space. Those tongue-in-cheek observations have probably not been valid for at least the last half century and certainly not over the last 25 years. In the UK, the military has faced a combination of increasingly diverse threats and resource reduction. It has been asked to do more with less. The same is true in HE as in the professions and many corporates, especially since the 2008 financial crash.

One way to maximise the possibility of continuing to do more with less is for individuals and organisations to learn and redevelop continually, with key responsibilities for leaders including horizon scanning and the assessment of both threats and opportunities. At a strategic level, the military (as is the case for HE) needs to interact constructively with politicians, whose time horizons may be very different but who ultimately hold the purse strings.

This learning and redevelopment requires a review process, whether at regular intervals (monthly, quarterly, etc.) or at significant milestones (project completion for example). A problem with many reviews is that the focus is on what went wrong or could have been done better, thus generating an unhelpful combination of a blame culture and defensiveness.

To overcome this, the military routinely uses the 'after-action report'. The process is simple. All those who took part in a given project (to put it in a HE context), whether directly or indirectly (in support roles for example), meet as soon as practicable after the project is complete. The meeting may usefully be facilitated by someone who was not involved. First, the facts are established: what actually occurred. Next there is a discussion of what went well. Last, there is a discussion of what could have been done differently or better. No blame is given; the purpose is to learn and to consider how to improve for the future.

If something blameworthy does come out of the conversation, it is handled separately. The learning points are recorded and shared, either within the unit or more widely as appropriate. Experience indicates that participants in the after-action reporting process tend to assess their actions objectively and may be tougher on themselves than their colleagues might have been when it comes to considering things that could have been done better.

> **Questions to consider**
> - How well does your organisation learn from itself?
> - How could it learn more?
> - How could you encourage organisational learning without a blame culture?

This is of course simply a variation of the long-standing Plan–Do–Review process used in the manufacturing industry and in many change management projects. It could also be thought of as a variant of the Toyota Manufacturing System with its Quality Circles approach. The exact approach to implementation can be adjusted as needed to fit with the context, including the culture of the organisation. However, some form of ongoing, formalised organisational and individual learning and review process is hugely valuable in any organisation.

The pros and cons of elites

There has long been a debate in military circles concerning the value of elites such as Special Forces. The main arguments focus on, on the one hand, the cost to select, train, and deploy Special Forces effectively and, on the other, the fact that some types of operation can only be carried out effectively by a Special Forces-type unit.

In order to develop an elite group, a military institution must have adequate scale. If only around 1% of serving military personnel have the capability to serve effectively in a Special Forces environment, there needs to be a pool of adequate size from which to select in order to maintain such[10] a force of a size that can operate effectively and in more than one location simultaneously.

Special Forces have long approached selection based on the attitude of the individual first, aptitude second. Only if the first two are in place will training be able to produce individuals with the skills and capabilities necessary. Attitude and aptitude are simple but effective filters to reduce the dropout rate in training. A further filter is that, in most cases, those aspiring to join Special Forces must have a minimum time in service (to ensure adequate experience) and a recommendation from their boss and boss's boss (their 'senior rater') as part of their periodic performance evaluation.

In the HE context, the issue of elites remains relevant, although the considerations are very different and arguably more nuanced. What defines an HE elite? Is it the nature of the institution in which an academic works – Russell

Group/Ivy League* versus so-called 'red brick' or post-92 universities, for example? Is it instead the perceived excellence of an individual academic in their field? Is it still the case that an institution not generally recognised as one of the 'great universities' can be regarded as a centre of excellence in a given field and hence able to attract the best academic talent, both in teaching and as students?

A more important issue in both the military and HE fields is how to enable the wider dispersion of capabilities developed within an elite (however that may be defined). In the military, a proportion of Special Forces personnel will return to normal duties after a period of time. They bring with them skills and attitudes that serve to raise the standards of the unit to which they return. It is arguable that academics who have helped to create a centre of excellence in research, for example, and who move on after completion of the research project to take up a teaching post elsewhere achieve the same effect.

Questions to consider

- How effectively does your organisation harness its internal elites to bring about general improvement?
- Is yours an elite organisation? What makes it so?
- Why does it matter (for you)?

Whilst there is something of the chicken and egg in the question of elites, it seems likely that their existence serves as an aspirational benchmark for others – something to strive for or by which to judge one's own efforts. It is akin to the role of elites in sports: one might not have the capability to equal the success of Steve Redgrave or Jessica Ennis-Hill, but such figures set a benchmark for success and serve as exemplars of the need for passion to perform and hard, focused work to achieve that success over and above raw talent.

Leading under stress

There is an old saying that, in fair weather, anyone can steer the ship. Leadership in times of stress is always challenging and the greatest enemies of success are complexity and distraction. Whatever the cause of stress, success is more likely if leaders are able to focus on the job in hand and reduce the number of variables they must handle. This is one of the valuable aspects of creating a clear 'Commander's intent' on which leaders at all levels of the organisation can focus.

There will inevitably be competing distractions. However, anything that does not deliver that objective can be ignored, at least temporarily – an idea discussed in the 2005 book *Will it Make the Boat Go Faster?* by Hunt-Davis and Beveridge. It can of course be hard to identify what is on the so-called critical path and what can be sidestepped. Adaptability and resilience are essential leadership traits because they enable such decisions to be taken more easily. In most cases, experience indicates that deciding what *not* to do can deliver greater value than deciding what to do.

Note

* The 'Russell Group' comprises 24 UK universities that are research-intensive and consider themselves world-class in both research and teaching. In the US, 'Ivy League' has similar connotations. So-called 'red brick' or 'post-92' universities in the UK have come into being relatively recently or were created in 1992 by re-categorising former polytechnics as universities. Whilst they may lack the cachet of their Russell Group counterparts, many are now recognised as centres of excellence in their own right.

References

[1] von Clausewitz, C. (1832/1976). *On War.* New Jersey: Princeton University Press.
[2] Svechin, A. (1992). *Strategy*, ed. Kent D. Lee. Minneapolis: East View Publications.
[3] Slim, W. (1957). *Courage and Other Broadcasts.* London: Cassell & Co. Ltd.
[4] Miller, G. (1956). The Magical Number Seven, Plus or Minus Two Some Limits on Our Capacity for Processing Information. *Psychological Review* 101(2), 343–352.
[5] Halford, G., Baker, R., McCredden, J., & Bain, J. (2005). How Many Variables Can Humans Process? *Psychological Science*, 16(1), 70–76. 10.1111/j.0956-7976.2005.00782.x.
[6] Maccoby, M. (2004). Narcisstic Leaders: the Incredible Pros, the Inevitable Cons. *Harvard Business Review.* 82(1), 92–101.
[7] Peterson R. & Wiley Wakeman, S. (March 6 2017). *The type of narcissist that can make a good leader.* Harvard Business Review Digital Articles. Available at: https://hbr.org/2017/03/the-type-of-narcissist-that-can-make-a-good-leader (Accessed 7 June 2020).
[8] Collins, J. (2001). *Good to Great: Why Some Companies Make the Leap.. and Others Don't.* New York: Random House.
[9] Katzenbach, J. & Smith, D. (1993). *The Wisdom of Teams.* Harvard: Harvard Business School Press.
[10] Hunt-Davis, B. & Beveridge, H. (2011). *Will It Make the Boat Go Faster? Olympic-Winning Strategies for Everyday Success.* Kibworth: Troubador Publishing.

CHAPTER 11

Leadership in sport

Kendall Jarrett with Victor López-Ros, Andy Siddall, Serge Eloi, Matthew Hobbs, and Lukas Marek

As a society we have come to recognise effective leadership in sport as being the catalyst for successful sporting performance. Whether it's the backroom decisions of an administrator, the off-court instructions of a coach, or the on-field actions of a player, effective leaders in sport are known not just for their impact on successful performance and the development of other leaders, but also because of the circumstances within which their leadership led to success. Circumstances synonymous with sporting success include the overcoming of adversity (e.g. swimmer Yusra Mardini's selection for the Refugee Olympic Team in 2016), sustained achievement (e.g. New England Patriots' nine Super Bowl appearances in 18 years), and 'against the odds' triumphs (e.g. Leicester City FC winning the English Premier League in 2015/16).

Within all circumstances that lead to sporting success, the right leadership behaviours are 'critical and highly relied upon' (Cummins & Spencer, 2015, p. 174) to garner a common sense of purpose, a commitment to task, and an appreciation of requirements. Sporting success, especially in a team sport environment, is rarely achieved if such foci remain unknown, ill-defined, and/ or under-resourced.

Typically, what sporting success *is* (e.g. what the outcome or goal is), is known to all those involved (e.g. winning the championship). In HE it is often the case, however, that circumstances within which leadership operates and within which success is defined, remain deliberately out of view from those who are being led. What can often be even more frustrating is that the strategies and behaviours known to lead to success can be nigh on impossible to enact due to the hurdles created by an abundance of meaningless policy and/or the perfunctory nature of leadership. So, what can we learn about effective[1] and successful[2] leadership in sport that can enhance our capacities as leaders in HE?

On-field leadership

On-field leadership means different things to different people. In cricket the formal leadership position of captain brings with it play-by-play tactical decision-making responsibilities. It is a leadership *and* management role all in one, requiring empathy, resilience, and competitive drive (Cotterill & Barker, 2013). As former Australian Test Cricket Captain Sir Don Bradman once stated:

> A captain must make every decision before he [sic] knows what its effect will be, and he must carry the full responsibility, not whether his decision will be right or wrong, but whether it brings success.
> (Mukherjee, 2016, p. 86)

Conversely, in other team sports the responsibilities of a formal captain may be viewed as more ceremonial, e.g. the tossing of the coin, the wearing of an armband. This does not mean one type of formal leadership role is any less important than another, but it does highlight the range of on-field responsibilities a formal leader might have (Cotterill & Cheetham, 2017). It is also important to recognise the on-field contribution of informal leaders within sport. Effective informal leaders, described by Norwegian sport psychologist Willi Railo as the cultural architects of a team based on their abilities to change the minds of teammates, can be equally as pivotal as formal leaders in taking a group forward to achieve on-field success (Railo, 1986).

Formal and informal leadership opportunities in sport

Playing sport from a young age acts as a nursery for the development of leadership skills. As a captain (e.g. in cricket), a specialist (e.g. libero in volleyball), an official (e.g. 'calling your own fouls' in basketball), and a coach (e.g. guiding a peer who is new to archery), athletes are consistently exposed to opportunities to develop their leadership skills. As sport becomes more competitive, the naming of a formal leader or captain can follow, and it is at this stage that the multifaceted nature of team sports leadership reveals itself. Cotterill and Fransen (2016) define four separate team sport leadership roles:

- a task leader (e.g. on-field tactical instruction);
- a motivational leader (e.g. on-field motivator);
- a social leader (e.g. tasked with maintaining positive team relations off the field);
- an external leader (e.g. one who communicates with management, sponsors, media).

> **Question to consider**
> - What do you do now (or not do now) as a leader that can be traced back to experiences of sport leadership?

As previously stated, not all team sport leadership roles will (or should) be filled by the formal, nominated leader. Indeed, the importance of informal leaders spread throughout a team was highlighted in a study by Fransen et al. (2014) exploring athlete leadership. Their survey of 4,451 players and coaches across nine different team sports found that the leadership qualities attributed to the nominated captain of a sports team were 'overrated' and that almost half of those surveyed 'did not perceive their captain as the most important leader, neither on, nor off the field' (p. 1394). As such, the role of the informal leader is a significant one as their influence can be felt through either the strengthening of a shared vision or the spreading of discord throughout the team (Cotterill & Fransen, 2016). Gaining exposure to this formal/informal leadership dynamic and becoming accustomed to the different types of leadership roles available within a team can provide all those who participate in sport with a better understanding of the complexities of leadership and a better sense of the skills required for effective leadership.

Leadership development support

The development of effective on-field leaders in sport is the product of a series of interactions between the coach, the athlete, and the sports environment requiring continuous planning and evaluation (Argent, 2005). To assist with this dynamic, on-field leaders are often provided with access to former sports leaders in a mentor–mentee arrangement. Clubs invest in such arrangements to help cultivate within its leaders a greater sense of belonging to the role as well as a better understanding of the leadership practices typically required for on-field success.

> **Question to consider**
> - What leadership development environments are afforded colleagues within your institution?

The unique circumstances within which the playing of sport is conducted means it is commonplace to have consistent access to development environments to hone leadership skills, e.g. weekly practice sessions and/or pre-season competitions. Such 'training' occasions lend themselves to leadership behaviours being trialled, evaluated, reflected upon, and subsequently developed in readiness for the pressures of game-day leadership. Thus, there is an onus on coaches to design intentional development practices for their leaders within such training occasions. One such framework coaches might consider when developing a programme of leadership development is the use of Newman, Lower, and Brgoch's (2019) *Model for Developing Sport Team Captains as Formal Leaders*. The model outlines the following five processes:

1. fostering a team culture of leadership;
2. determining the role(s) of team captains;
3. identifying and selecting team captains;
4. developing and supporting team captains (e.g. setting expectations and standards, empowering them to make important decisions, providing role models, encouraging reflection, maintaining positive coach–captain relationships);
5. evaluating and reinforcing team captains.

Adherence to this or other models for formal leadership development in sport (e.g. Jones & Spamer's (2011) the Leadership Styles Competency Framework for Governing Bodies in Sport) can help to condition on-field leaders to the requirements of working closely with their coach/manager, and vice versa. And if this relationship is to be effective, mutual trust and respect, sustained via frequent, candid, and honest communication, is paramount (Janssen, n.d.). Any disconnect between captain and coach can ultimately exacerbate the disconnect felt by the rest of the team, as a study of US collegiate coaches' time investment in their captains revealed. The study, completed by the Janssen Sport Leadership Centre, found that 77% of coaches surveyed thought they spent sufficient time with their captains, whilst only 38% of captains thought the same. This perceived leader distance, evidenced by way of discrepancy in time investment, can have a significant impact on the overall development of on-field leadership behaviours (Arthur, Wagstaff & Hardy, 2016).

Off-field leadership

To explore what effective off-field leadership in sport actually looks like first requires a degree of perspective. We know from our experiences of sport, and the many celebrations of sporting success we have been privy to, that the requirements of sporting success are as varied (e.g. the contexts within which success is achieved) as they are the same (e.g. the types of behaviours that lead to success). We know that sporting success, by its very definition, requires others to fail or (to frame defeat in a more digestible form) come up short in their attempts to achieve the same outcome. We also know that in the world of competitive sport, individuals and organisations will go to great lengths (and expense) to seek every advantage possible, even if it means deliberately breaking the rules. In such a complex and value-laden environment where luck and chance also play their part, effective off-field leadership by sport coaches and sport organisation administrators 'can be a source of significant competitive advantage' (Frawley, Favaloro & Schulenkorf, 2018, p. 123) or the defining factor in on-field failure.

Sport coaches and leadership

With over two decades of experience as a sport coach, team manager, and sport masseur working with athletes and teams from participatory to elite level, I have witnessed a range of leadership behaviours influence a range of sporting outcomes. In Japan, whilst working for a prefecture's board of education, I watched dedicated high school students diligently repeat the exact same training session every evening for a month for no discernible performance improvement. In Australia, whilst working for the Hockey SA Women's Team, I saw coaches empower players to develop off-field culture for the benefit of on-field performance on a national stage. And in South Africa and Sri Lanka during international cricket tours for English school and university cricket teams, I have been privy to the lengths to which coaches will go to imbue within their athletes the pursuit of goals in the face of adversity. As such, the impact a sports coach can have on individual and team performance and development, within and outside the confines of the chosen sporting endeavour, is immense.

> ### Questions to consider
> - How accessible are leadership coaches at your institution?
> - What emphasis is placed on the need for coaches as a means to develop incumbent leaders in HE?

Whatever the coaching circumstances, 'it is crucial for effective coaches to employ their own leadership approach [whilst remaining] cognizant of player preferences for specific leadership styles' (Bennie & O'Connor, 2012, p. 87).

This cognisance also refers to an appreciation of contextual factors, such as the sport being played, the level of play (e.g. participation right through to elite level) and the age and background of athletes (Bennie & O'Connor, 2012). In addition to this, Bandura and Kavussanu (2018) suggest that by remaining authentic as a leader (e.g. self-aware, honest, trusting, athlete-centred, acting with moral purpose), athlete enjoyment and commitment can be heightened. It is obvious then that the responsibilities of sport coaches in any sporting context are numerous and far reaching. For example, Constandt and Willem (2019) state that sport coaches have a responsibility to model ethical behaviours within sporting organisations and as such should act as 'go-betweens to transfer perceived organizational ethical leadership to the players' (p. 413). With all these requirements and responsibilities for sport coaches being alluded to, it becomes ever more inviting for sport coaches to gravitate towards lists of prescriptive coaching dos and don'ts. Yet such lists and resources should always be read through a filter of context.

As with any goal-oriented environment, practices of leadership in sport should be tempered around the context of their application. An example of this is Steve Kerr and his tenure as Golden State Warriors (GSW) head coach in the NBA. From 2015 to 2019 the GSW played in five consecutive NBA finals series, winning three championships. During this time the team comprised multiple All-Stars and future Hall-of-Famers – current icons of the game. Due to player injury, retirement, and trading, though, the team to take the court at the start of the 2019/20 season was vastly different in age, experience, and talent. For Steve Kerr to adopt the same coaching rhetoric and focus for the 2019/20 season as in previous seasons would be nonsensical.

For coaching success (however defined at the time) to occur in such times of transition, either of two decisions are often made: (1) the coach adapts their coaching mentality and focus; or (2) the coach is replaced by a perceivably better-suited coach. A remarkable example of what a change in coach can bring can been seen in the rise of Leicester City Football Club, who in 2015/16 under a newly appointed coach, Claudio Ranieri, went from near relegation the previous year to English Premier League champions. Making the decision to replace a coach, and who to replace them with, is the domain of sports administrators (e.g. team owners, sporting directors, club committee members).

Sport administrators and leadership

In any one day, sports administrators 'can be thanked for team success or be accused of failure' (Matusitz & Simi, 2019, p. 154). The decisions made by sport administrators can affect a generation of sporting dreams. As the 199th pick in the 2000 NFL draft, Tom Brady's selection by the New England Patriots was viewed by some as just filling a roster spot. Nine Super Bowl appearances and six championship rings later, he is the most successful quarterback in NFL history. Erin Phillips, the former WNBA player turned Australian Rules Footballer, is another whose selection as a rookie listed player by Adelaide Football Club administrators for the inaugural 2017 season (having not played the sport competitively for 13 years prior) was seen as a 'punt' by many. Her recruitment, though, translated into two League Best and Fairest wins (2017, 2019) and two team premiership wins (2017, 2019). Indeed, many of the decisions made by sports administrators should be commended for their bravery in committing to the realities of risk versus reward decision-making. The roster changes made by Toronto Raptors president Masai Ujiri ahead of their NBA title-winning season of 2018/19 are an example of what brave leadership can accomplish.

The opposite is also true. In 2017 Alexis Sanchez moved from Arsenal to Manchester United on a reported £391,000 a week wage package. Eighteen months later the team had failed to improve on-field performances and with Sanchez costing the club £11 million per goal and £19,800 a minute playing time, he was unceremoniously jettisoned to another club (Ruszkai, 2019). The risk versus reward gamble had not paid off, which ultimately intensified scrutiny of recent personnel changes in off-field leadership (e.g. appointment of a new chief executive along with the hiring and firing of a series of managers after a prolonged period of great stability and on-field success). This apparent power vacuum left by serial leadership change, though, is not uncommon and is often exacerbated by a win-or-bust mentality. Burton and Leberman (2017) wrote that 'with a focus on winning, and winning at all costs, leadership may take on more destructive forms' (p. 151). Thus, the value of authentic and ethical leadership, particularly at board level, should not be underestimated. Honest, open relationships between the CEO and other organisation hierarchy, set the moral compass for a sporting organisation and can provide the foundation for organisation success (Takos, Murray & O'Boyle, 2018). So how can sporting administrators be developed as such?

> **Question to consider**
>
> - What impact does the 'moral compass' of your institution's board have on your or others' leadership practices within your institution?

In a study of 15 senior managers in Australian professional sports organisations, the authors (Frawley, Favaloro & Schulenkorf, 2018) found that whilst formal education opportunities were of benefit, ultimately 'there's a whole series of things that you can only learn by experience' (p. 127). Further comment stated that for senior managers 'there was no specific turning point [relating to their development as sport administrators] but instead a series of significant events and experiences that led to them becoming competent and confident leaders' (p. 127). By accessing experiences that exposed leaders to the context and requirements of decision-making, by learning from one's mistakes and becoming more self-aware of decision-making options available, by building and relying on networks forged, the leadership skills and knowledge of sport administrators can benefit considerably (Frawley, Favaloro & Schulenkorf, 2018).

Characteristics of effective sporting leaders

In a study by Smith et al. (2017) exploring perceptions of transformational leadership behaviours exhibited by formal team captains and head coaches, the following effective leadership behaviours were identified:

- high performance expectations (e.g. maintain exemplary levels of behaviour and conduct off the field as well as effort in training);
- inspirational motivation;
- individual consideration;
- appropriate role-modelling;
- intellectual stimulation;
- fostering acceptance of group goals.

It is apparent, though, that not all successful captains, coaches, and administrators exhibit all (or any!) of these characteristics. Research by Arnold, Fletcher and Hobson (2018) exploring Olympic athletes' perceptions of leaders and managers with dark trait characteristics[3] (e.g. inauthentic, success-obsessed, self-focused) highlighted the range of positive *and/or* negative effects such characteristics can have on athletes' behaviour and performance. The implications of their research are that leaders should be aware of their own dark characteristics and the impact these can have on others and that 'to emerge as a leader and be effective in that role, it is not as straightforward or simplistic as developing and nurturing characteristics of a bright nature [e.g. conscientiousness, openness, intelligence] and avoiding those that are dark' (p. 461). As such, sporting leadership effectiveness is a difficult beast to control. There is a fine line between challenging athletes to perform at their maximum, maintaining appropriate boundaries, and providing effective emotional and performance support (Smith et al., 2017). That is why, though, we can learn so much in HE from leadership in sport.

Global stories of leadership in sport

The sporting world provides a plethora of narratives on leadership. From the first taste of leadership responsibility on a junior team right through to locker room rallying addresses televised to millions, stories of sporting leadership are used to inspire and for dissection with the hope that lessons learned can advance the search for success. The conveyor belt of sporting autobiographies that grace then vacate our bookshop shelves tend to hold within them stories of leadership that define a sporting dynasty, event, or career. From the inspiration of Gareth Thomas's *Proud*, Jessica Long's *Unsinkable*, and Ben Hunt-Davis's *Will it Make the Boat go Faster?*, to the revelations of Tony Adams' *Addicted* and Tyler Hamilton's *The Secret Race*, the sports autobiography genre provides the reader with a glimpse into the life of a sporting leader. To extend this genre of writing from which so much of our understanding of leadership success is built, five sporting leaders (within four separate stories) now share their stories of leadership in sport. Each was asked to outline their sporting leadership experiences and to present key lessons about leadership pertinent to their chosen sporting/recreation field. The purpose of sharing these stories is to help readers develop and consider takeaway messages held within stories to enhance their own leadership in HE.

Story 1 – Leadership in cricket with Andy Siddall (UK)

I have had 20 years' experience of leading in several cricketing environments. These started as a university student captaining the Leeds Bradford MCCU (one of six national cricket centres of excellence in the UK). I discovered captaincy and leadership was something I naturally gravitated towards and the natural desire to lead, achieve, and grow resulted in me becoming captain of a men's club 1st XI, where we had some successful times. Looking back this was a significant time of growth as leading men, often older than myself, from such diverse backgrounds, working in diverse fields and some being deeply experienced and successful in their own lives was invaluable. Getting an entire club of three senior and four junior teams, with committees, structures, and history, to get onto my page as a 23-year-old helped me start to grow my leadership toolkit. My journey then took me into a number of other environments, including seven years as head coach at a university cricket programme followed by eight years at Leicestershire County Cricket Club as academy director.

All these experiences meant, at various times, having to deal with significant emotional shifts for my teammates and myself. It is important to understand that as time passes, all these experiences have proven to be invaluable. All of them have shaped my philosophies, standards, behaviours, principles, values, beliefs, and understanding of self, which in turn has grown my leadership skill set and allowed me to be credible and equipped for new roles and challenges. One thing that is evident is that being 18 years old and expected to make decisions – whether large or small – on people, structures, systems, and budgets, and then communicate them, has meant that for as long as I can remember I have felt comfortable making decisions and living with the consequences of them.

In my first full-time professional leadership role, I was surrounded and mentored by some excellent people – men and women who were very positive yet realistic, who possessed high levels of emotional intelligence, management skill, and various leadership qualities. My experiences during my second professional role allowed me to see a different side to leadership and learn from the shortfalls and failings of other leaders. This learning and cross-examination was magnified by working under so many different styles given the high turnover of leaders.

Like other people, my own understanding of leadership is constantly growing and is a mix of both complex, nuanced messages as well as incredibly simple ones. For me what is key as a leader in sporting environments is:

1. Vision and direction – the ability to 'see' the future and convince others to get on board.
2. Trustworthiness – don't bullshit people, you will get found out.
3. Authenticity and vulnerability – show vulnerability in order to create vulnerability-based trust.
4. Credibility – people must believe in the messenger. Credibility is eroded if you don't know what you stand for.

In addition, my leadership in sport is guided by the following statements:

- People are key – apply the principle of first *who* and then *what*.
- Understand your values, principles, and non-negotiables and model them.
- Read, listen, share ideas – don't be ignorant, but do not become guilty of serially jumping from *this to that*.
- Leadership at the highest levels is not just 9-to-5. It is 24/7, 365 days a year. Partners must be supportive and understand the commitments required, otherwise you are not at your best.
- Be humble – think lightly of yourself, but deeply of the world.
- Do not expect your players to get better day-by-day if you do not expect the same of yourself.
- Celebrate success.
- Review and reflect at every opportunity.
- NEVER underestimate your opponent.

Story 2 – Leadership in athletics with Victor López-Ros (Spain)

Since 2016 I have been working as part of a 'performance team' with an Olympic middle-distance runner. This team includes a head coach, a physiotherapist, a medical doctor, a biomechanist, and me as a strength and conditioning coach and head of performance. My work in this team includes specific tasks on strength and conditioning, technique, and peak performance planning. I am at all times trying to reduce the gap between research and practice, between laboratory and field. My professional responsibility to the athlete is to be available and to work under pressure.

Every member of the team leads a key function critical to overall performance success. When you are working with a high-performance athlete, everything is important, as the smallest detail can be the difference between success and failure. As a leader I must have all aspects of the training process in my mind at all times in order to effectively analyse and respond to any change or detail. I also need to think clearly under pressure in order to make the most correct or beneficial decision the situation requires.

It is important to also remember that sometimes, especially when working with information provided from so many different fields (e.g. physiology, anatomy, nutrition, biomechanics, psychology), the 'correct answer' does not exist. When faced with multiple possibilities I need to decide what is best for my athlete, at this time, in this specific context.

In terms of athlete leadership, everything is easier if you work with people who share common traits and goals. If your athletes are confident and responsible, honest and generous, the experience, for me, is all that more rewarding.

When working with other leaders in a team I have learned:

- It is important to always be aware of who is the protagonist in any one moment, and to respond always with the athlete in mind.
- The developing and sustaining of confidence between team members should not be trivialized.
- The realities of leadership are that leaders make decisions, those decisions have outcomes, and that a leader should have a greater awareness of that fact.

Story 3 – Leadership in volleyball with Serge Eloi (France)

For 15 years I was fortunate enough to work as a professional coach in the French Ligue A volleyball competition. My career consisted of two phases: the first phase as an assistant coach followed by another phase as a head coach. I also spent time as a national coach for the French Volleyball Federation (FVF) as the head of statistics and game plans. As a coach I experienced a range of highs and lows. The highs were placing fourth at the 1997 European Championships with the French Men's team, winning the French League (five times), Coupe de France (twice) and the Champions League, coaching at an amateur club, and coaching at a professional women's club. The lows were being fired without justification, seeing colleagues fired without justification, and being the fall guy for club administrators who after five months changed their minds about my appointment.

> **Question to consider**
> - Who do you have access to as a leader that invigorates and innovates your leadership practices?

Working with innovative coaches and dedicated players at the forefront of European volleyball was fantastic. As an assistant coach, my leadership was more informal, with players coming to me for various on- and off-court needs. My role as assistant coach allowed me to make a lot of innovations (e.g. development of game analysis software, training situation, game strategies). The limitation of this position was that I always had to fight to make my point and that was sometimes exhausting.

As a head coach, the status this position has always led me to more formal leadership practices aligned to telling and showing. As such, I was responsible for both controlling events whilst at the same time responding to them, as all problems came directly to me (e.g. player injuries, jealousy between players, issues with ego, press, delayed planes). I was a direct coach, by necessity. The need for results left little time to change behaviours and practices or open up new perspectives to players. I had to show that I knew my job very quickly, which is what the players also expected. What this also meant was that most athletes I worked with preferred to be guided and didn't want to take on responsibilities. This seems to run counter to theories that decision-making should be collective; although with that said, I became aware that the players I was coaching at the time were not trained to be leaders themselves. I hope that in future new players will be trained to become more involved as decision-makers, as making decisions means positioning yourself in the face of a problem.

Story 4 – Leadership in surfing with Matthew Hobbs and Lukas Marek (New Zealand)

We are spatial scientists, but also amateur surfers. Having surfed individually in the UK, Australia, New Zealand, Thailand, Wales, and Indonesia, we now both surf together in and around Christchurch. Leadership in surfing can be both formal and informal. Formal leadership, by a surf instructor, is common when learning how to surf. Instructors provide essential advice on how to paddle, stand up, and behave while surfing. However, as surfers become more experienced, leadership often becomes mostly informal, e.g. by following the example of local surfers or (more) experienced friends.

The New Zealand surf landscape often comes with isolated surf spots, dangerous rips, submerged rocks, winding unpaved roads with steep drops either side, and a variety of wildlife to share the water with. Successfully leading informal surf excursions in this environment, for instance by helping others surf safely, can be extremely rewarding. However, it requires a unique skill set. For instance, first, it is essential to spend time researching the correct surf spot. Second, you must respect the conditions on the day: is the surf much bigger than forecasted? Where are the rips? Are there any rocks you need to be aware of? What happens if you come across any wildlife? Do you need a farmer's permission to cross their land? Third, once you feel comfortable taking you and your group into the swell, does everyone know about surf etiquette? Do they know who has right of way on the wave? For beginner surfers, the likelihood is no (which can often be a bit more difficult than expected).

Surfing requires both resilience and patience to progress. People often say, 'surfing is harder than I expected.' Beginners are often seen fighting near the shoreline with small messy waves while they become familiar with the surfboard and technique to stand up. However, with resilience, you become stronger and more experienced. Once the surfer builds the strength and skills to get through the breakwater, they can paddle to the line-up 'out back'. Surfing is difficult and getting to this stage is no easy feat. The water can be wild and the route to the line-up is often blocked by breaking waves. This requires patience. You also rely on the wind and the waves to surf; however, there are often periods with no wind and no waves. The only thing you can do is wait, meaning not everyone is able to progress quickly.

Similar to leading in academia, surfing is a difficult and complex activity. Improvement in some cases may be slow or even hard to observe for an individual when compared with others. Indeed, while some surfers and leaders are able to improve very early and quickly, others need a slower pace to build to become more comfortable in order to enjoy the experience. Both surfing and leadership in academia are activities that are attractive. However, the dropout rate in both can be high. Once a person starts, they often find out that the activity is more challenging than anticipated. It is important that beginners feel comfortable and are supported regardless of the pace and challenge.

To conclude, successfully leading a surf excursion could be compared to leading colleagues in the writing of a journal article. Did you conduct your background research to ensure you are surfing in the right spot (literature review)? Do you have the right tools, i.e. surfboard and wetsuit for the conditions (methods)? Did you enjoy it, how many waves did you get (results)? Reflecting on the session, was everyone happy with the trip (discussion)? With experience you will know which wave to catch, and which one to let go; if you do catch the wave you want, think about where it might take you, and if it will be a fun ride along the way.

Final thoughts

From the stories shared above, it is important to acknowledge the very different contexts surrounding each experience of leadership. What works for a career cricket coach working with professional cricketers in the UK may not yield remotely the same outcomes as occasional leaders in the surfing community in New Zealand. Indeed, finding commonality in the requirements for leadership effectiveness and success in sport is a continuous undertaking. One attempt to uncover this commonality can be found in Sam Walker's (2017) *The Captain Class*, where seven traits of elite sports team captains were identified (p. 91):

1. extreme doggedness and focus in competition;
2. aggressive play that tests the limits of the rules;
3. a willingness to do thankless jobs in the shadows;
4. a low-key, practical, and democratic communication style;
5. motivates others with passionate non-verbal displays;
6. strong convictions and the courage to stand apart;
7. ironclad emotional control.

As highlighted in the stories of leadership shared in this chapter, effective leadership in sport requires acceptance of certain givens. For example, on occasion time will be against you, the ball won't bounce your way, the playing ground will shift beneath you, or you might have to compete with a player down. Such sporting analogies hold true in the world of academic leadership too, along with the realisation that at times even the goal posts will move! It is important to remember, though, that effective leadership is rarely a one-person concept and that the consideration of the leadership stories of others, no matter what the context, can be the catalyst for leadership success.

Notes

1 Effective leadership in sport pertains to developing a team and/or individual through cognitive/attitudinal/behavioural/skill/tactical improvement.

2 Successful leadership in sport pertains to the achievement of a desired sporting outcome, e.g. winning.
3 Also see comments on 'productive narcissism' in Chapter 3.

References

Argent, E. (2005). From the locker room to the boardroom: Developing leaders through sport. PhD thesis. Loughborough University Institutional Repository. https://ethos.bl.uk/OrderDetails.do?uin=uk.bl.ethos.505374

Arnold, R., Fletcher, D. & Hobson, J. (2018). Performance leadership and management in elite sport: A black and white issue or different shades of grey? *Journal of Sport Management*, 32, 452–463.

Arthur, C.A., Wagstaff, C.R.C. & Hardy, L. (2016). Leadership in sport organizations. In C.R.D. Wagstaff (ed) *The Organizational Psychology of Sport: Key issues and Practical Applicants*. Abingdon: Routledge, pp. 153–176.

Bandura, C. & Kavussanu, M. (2018). Authentic leadership in sport: Its relationship with athletes' enjoyment and commitment and the mediating role of autonomy and trust. *International Journal of Sports Science & Coaching*, 13(6), 968–977.

Bennie, A. and O'Connor, D. (2012). Perceptions and Strategies of effective coaching leadership: A qualitative investigation of professional coaches and players. *International Journal of Sport and Health Science* 10, 82–89.

Burton, L. & Leberman, S. (2017). New leadership: Rethinking successful leadership of sport organizations. In L. Burton & S. Leberman (eds) *Women in Sport Leadership: Research and Practice for Change*. London: Routledge. pp. 148–161.

Constandt, B. & Willem, A. (2019). The trickle-down effect of ethical leadership in nonprofit soccer clubs. *Nonprofit Management and Leadership*, 29, 401–417.

Cotterill, S. & Barker, J. (2013). *The Psychology of Cricket: Developing Mental Toughness*. Birmingham: Bennion Kearny.

Cotterill, S. & Cheetham, R. (2017). The experience of captaincy in professional sport: The case of elite professional rugby. *European Journal of Sport Science*, 17(2), 215–221.

Cotterill, S. & Fransen, K. (2016). Athlete leadership in sport teams: Current understanding and future directions. *International Review of Sport and Exercise Psychology*, 9(1), 116–133.

Cummins, P. & Spencer, J. (2015). Sports coach leadership models. In I. O'Boyle, D. Murray & P. Cummins (eds) *Leadership in Sport*. London: Routledge, p. 174.

Fransen, K., Vanbeselaere, N., De Cuyper, B., Vande Broek, G. & Boen, F. (2014). The myth of the team captain as principal leader: Extending the athlete leadership classification within sport teams. *Journal of Sports Sciences*, 32(14), 1389–1397.

Frawley, S., Favaloro, D. & Schulenkorf, N. (2018). Experience-based leadership development and professional sport organizations. *Journal of Sport Management*, 32, 123–134.

Janssen, J. (n.d.). 10 strategies to strengthen the critical coach-captain connection. Janssen Sports Leadership Centre. Accessed June 7, 2020, at: www.janssensportsleadership.com/resources/janssen-blog/10-strategies-to-strengthen-the-critical-coach-captain-connection/

Jones, G. & Spamer, M. (2011). A leadership styles competency framework for governing bodies in sport. *African Journal for Physical Activity and Health Sciences*, 17(2), 340–356.

Matusitz, J. & Simi, D. (2019). Pathways to sports leadership for Latinas in U.S. higher education. *Journal of Latinos and Education*, 18(2), 151–163.

Mukherjee, S. (2016). Leadership network and team performance in interactive contests. *Social Networks*. 47. 85–92. doi:10.1016/j.socnet.2016.05.003

Newman, T., Lower, L. & Brgoch, S. (2019). Developing sport team captains as formal leaders. *Journal of Sport Psychology in Action*, 10(3), 137–150.

Railo, W. (1986). *Willing to win*. Utrecht: Amas.

Ruszkai, A. (23 August 2019). £11m per goal! Alexis Sanchez has cost Man United £55m so far - with £97m to come. Accessed at: www.goal.com/en/news/11m-per-goal-alexis-sanchez-has-cost-man-united-55m-so-far/1hpkixxwcjlhyz9xiob5qwvhl

Smith, M., Young, D., Figgins, S. & Arthur, C. (2017). Transformational leadership in elite sport: A qualitative analysis of effective leadership behaviors in Cricket. *The Sport Psychologist*, 31, 1–15.

Takos, N., Murray, D. & O'Boyle, I. (2018). Authentic leadership in Nonprofit sport organization boards. *Journal of Sport Management*, 32, 109–122.

Walker, S. (2017). The captain class: The hidden force behind the world's greatest teams.

White, J. (21 May 2001). An interview with Willi Railo. www.theguardian.com/football/2001/may/21/sport.comment2

CHAPTER 12

Leadership in the public and third sectors

Kendall Jarrett with Karl Waddell, Christina Curry, Rev Tim Smith, Gabriel MacGregor, and Jan Hawkes

My involvement as a leader in the charity and volunteer sectors is vitally important to me. Working with friends and colleagues to support causes that have a positive and lasting impact on the lives of others is as rewarding as any other vocational leadership endeavour I have grappled with. From my experiences of co-founding and co-directing a small international fundraising cause[1] to volunteering as an event leader within a service club network of over a million members,[2] the *leadership jacket* I wear during such times has had a significant impact on how I go about fulfilling my vocational leadership responsibilities as an academic. So, what are the synergies between leadership in HE and leadership in the public and third sectors, and how does the wearing of the *leadership jacket* in one sector relate to another?

The leadership jacket

We all wear the leadership jacket[3] at some stage in our vocational lives. Some people are more reluctant than others to try it on, whilst some find it hard to take off once on. Some people are handed the leadership jacket whilst others buy it. Some wear it only for a short time. Some put on the same jacket time and time again, whilst others try out multiple, new jackets. Some jackets fit better than others. Some are tailored to fit perfectly, some are ragged, ill-fitting or require constant alteration. Some have deep pockets, whilst some have hidden pockets. Some have no pockets to hide anything at all. Some jackets are too big or too cumbersome to wear. Other jackets might make the wearer too hot. Sometimes a wearer might be asked to take off their jacket in public. Sometimes a wearer might be given private assurances they can wear a new jacket somewhere else. Sometimes the same jacket can be worn for too long preventing others from trying it on. And on and on the metaphor goes…

At any one time, all of us in HE either wear the leadership jacket or observe someone else wearing it. For leaders in the public and third sectors it is no different. It is the context that is different. The cyclical nature of Government policy change that affects HE provision (e.g. the change in tertiary funding and competition legislation that has occurred in the United Kingdom over the past three decades) often brings with it considerable media attention. As such, leaders in HE are often required to respond to questions about brand association, generation of income, historical injustices, and communication transparency (just to name a few). Arguably, such requirements are seemingly ever-present in the spheres of public and third sector leadership. So, what can we learn about leadership in the public and third sectors that can inform our duties as 'jacket wearers' in HE?

Leadership and public office

The role of the public sector, typically comprising government and public enterprises, is to 'focus on regulatory implementation of legislation and service delivery to citizens' (Ferguson, Ronayne, & Rybacki, 2014, p. 1). Within the public sector, the many thousands of projects commissioned every year require leaders 'who can navigate complex, highly visible positions while prioritizing long-term initiatives over short-term politics' (Daniel, Remedios, & Pigni, 2019). As such, the requirements of leadership within the public sector are often said to be harder than leadership requirements in other sectors, as supported by comments made by Sir Donald Brydon, former chairman of Royal Mail and the London Stock Exchange Group:

> Leadership in the private sector is easier in that there is a clear unifying financial goal. This is often not so clear in the public sector where, as a result, there is a greater need for consensus building if decisions are to hold.
>
> Blagg (2013)

In the UK in the mid-1990s, the Committee on Standards in Public Life set about establishing a list of seven principles of public life to guide the ethical behaviours of all public officers. The principles of accountability, honesty, integrity, objectivity, selflessness, openness, and leadership – better known as the Nolan Principles – were devised to help govern the actions of all those holding public office. The inclusion of leadership as a key principle promotes the idea of leadership as a function for all, not just the domain of those in formal positions of responsibility. And in referring to leadership as a key principle of public life, the inference made is of expectation and action:

Leaders [in public office] must be visible in the organization to provide a good working environment for employees and to deliver sound leadership practices such as being supportive, acting as a coach and a mentor, [and] showing direction.

(Løkke & Krøtel, 2020, p. 97)

> **Question to consider**
>
> - What need is there for more or less visibility in your leadership role?

As van Eeden Jones and Lasthuizen (2018) contend, having leaders who are visible in terms of who they are and how they act is vitally important as a function for 'creating, maintaining and changing ethical culture' (p. 179), because without ethical leadership practices, the associated weak standards of public office can result in widespread corruption. Corruption, though, is just one of many hurdles a leader in the public sector might have to contend with. There is also the Peter Principle.

The Peter Principle relates to the promotion of workers based on current job performance into roles they may not be suited for, nor have the capacity or desire to be successful. Workers reach their level of incompetence from which no further promotions result (Peter & Hull, 1969). As Turney (2009) writes, 'if ever there was a perfect example of the Peter Principle, it would be government.' Over time, the foreseeable outcome is underperforming leaders in a hierarchical stalemate. The presence of the Peter Principle in HE hierarchies is also noticeable. 'He wrote such good papers until we gave him tenure' (Lazear, 2001, p. 1) is a worryingly common phrase uttered in HEI. Apart from adopting promotion protocols that decrease the chance of the Peter Principle taking effect, Reh (2019) suggests that if an issue is recognised, inverse promotion, additional training, and access to mentoring should be considered.

Thus, the challenges that leaders in public office face are both unique in terms of context and complexity, but also shared in terms of relatability to other sectors. And it is this relatability that underpins the sharing of three micro-stories[4] of public sector leadership.

Story 1 – Gabriel MacGregor

> By the time I become a manager/leader in local government I had been employed in the public sector for 22 years. Leadership development programmes were only made available after I became a leader. It's a bit 'cart before the horse', but once I was a leader there were

lots of development opportunities made available to me. Prior to that it was about being willing to take opportunities and 'act up', e.g. if someone was away I'd say 'I'll do that'. For me it was about sticking my head above the parapet.

When becoming responsible for managing colleagues I had previously been at an equal level with, most were happy to look to me for leadership because I had previous 'acting up' experience. For some people this was a more difficult relationship, but I myself had a very good manager who I could always ask for guidance.

I wanted to emulate their style of management so I would learn just by observing them, by hearing them on the phone, hearing how they managed difficult situations. The greatest advantage was of course if they weren't around and someone asked a question, I had a good idea of what was going on. So much of what goes on in public office is about what's *not* written down as opposed to what *is* written down.

I worked with a relatively small team, so I knew my vision of leadership should be based around devolved leadership. I could not do the role I did if I didn't have full confidence in each member of my team.

Being able to talk to people in the language of their discipline is very important. People aren't stupid. When things are bad, they know things are bad, so I didn't try to spin it too much.

Maybe sometimes I tended to assume people would adhere to the same values that I did.

Knowing what I know now as a leader, I would have been more confident in my knowledge that I was a good leader.

Story 2 – Jan Hawkes

Following a career in the private sector, where the 'cut and thrust' of profit margins, cash flow, and staying one step ahead of competitors were ever present, it was time for a change. I was intrigued and excited to bring private sector knowledge and experience into the public sector.

Driven in part by the austerity measures, public sector organisations are much more commercially aware, innovative, and creative in terms of service design and delivery, maximising best value for every pound spent of the public purse.

The future leader of the public sector needs to be collaborative, resilient, provide autonomy, invite contribution and challenge, be adaptive to an ever-changing environment, engage with stakeholders across formal boundaries, and develop commercial leadership prowess and judgement. Evidence-based decision-making and relationship management in a complex environment are also key.

The public sector workforce has a huge 'want to serve' mindset. As a leader it is important to reflect this mindset and culture across the broad range of organisation development strategies, activities, and interventions I am responsible for.

I support an action learning approach to CPD engagement whereby leaders from across formal boundaries come together to reflect on and develop their leadership style and capabilities, whilst at the same time working collaboratively to inform and influence strategic organisational issues.

Millennials have their own views and ideas on how they should be perceived and developed, and we need to ensure that we keep up with their expectations and build organisations that cater for their needs; otherwise we will not be their employer of choice and attract the best talent into the organisation.

Leaders in the public sector need to be fully aware of and understand the political environment in which they operate and should be developed to work with ambiguity and complex structures.

Within the large organisation I work in, the cascade of messages can get distorted. Consistent clear communication is vital along with a range of push[5] and pull[6] communication techniques.

Continual research engagement and keeping up with political and legislative changes are important. I would have paid much more attention to the softer skills earlier on (e.g. culture, behaviour, mindset change) as they really are the keys to making step change in organisations successful.

Story 3 – Dr Christina Curry

In 2017, significant changes were introduced to reform local government across some states in Australia. This included mandatory training for all people elected to office. An intensive compulsory programme must now be completed in the first few weeks of term. Councillors are also required to continue professional development throughout their term. I was elected originally in 2012 prior to this reform. I relied on the informal mentoring of my councillor colleagues and attending professional development opportunities through my own desire to develop the necessary skills for public office.

In local government I believe it is vital to be an active member of the community and have demonstrated commitment to areas of the community. I always felt I was able to work well with councillor colleagues and the community.

The challenge is knowing when to advocate and what is in the best interests of the community. I am elected to advocate on behalf of the community I represent and to work with them to make our area a better place to live, work, and play. It requires working with others, negotiating with others, and sometimes challenging the agenda of others.

Leadership involves letting some people know that what they want is not always what is in the best interests of the whole community. This is not always accepted and can sometimes result in negative responses. An important lesson is never listen to the loudest, but seek the view of the majority.

Ultimately I am guided by my values.

A challenge I have found is that many people do not understand the role of local government or councillors or simply do not care.

You have to find ways to engage with the broader community to ensure you are representing the majority. Mobile offices work, and door knocking allows opportunities for discussion to determine if something in an area is really an issue for most or just a few. Social media is tricky as the majority view can be skewed. Making the time to mix and hear from different people within the organisation and broader stakeholders is invaluable.

The sharing of these micro-stories provides insight into the experiences of leadership in large local government organisations. Yet despite organisational similarity, each leadership story held within it a different style of leadership being utilised. With Gabriel's use of devolved leadership,[7] Christina's commitment to servant leadership,[8] and Jan's investment in transformational leadership,[9] each story of leadership from the public sector promotes an awareness of the different styles of leadership relatable to use in HE (see Chapter 1). It is also worth noting that Story 3 shared by Christina relates to elected leadership in the public sector, which brings with it (as alluded to in her micro-story) the dilemma of majority representation against personal values.

Elected leadership in the public sector

> We all know what to do, but we don't know how to get re-elected once we have done it.
>
> Jean-Claude Juncker Former President of the European Commission

The quote above highlights a fundamental issue associated with the leadership of elected public officials. From federal politicians and local government councillors, to school superintendents and trade union representatives, elected leaders within the public sector are faced with daily consideration of *leadership action* versus *community reaction*. Thus, for elected officials in the public sector, a strategic game is afoot with decisions made increasingly being viewed against a backdrop of choice between personal/party gain or social good.

With a growing emphasis on the development of public and private sector leaders, Silvester and Wyatt (2015) question why formal support is not more readily available for aspiring and incumbent politicians. Yet a dilemma exists. As Silvester and Wyatt (2015, p. 368) go on to discuss:

> Unlike other professionals political candidates are not expected to possess a specific body of knowledge or skills. We do not insist that our politicians pass certain exams in order to be elected. In fact, the very nature of democratic process means that we assume elected representatives should be able to rely on the knowledge and expertise they have already acquired outside politics to help them perform their political roles.

Question to consider

- What assurances of ethical leadership practice are utilised in your institution?

One argument that supports the need for political training concerns the development of ethical leaders. In Afridi et al.'s (2017) study of women elected to village councils in India, the view was shared that 'as experience accumulates, governance improves' (p. 28), which was reflected in data detailing a decrease in the number of corruption-related irregularities the longer the leader was in post. One of the findings from the study underlined 'the need for capacity building and institutional support to reduce corruption' (p. 5). On a more positive note, one of the many benefits of having elected leaders is their typically high visibility and profile, which can translate into being better facilitative leaders in times of need (Saminaden, 2014).

The growing emphasis on leadership development in the public sector

The global commitment to developing public sector leaders continues to gather pace. In 2019 the first cohort of public sector leaders were welcomed into the UK's new National Leadership Centre (NLC). Through a development framework comprising a residential programme exploring system leadership, networking opportunities, and research suggesting that the most effective public sector leaders are adaptive, connected, questioning, ethical, and purposeful, it is proposed that the NLC develops over 100 senior public service leaders annually (Gov.uk, 2019).

In the US, the Boston Consulting Group (BCG), known for assisting organisations around the world with aspects of business strategy, have developed the BCG Public-Sector Leadership Framework to help government agencies coach their leaders across three key areas – personal skills (e.g. how to be a transparent leader), network leadership, and impact on society (Daniel, Remedios, & Pigni, 2019).

In 2016 the Asian Productivity Organisation[10] began developing a public sector leadership framework to aid in the development of leadership capacity across the region to help overcome challenges specific to the public sector context. Within the framework, desirable leadership competencies and capabilities are stated, along with specifics around expected productivity outcomes, strategies, milestones, and resources. Key within the framework is the idea that 'public-sector leadership is a shared responsibility' across all levels of the organisation (Mau, 2018, p. 5).

In Africa, there is also an increased focus on public sector leadership development as evidenced by commitments made by organisations such as the Africa Governance Initiative, although the long-term effectiveness of such interventions is yet to be determined (Yanguasa & Bukenyab, 2016).

Leadership in the third sector

According to the National Audit Office in the UK (n.d.), third sector organisations (TSOs) are those that can be categorised as belonging to neither the private (e.g. driven by profit) nor public (e.g. funded by taxes) sectors. TSOs include voluntary and community organisations such as charities, community groups, social enterprises, cooperatives, and churches and other religious bodies. They are typically not-for-profit organisations run by voluntary trustees.

TSOs are a valued part of society (Anon, 2015), although since 2008 the sector in Europe 'has been operating under the shadow of austerity' with this shift meaning an emphasis 'on survival and resilience' (Hodges & Howieson, 2017, p. 69). A similar trend can also be seen in other parts of the world over this time period (CAF, 2019). The very same circumstances are also shaping the operations of HEIs around the world, with significant implications for TSO and HE leaders – including institutional hiring habits, how visions of leadership effectiveness are devised, what collaborations are prioritised by leaders, and how leadership performance might be measured. As Moss (2020) discusses, there is challenge for TSO leaders in how one responds to financial constraints and limited funding control, and there are pressures with supporting distressed service users and requirements to work more in partnership – all this within a competitive sector where 'behind the mutual back-patting, sinews are strained to gain an advantage' (Stanford, 2014, p. 55).

Leadership in the third sector, just like in HE, has its challenges. But also its rewards. Presented below are two leaders' micro-stories that not only include reflection on the challenges of leadership in the third sector, but also the reward of leadership and the meaning one can find as a leader.

Story 4 – Rev Dr Tim Smith

> Development of leadership skills within the Anglican Communion has been progressive. There has been much change in the nature and purpose of the organisation as the generations have changed. Consequently, there has been a shift in leadership from being the pastoral care giver to being a leader who is inspiring and equipping volunteers for the purpose of rebuilding congregations. This has meant that the institutional organisation has taken responsibility to provide formal and ongoing training of leadership.
>
> There has been a shift from 'Get on with it', to 'What are your plans, what do you need in order to achieve it, and how can we assist you?'
>
> Internal issues and external influences have also changed the nature of leadership and the necessary training. The Royal Commission into Child Sexual Abuse within Institutions, completed here in Australia last year, resulted in recommendations by the state on institutions regarding professional standards. So ongoing training about child protection, and being a safe faith community, is required.
>
> When commencing ministry, however, I had no idea what my model of leadership was to be. A part of this was the result of a structure of training that placed a new priest under the leadership of a senior priest, meaning that a new priest is required to operate under their

leadership style. This in itself was important in developing a vision of leadership because it raised awareness of conflict with our own developing vision for leadership, even if that could not be named at the time.

My experience has led me to understand that leadership needs to be a broad thing. This means sometimes being an autocrat, or a benevolent dictator, or just benevolent.

The most important communication challenge is to provide a means for communication: leadership to congregation as well as congregation to leadership.

Establishing regular times to come together provides an opportunity to identify the validity of any disturbance, the needs that are not being met, what the need is, and a means to meet that need if it is real.

It is my understanding that I have come to my present position to help this congregation develop its vision for its life together. I have taken some risk by immediately instituting changes, without consultation, which reflect the direction I understand the parish wants to go. The work ahead will be to lead them to create a vision to help that direction become a reality.

Story 5 – Karl Waddell

I was selected as the inaugural leader of the organisation by virtue of demonstrated performance in a volunteer capacity. Just as importantly, I was appointed by way of my emotional connection to the SIDS (Sudden Infant Death Syndrome) cause. Our organisation was founded and conceived out of the loss of our first-born child, our 4-month-old son River, to SIDS. The emotional parallel with our mission and objectives lend to my capacity to drive an emotion-fuelled pursuit of change in the community.

My ability to speak in public, drive critical messages, and bring a team of fundraisers with me is critical to my appointment.

When starting the role as GM of River's Gift, the vision of the organisation, to 'Stamp Out SIDS', had already been clearly articulated amongst community circles. I made it a priority of mine to continually grow, refine, and publicise our message across all levels of community.

> By nature of the physical 'separation' between myself and many of my peers (including families affected by SIDS, volunteers, donors, fundraisers), it's become increasingly evident that the power of 'personal touch' can never be underestimated – particularly in a world where humans have grown to rely so heavily on digitalisation for communication and interaction. The phone calls to express thanks and gratitude, the personally written cards, the personally addressed emails – this is where communication with peers can be performed in its finest form.
>
> I'm continually learning to evolve as a leader within an organisation and an industry that I feel very fortunate and blessed to be working in. Over time, I've developed my capacity to listen to my peers (staff, volunteers, supporters) and have them feel that their input is valued. But I often find it a challenge to combine my focus both 'on the business' and 'in the business'.
>
> Out of the tragedy of personal experience, in the loss of my own child, has come an enlightenment to shed positive light, education, and colour on the world I live in. I thrive on leading our organisation, and the impact that we can make on the community by helping inform, educate, and instil change that leads to the enhanced preservation of infant life.

In both micro-stories above, each leader was driven by an internal compass to do good in the community. For successful leadership to prevail, both storytellers commented on the power of personal touch and connection with peers through conversation. Just as Stanford (2014, p. 55) writes:

> We are humans, not calculating machines, and we respond better to a leader who engages and entertains us than to one who resorts to flow charts, graphs and computer projections.

For both storytellers, their development as a leader in the third sector reflected a keen desire to learn about one's self as a leader for the advancement of cause. In increasingly complex and crowded markets, effective leadership development becomes an even more important priority.

Developing leaders in the third sector

With regards to third sector funding, in recent times all round the world there has been a shift from public sector grants to contracts (Thompson,

Williams, & Kwong, 2017). Thus, third sector leaders are now having to compete with the private sector for access to funds. This requires greater emphasis to be placed on the additional social contribution TSOs offer and better use of boundary-spanning activities (such as resource allocation and networking) if contract attainment is to be achieved (Lu, 2015; Thompson, Williams, & Kwong, 2017). There are implications, then, in terms of leadership development and the type of leader drawn to such opportunities, as their leadership may invariably be constrained by limited budgets, access to fewer and fewer resources, and a reliance on collaboration. For leaders in HE, these circumstances of leadership might sound familiar! So how have third sector leaders gone about developing their skill set in such challenging times?

> **Question to consider**
> - What has been the impact of austerity measures on your access to leaders?

One method, as reported by Moss (2020), has been the involvement of leaders in action learning interventions. These group-based, discussion opportunities provide a judgement-free space for leaders to take a step back and make sense of the complexity of their roles. Periodic meetings between leaders followed a format of checking in, bidding for time to present an issue, listening to colleagues, and then asking open questions to encourage 'movement towards insight and action and reflection on change' (p. 129).

With third sector leadership, as with other sectors, 'there is a need to ensure leadership is enacted in an ethical way' (Hodges & Howieson, 2017, p. 75). The development of ethical leaders in TSOs is vital to organisation integrity, as moral failures can impact large numbers of a variety of people for a significant amount of time (Ciulla, 2005). So how can TSOs find morally driven leaders? Gardner and Holloway (2019) suggest the promotion of ethical leadership can be achieved through the employment of *cultural creatives*. Cultural creatives are leaders who have a value-driven identity built on authenticity, being engaged throughout the whole process, having a world view, and being anti-materialistic. Such leaders according to Gardner and Holloway (2019, p. 10) are 'a good fit for work that involves wicked problems, influence and persuasion' – arguably three key bedfellows of leadership in HE.

> **Questions to consider**
> - Who would you consider to be a cultural creative in your institution?
> - What sets this leader apart from other leaders in terms of how their leadership is enacted?

Learning from leaders in the public and third sectors

As Hodges and Howieson (2017) utilised in their article exploring the challenges of leadership in the third sector, this chapter includes written narratives of leaders reflecting on their own understanding and experiences of leadership. From these narratives, questions are drawn with the intent for readers to make links to their own leadership landscape in HE. This chapter's exploration of *leadership in practice* also utilises global research into public and third sector leadership to complement individuals' views on leadership. Typical within both the micro-stories shared and the research are suggestions for formal leadership development opportunities, the recognition of context as a key determinant of leadership effectiveness, and a desire to be closer and 'more hands-on' with those being led. Far from being a prescription of dos and don'ts, discussion in this chapter aims to present a view on what to *think about* rather than what to *think* when investing attention on other-sector leadership. To bring discussion full circle, then, when putting on the leadership coat it is important to recognise the barriers to leadership development effectiveness that may present themselves to all leaders as well as the impact of alternation in leadership, regardless of sector.

> **Questions to consider**
> - What has reading this chapter made you think about as a leader?
> - How might your consideration of this issue/theme influence your practice as a leader?

Barriers to leadership development success

As Gurdjian et al. (2014) allude to in their article 'Why leadership development programmes fail', the design of leadership development programmes should recognise all potential barriers to success. These barriers include:

1. overlooking context;
2. the gap between 'reflection-on-leadership' and 'real work';

3. underestimating mindsets;
4. failing to measure results.

Ever present also are the institutional barriers that can curtail leadership development programme success. An evolving work agenda, a change in resource availability, and a reluctance for organisations to change to accommodate the products of leadership development can all stymie programme success. 'If the system does not change, it will not support and sustain individual behavior change – indeed, it will set people up to fail' (Beer, Finnström, & Schrader, 2016).

> **Questions to consider**
> - What is the biggest system change required at your institution and how will/does your behavior as a leader drive that change?

Alternation in leadership

As Williams and Baghurst (2014) discuss in their study of the management impact of elected law officials, alternation in leadership has its costs. Their study found that inconsistent levels of communication when starting a new role and transitioning out of one, alongside staff perceptions of disconnection with incoming officials, can lead to significant 'obfuscation of the agency's goals and progress' (p. 8). However, the transitioning of leaders does not always bring with it negative outcomes. For example, when researching the impact of leadership change in sub-Saharan countries, Carbone and Pellegata (2017) confirm that the alternation of governments and government leaders saw a positive effect on social welfare performance when achieved through multi-party elections. Thus, although democracy implies an element of 'institutionalised uncertainty' (Carbone & Pellegata, 2017, p. 1970), new leadership can elevate agendas of social good.

Notes

1 *Education Ethio* is a registered international fundraising cause supporting Ethiopian university graduates access postgraduate learning opportunities abroad.
2 Rotary International.
3 The wearing of the leadership jacket does not just refer to having a position of responsibility in an organisation. The leadership jacket can also be worn by

those influencing others by means of pedagogical leadership, wellbeing leadership, assessment leadership, etc.
4 A micro-story is typically no more than 400 words in length.
5 Push – focuses on delivering specific learning content to learners e.g. a leadership development programme.
6 Pull – directs leaders to learning resources that they can access at any time e.g. a learning portal
7 Devolved leadership – the distribution of leadership responsibility amongst a team.
8 Servant leadership – leaders who put the needs of others ahead of their own needs.
9 Transformational leadership – leadership that inspires change in others.
10 The Asian Productivity Organisation is an intergovernmental organisation committed to increasing productivity in member countries across the Asia-Pacific region.

References

Afridi, F., Iversen, V. & Sharan, M. (2017). Women political leaders, corrucption, and learning: evidence from a large scale public program in India. *Economic Development and Cultural Change*, University of Chicago Press, 66(1), 1–30. DOI: 10.1086/693679

Anon. (2015). *The Third Sector: Value Driven, Transparently Managed.* Good Governance Institute. Accessed at: www.good-governance.org.uk/wp-content/uploads/2017/04/The-third-sector-value-driven-transparently-managed.pdf

Beer, M., Finnström, M. & Schrader, D. (2016). Why leadership training fails – and what to do about it. Accessed at: https://hbr.org/2016/10/why-leadership-training-fails-and-what-to-do-about-it

Blagg, M. (May 1, 2013). Leadership in the Public v Private Sector. *Blog post to Criticaleye.com.* Available at: https://criticaleyeltd.wordpress.com/2013/05/01/leadership-in-the-public-v-private-sector/ (Accessed June 7, 2020).

Carbone, G. & Pellegata, A. (2017). To Elect or Not to Elect: Leaders, Alternation in Power and Social Welfare in Sub-Saharan Africa. *The Journal of Development Studies*, Vol. 53(12), 1965–1987. DOI:10.1080/00220388.2017.1279733

Charity Aid Foundation. (2019). CAF charity landscape 2019. Accessed on 21 February 2020 at: www.cafonline.org/docs/default-source/about-us-publications/charity-landscape-2019_web_2620a_290319.pdf?sfvrsn=65ca9b40_0

Ciulla, J. B. (2005). The state of leadership ethics and the work that lies before us. *Business Ethics: A European Review*, 14(4), 323–335.

Daniel, C., Remedios, S. & Pigni, D. (7 August 2019). The new public-sector leader. Accessed at: www.bcg.com/capabilities/people-organization/new-public-sector-leader.aspx

Ferguson, J., Ronayne, P. & Rybacki, M. (2014). *Public Sector Leadership Challenges: Are They Different and Does It Matter?* White Paper, Centre for Creative Leadership.

Gardner, P. & Holloway, M. (2019). Organizations need ethical leaders: how to attract and nurture cultural creatives into positions of leadership and influence. *Development and Learning in Organisations*, 33(5), 8–11. DOI: 10.1108/DLO-02-2019-0047

Gov.uk. (12 September 2019). National Leadership Centre programme launch. Press release. Accessed at: www.gov.uk/government/news/national-leadership-centre-programme-launch

Gurdjian, P., Halbeisen, T. & Lane, K. (2014). Why leadership development programmes fail. Accessed at: www.mckinsey.com/featured-insights/leadership/why-leadership-development-programs-fail

Hodges, J. & Howieson, B. (2017). The challenges of leadership in the third sector. *European Management Journal*, 35(1), 69–77. DOI: 10.1016/j.emj.2016.12.006

Lazear, E. (2001). The Peter Principle: promotions and declining productivity. *NBER Working Paper Series*. DOI:10.3386/w8094

Løkke, A.-K. & Krøtel, S. (2020). Performance evaluations of leadership quality and public sector leaders' absenteeism. *Public Management Review*, 22(1), 96–117. DOI: 10.1080/14719037.2019.1638441

Lu, J. (2015). Which nonprofit gets more government funding? Nonprofits' organizational attributes and their receipts of government funding. *Nonprofit Management & Leadership*, 25(3), 297–312.

Mau, T. (2018). *Public-Sector Leadership for Innovation and Productivity: APO Framework and Resource Guide for Public-Sector Leadership*. Technical report. Asian Productivity Organisation. DOI: 10.13140/RG.2.2.28304.10242

Moss, S. (2020). Exploring the challenges of system leadership in the voluntary and community sector. *Action Learning: Research and Practice*, 17(1), 125–137. DOI: 10.1080/14767333.2020.1712851

National Audit Office. (n.d.). What are third sector organisations and their benefits for commissioners? Accessed on 20 Feb 2020 at: www.nao.org.uk/successful-commissioning/introduction/what-are-civil-society-organisations-and-their-benefits-for-commissioners/

Peter, L. J. & Hull, R. (1969). *The Peter Principle: Why Things Always Go Wrong*. New York: Morrow.

Reh, F. (15 November 2019). The Peter principle and how to beat it. Accessed at: www.thebalancecareers.com/the-peter-principle-2275684

Saminaden, M. (2014). Are directly elected mayors better facilitative leaders than indirectly elected leaders? PhD thesis, University of Bristol. Accessed at: https://ethos.bl.uk/OrderDetails.do?uin=uk.bl.ethos.658201

Stanford, P. (2014). Can we learn instinctive leadership? *Thirdsector*, October 55.

Silvester, J. & Wyatt, M. (2015). Developing strong and diverse political leaders. *The Psychologist*, 28(5), 368–371.

Thompson, P., Williams, R. & Kwong, C. (2017). Factors holding back small third sector organisations' engagement with local public sector. *Nonprofit Management & Leadership*, 27(4), 513–531. DOI: 10.1002/nml.21260

Turney, M. (6 November 2009). The Government Peter Principle. Accessed at: https://townhall.com/columnists/meredithturney/2009/11/06/the-government-peter-principle-n875704 van Eeden Jones, I. & Lasthuizen, K. (2018). Building public sector integrity in Indonesia: the role and challenges of ethical leadership. *Asia Pacific Journal of Public Administration*, 40(3), 175–185. DOI: 10.1080/23276665.2018.1515392

Williams, M. & Baghurst, T. (2014). The Management Impact of Elected Leaders: Attorneys General. *SAGE Open*, 4, 1–10. DOI: 10.1177/2158244014531769

Yanguasa, P. & Bukenyab, B. (2016). 'New' approaches confront 'old' challenges in African public sector reform. *Third World Quarterly*, 37(1), 136–152. DOI: org/10.1080/01436597.2015.1086635

PART 2

Summary

Stephen Newton and Kendall Jarrett

This part explores a variety of leadership perspectives from within and outside the HE sector. Although each chapter covers very different ground, both in terms of topic and geography, there is a considerable degree of commonality as regards learning points.

These include:

- making the most of opportunities;
- the need for mid-course adjustments as a leader;
- adaptability and resilience;
- being willing to take tough decisions regarding the capability and performance of colleagues and hence their suitability for particular roles;
- the need for self-awareness and a strong sense of values (we refer to this as *self-leadership* in Chapter 1);
- the need for, and power of, self-reflection;
- the need to adapt knowledge to the context in which one operates (including organisational conditions and culture);
- recognition that every project becomes someone else's from the moment you depart and that it is not always possible or desirable to leave a lasting imprint on an organisation

In Chapter 4, Richard Light considers the influence of experience and culture on his leadership approach. Like many young adults, Richard did not seek leadership opportunities. However, when he discovered a passion for, and a talent in, martial arts, he felt able to translate that into establishing and running a successful, multi-site business in his native Australia teaching karate and kickboxing. That led to work as a rugby coach in Japan, which required catering to a strictly hierarchical culture in which *tatamae* (effectively telling the boss what he wants to hear) contrasts with *hone* (what the individual actually thinks).

Work at Leeds Beckett University gave him experience of initiating and managing complex change and the opportunity to learn a different leadership approach. Patience was an issue for Richard and he felt that he could have spent more time watching and waiting before initiating a significant change programme. A move to a head of school role in New Zealand proved to be challenging due to Richard's assumption that Australian and New Zealand cultures would be very similar – something that proved to be unfounded and led to what he felt was a failure to deliver change and to achieve goals. Reflection served to alter his perceptions and hence to the success of his role as Head of Research.

In Chapter 5 Kathleen Quinlan explores effecting change by building on values and expertise. She uses several real-world examples (anonymised) to illustrate her key ideas. She highlights the value of distributed leadership versus an unduly structured approach – setting out a vision and influencing others to engage around it rather than the 'heroic leader' setting goals to be accomplished. She refers to the need to acknowledge existing cultures (as does Richard Light in Chapter 4) without necessarily perpetuating them. She also recognises that leadership occurs at multiple levels in any organisation and explores the power of emotional authenticity. A key point is to link 'instructional leadership' (knowledge of how to teach) to the influencing of change in teaching approach by reverse-engineering assessment criteria to determine what to teach.

Chapter 6 allows Kendall Jarrett and John Baumber to examine leading complex systems, via the lens of multi-academy trusts in the UK and similar educational partnerships in Sweden and South Africa. Clearly there are significant cultural differences at play. However, John makes the point that success in such partnerships is driven by achieving the benefits of alignment (in terms of processes, systems, etc.) whilst allowing individual schools to retain a distinct identity. This occurs through a sophisticated governance regime that is culture-based and acknowledges the distinction between 'institutional' leadership of a single school versus 'educational' leadership of a number of institutions, which is far more strategic.

John acknowledges the need to drive out underperformance without overwhelming pre-existing cultures. He describes this as 'creating conformity and synchronicity in a partnership … but not at the expense of reducing talent'. However, whilst persistent non-conformers/underperformers may need to be removed, there needs to be a 'system leader development' framework to enable talented individuals to become the kind of leaders who will thrive within the system.

Chapter 7 is a 'ghost chapter' in that it proved impossible for the person who had agreed to contribute their experiences as an academic leader in exile to do so. The stress and complexity of a life that had become focused on basic survival for themselves and their family was too great. Accordingly, Kendall and I offered some thoughts and questions to consider in this context.

Chapter 8 covers the concept of legacy. As outlined in Chapter 15, one might argue that your legacy as a leader exists only in terms of the perceptions of others. It is hard to pre-plan what it might be whilst acting in the moment and harder yet to control events to ensure it is achieved. Sally Brown and Pauline Kneale offer some valuable ideas on preparation for eventual retirement and what might come next, including making the point that experience in academic leadership is valuable in many other fields and to so many others. They also outline some practical aspects to consider immediately prior to departure, including how to dispose of data, papers, etc., and whether/how best to remain involved in HE or engaged with one's subject.

Within Chapter 9 Stephen Newton explores corporate leadership from the perspective of 'good' versus 'bad'. Prior to analysing the failings of leadership that have occurred in industries such as oil and gas, technology, and energy trading and the audit profession, he presents commentary on the many core competencies and skills required for effective leadership as well as the indicators for 'problems ahead' that organisations should be mindful. Questions posed throughout the chapter not only turn the lens of enquiry on self-as-leader, but also the organisation as a whole, which lends itself to the view that an effective leader rarely operates in isolation.

For Chapter 10 Stephen Newton provides an insight into military leadership and the view that leadership capability is considered a core competence. Honesty, loyalty, and trust are discussed as being central tenets of life in the military that prevail regardless of hierarchy. Respect for the chain of command is mentioned as giving rise to a more streamlined leadership process that enables a shift away from micromanagement and a leadership focus more on strategic aims and outcomes. With discussion of modern military action requiring 'a degree of (mental) agility and adaptability', our understanding of how military leadership operates extends beyond notions of pure autocracy to a more 'serve to lead' mentality. Exploration of the purpose and intention of after-action reports provides readers with an opportunity to reflect on how the process of evaluation occurs in HE and what improvements to the evaluation process could be made.

The focus of Chapter 11 is on leadership in sport with specific attention paid to the impact on performance of on- and off-field leadership. Written by Kendall Jarrett, this chapter discusses the impact that gaining exposure to informal–formal leadership dynamics in sport can have on leadership capacity development, along with the range of leadership roles available in sporting organisations. The importance of off-field administrative leadership was explored as well as the impact that remaining authentic as leader (e.g. being self-aware, honest, trusting, athlete-centred, acting with moral purpose) had on athlete enjoyment and commitment. The global stories of sport leadership included in the chapter provide readers with an opportunity to unpack the synergies that exist between experiences of leadership in sport and in HE and to reflect upon the characteristics of leadership that promote cultures of success.

Chapter 12 offers the reader a chance to connect the worlds of public and third sector leadership with the growing realities of leadership in HE. Through Kendall Jarrett's exploration of facets of leadership notably present within both sectors, discussion of underperforming leaders trapped in a hierarchical stalemate, alternation in leadership, and the enactment of leadership in ethical ways provides readers with a framework to consider their own leadership development and the skills required to operate effectively in complex and competitive marketplaces. The inclusion of five micro-stories of leadership from charity and church leaders and public officials provide relatable examples of leadership journeys laced with information about communication challenges, their overcoming, and the investment of self to 'do good' in the community.

PART 3
Stories of leadership in higher education

PART 3

CHAPTER **13A**

Becoming a leader
Rachel Masika

Professional biography

Before entering the learning, teaching, and educational development field in higher education, I held leadership roles initially in the charity sector and then the corporate world. I started out in the education field as a dual professional, combining research into learning, teaching, and educational development in HE with gender and international development consultancy work for governments and international organisations. Thus, my leadership trajectory has been a bit of a patchwork and bricolage, bringing with it the complexity and tensions of dual professional identities. My diverse exposure has, I believe, enabled me to appreciate nuances of approach compatible with differing organisational structures and ethos.

As a leader in the charity sector, I subscribed to the notion of servant leadership, but did not really articulate and understand my approach until I engaged with leadership theories whilst teaching. Servant leadership has been popularised by a demand for more ethical, people-centred management and leadership (Van Dierendonck, 2011). It has been described as a holistic approach that engages followers in multiple dimensions (e.g. relational, ethical, emotional, spiritual) and empowers followers to grow into what they are capable of becoming (Eva et al., 2019).

In the corporate sector I worked with business leaders to advance their organisation's corporate social responsibility. I saw first-hand the characteristics, behaviours, and practices of corporate leaders, and was particularly struck by the emotional intelligence and leadership effectiveness of senior personnel I met while operating in a cut-throat world. Emotional intelligence implies an approach to leadership centred on those led, whereas leadership effectiveness implies it is situational (Hersey et al., 2015) and contingent (Fiedler and Garcia, 1987). It is situational in that leadership styles shift according to the situation and are contextually contingent. On leaving the corporate sector I was invited to teach leadership on a business management programme at a research-intensive university, where I engaged with the literature and theories of leadership with relish. Finally, I was able to find the language to explain different characteristics, behaviours, styles, processes, and outcomes of leadership.

Currently, as a senior research fellow, I lead on research for a centre that aims to enhance teaching and learning. This entails leading on ethics, organising an annual research conference, strategic inputs to the leadership team, and enabling others to research. Research leadership may be defined as the influence of one or more people on the research-related behaviour, attitudes, or intellectual capacity of others (Evans, 2014). Unlike my experiences within the charity and corporate sectors, where leadership was sudden, it has been a more gradual process in the field of education. This gradual process has involved bringing to my role leadership ideas and skills gained whilst working in those other sectors.

What does effective leadership look like to me?

My notions of leadership are informed by my identity and experience as a woman of African origin living in Europe exposed to both collectivist and individualistic societies and worldviews and how I have been positioned in these contexts. I thus recognise the different emphasis or weight attached to different values, which is also the case for different organisations, as there are organisational cultural differences.

Effective leadership is about setting a direction and aligning and motivating people to the direction for the desired change. It also involves creating a culture of leadership since leadership is distributed, situational, and contingent. However, when reality confronts theory, a more personal understanding is required. For me, at the outset of any transformational path in any of my roles, a forensic and almost check-box approach has been useful. Key for me is a focus not on where one is leading, though that must be clearly understood, but why. Questions to be considered include: does the objective chime with institutional goals? Will the path and outcome be likely to enable participants to grow in the roles, to become personally and professionally invested? If their experience is simply of being led, that could represent danger to the project and a failure on my part. They may become disinvested, thwarted in their own ambitions, and less common-goal-oriented, as is often the case irrespective of organisational context. This is where the personal skills of applied emotional intelligence are essential. In my view these are allied to sensitivity and clear-sightedness, and the ability to communicate effectively in order to clarify, lead, and shape culture, values, and norms, as well as manage conflict. For this, a realistic appreciation of potential pitfalls should be at the back of one's mind at all times.

Sustained commitment and drive on the part of the leader are essential, the grace to undergo continual assessment of progress to fine-tune the approach, and the capacity to be nimble and agile in adapting to unforeseen events. Finally, effective leadership means that any ambitions of personal fulfilment must not be at odds with professional mores, and to me, as mentioned, underpinning all is a philosophy of leadership as service.

Inevitably, my impressions of what is effective leadership are informed by my experience and positionality. I single out a particular individual whose leadership approach was impressive, then a particular group of leaders. I was honoured quite early on in my career to work with an individual so gifted as a leader that I saw leadership exemplified. He was able to get a diverse group of people to work together through shaping norms and by the way he worked. He was able to command the respect and trust of others, both within the organisation and external stakeholders. I would describe him as a transformational leader who respected everyone's individuality and what they brought to the table. He always seemed to have time for everyone and a solution for everything based on asking people questions and then them contributing to the solution without even realising it.

Working with CEOs of large corporations on advancing corporate social responsibility within their organisations and wider spheres of their particular industry, I was particularly struck by their situational awareness, in terms of the ability to see the big picture, handle complexity, recognise opportunities, and pre-empt problems and provide solutions to avoid these problems. They also had the ability to inspire others.

Where is effective leadership required within my field?

In turbulent times for HE, effective leadership in the field of education requires leaders to be adept in anticipating, responding to, and navigating change while guiding people through. My specific field of higher education and the student experience has an increasingly diverse student body, a declining youth demographic with its implications for fees and sustainability of higher education institutions, research funding concerns, and political influences such as Brexit and immigration policies. The challenges these factors present for leadership are how to be strategic and manage the student experience in a shifting landscape. These changes and challenges are occurring within a broader context of marketisation/privatisation of HE, post-truth, culture wars, public scrutiny of HE, technological change, and global competition.

Effective leadership is therefore required around inclusivity, student welfare, protecting free speech, providing value for money, and keeping up with technological advancements. It entails a capability to address multiple influences with a clear purpose, direction, and vision for higher education and its place/role in society. Effective leadership therefore demands more than ever before discipline, listening, and ethical stewardship.

In terms of researching higher education, effective leadership is required in taking the lead in developing research that is increasingly flexible within inter- and multi-disciplinary contexts focusing on resolving major social, political, economic, and environmental issues. The ability to ask questions and think more critically are important conditions for adapting to a changing world for leaders.

As I am in the business of education, leadership in my field is also about enabling others to lead. It means enabling an active path to leadership for each participant, one with which they have agreed and to which they are continually committed. So, becoming a leader necessarily also involves enabling others to become leaders. Leadership is action in a particular situation that can be performed by anyone at any level at a given moment.

What decisions am I most/least proud of on my journey to becoming a leader?

In developing my leadership skills, displaying professionalism (practice discipline) was important for me in order to command trust and discipline and to be an effective leader. This to me meant establishing my reliability quickly: clarifying and communicating shared goals; keeping to deadlines; getting to meetings on time; and keeping appointments. Another important area in developing my leadership was seizing opportunities and taking on more responsibilities and trying to step out of my comfort zone.

I have also taken leadership development training courses for women, which were an eye-opener for me. These helped me reflect on my weaknesses and pay greater attention to developing these areas. Through personal interactions I learned to not feel threatened by people who disagree with me and appreciate and embrace what diversity of opinions brings. I learned to ask questions of as many people as possible, particularly from those who are less vocal, so that I can get a good feel for what they are thinking.

If I had my time again…

I would be bolder with my convictions and in articulating them to others. I would invest more in developing healthy working relationships. I would volunteer to take on more responsibilities.

What questions should one ask oneself when becoming a leader?

'Know thyself' is an important axiom for leaders. There are many approaches to leadership, leadership styles, and leadership characteristics or elements, so it important to be self-aware. So the first question I would suggest one asks is,

'Do I know my strengths and weaknesses?' One should always be authentic and also understand the context in which one is working – a situational awareness and an understanding of the organisational culture. One needs to be aware of how others perceive you and what to do to command trust and respect. Leaders are influencers, so need to understand what their leadership strengths are and what they need to develop to influence their followers. Leaders also need to understand the value of enabling others to lead, as leadership is situational and distributed. Following on from this, everyone who aspires to be a leader or who is a leader should continuously ask themselves these questions, as circumstances are always changing:

- What does it mean to be an effective leader?
- What can I do to become an effective leader in this context?
- Do I understand your organisational culture and the leadership it requires?
- What can I learn?
- How can I enable others to lead?

References

Eva, N., Robin, M., Sendjaya, S., van Dierendonck, D. and Liden, R.C. (2019). Servant leadership: A systematic review and call for future research. *The Leadership Quarterly* 30, 111–132. DOI: 10.1016/j.leaqua.2018.07.004

Evans, L. (2014). What is effective research leadership? A research-informed perspective. *Higher Education Research & Development* 33, 46–58. DOI: 10.1080/07294360.2013.864617

Fiedler, F.E. and Garcia, J.E. (1987). *New Approaches to Effective Leadership: Cognitive Resources and Organizational Performance*. New York: John Wiley & Sons.

Hersey, P., Blanchard, K.H. and Johnson, D.E. (2015). *Management of Organizational Behavior: Leading Human Resources*, 10th ed. Upper Saddle River, NJ: Pearson.

Van Dierendonck, D. (2011). Servant leadership: A review and synthesis. *Journal of Management* 37, 1228–1261. DOI: 10.1177/0149206310380462

CHAPTER **13B**

Becoming a leader

Emily Rumschlag Booms

Professional biography

I am an Associate Professor in Biology at Northeastern Illinois University, a designated Hispanic Serving Institution. I teach primarily first-generation college students and help prepare them for careers in the allied health sciences. I teach at levels ranging from general education, to majors, to master's students. My research training is in molecular microbiology and my research focuses on understanding how pathogens mediate entry to establish infection and identifying novel sources of inhibitors that can prevent infection. I hold a PhD in Microbiology and Immunology from the University of Illinois Chicago College of Medicine and a BA in Biology from Indiana University.

What does effective leadership look like to me?

As a freshly minted PhD graduate, I stepped into my first classroom as an instructor without any formal training in higher education pedagogy or practices. Fears of how would I fill nearly three hours of lecture time were soon followed by memories of my own college experiences when students quickly nodded off as the lights dimmed and the professor droned on while reading the lecture slides.

In preparing for my first semester, I spent a lot of time reading how to craft a strong syllabus, creating authentic learning experiences, and learning how to engage students in lecture. Soon I was focused on developing robust lecture slide sets, reading and rereading textbook chapters to be prepared to lead discussions as well as be able to answer any question my students might have. I quickly learned that all my preparation wouldn't be enough to lead a classroom full of students, especially a classroom so diverse as mine in culture, socioeconomic background, age, interests, and academic preparedness. Preparation for class was still key, but it wasn't enough. Without realising it, I began to draw on my experiences as an athlete to become an effective leader in the classroom.

Like an athlete, you must have a desire to lead a classroom full of students. I can recall teammates throughout my athletic career that exuded raw talent, but lacked the passion and desire for the sport. They played because they were good and it was expected that they would play, but without their heart in it, they never rose to the next level. In a similar manner, I've worked with researchers and scientists that were extremely intelligent, but were ineffective in their teaching because they didn't want to be teaching, but had to fulfil that obligation for one reason or another. Wanting to be in front of a room full of students is the first step to becoming an effective leader in the classroom. That desire pushes you to prepare for the semester and for each class, just as an athlete prepares for their season and each competition. The athlete reflects after each competition on how they can improve and better themselves, and their team, for the next competitor they will face. Effective leaders in the classroom want to be there and strive for excellence and to improve consistently.

Where is effective leadership required within my field?

Leadership is as much about the desire and preparation as it is about adaptability, being able to read your audience, and developing a sense of community and teamwork within the classroom. While the first week of class is always full of excitement, anticipation, and energy, the population of students is uniquely different from the previous semester and these nuanced differences can greatly impact how the classroom functions. Leading a classroom means recognising these differences and modifying one's approach to maximise student learning. These modifications may need to be made week-to-week or semester-to-semester. For example, in the sciences, students need to have a maths skill set that allows them to learn how to perform laboratory calculations, compute statistics, and analyse data. In some semesters, my class merely needs more practice problems to master these new skills. Based on the particular needs of that class, I can create a set of practice problems tailored to their needs and provide them on our learning management system. In other semesters, I can read the students' expressions and see that we need a more rudimentary review of math concept(s) that are foundational to the new skills. This situation requires me to modify our class time on the fly, and possibly the remainder of that day's discussion plan and/or the next lecture session.

While this type of situation initially rattled me and would throw me off for the remainder of my lecture, over time, I embraced these learning opportunities. I became aware that my students appreciated my investment in having the entire class engaged and learning. Once I adopted this teaching approach,

I also noticed a greater sense of community within my courses. Leading a class was no longer about what I thought we needed to cover in a particular timeframe; rather it became about ensuring that the class as a whole was learning, which then enhanced their learning as they began to work together more. It shouldn't be the professor on one side and the students on the other. Leadership in higher education should be more like being the team captain of the classroom. Your commitment to the goal of learning and reaching the entire class, rather than just the few at the top, inspires the class to then work as a unit. The students at the top will often work with students that need additional help, bringing them up to play at a higher level. This commitment to meeting your students where they are and working together to get them where they need to be demonstrates leadership.

What decisions am I most/least proud of on my journey to becoming a leader?

Being a leader also means not going it alone. The most effective leaders surround themselves with a strong support system of other faculty and administrators that share their vision for effective teaching. This support system also serves as a source for new ideas, for critiques, for feedback, and for collaboration. A leader in higher education recognises the limitations of their specialisation, in both teaching and research, and embraces the expertise of those around them, rather than viewing their colleagues as competitors. One of the best decisions I've made is to seek out feedback from my colleagues, which has enhanced my teaching and how I approach teaching, and to draw on the expertise of those around me to also enhance my research. It has also made me a more effective leader in the classroom when it comes to handling student dynamics, classroom dynamics, and other interactions that can impact the student learning environment. My biggest recommendation would be to engage your colleagues, within your discipline and outside your discipline, in conversations about teaching and student learning, in addition to research, because you can learn so much from others rather than trial-by-fire on your own.

If I had my time again...

If I had my time again, I would have engaged in more professional development in pedagogy and assessment in my first year or even before I began teaching, and I would have focused on techniques specifically suited for my type of university and student population. I think my first years of leading a classroom would have been less stressful and taxing if I had acquired a deeper toolkit on which to draw, rather than learning on the job. So many of my early thoughts on teaching were formed from my own experiences as a traditional college student at a large, state university. But I am not at this type of teaching institution and I am not teaching traditional college students. It took some time to break away from these impressions, to recognise the needs of my students, and to develop a more appropriate approach to maximally engage my students.

CHAPTER **13C**

Becoming a leader
Dave Thomas

Professional biography

I am an occupational therapist and public health specialist, with a remit in social justice, registered with the Health and Care Professions Council (HCPC) in the United Kingdom. I am currently reading for a PhD in higher education at the University of Kent. I am interested in how Westernised ontology, epistemology, and pedagogy shapes educational trajectories, outcomes, and interest for black students in higher education. I am also a project manager on the institutionally funded Student Success Project in the School of Sport and Exercise Sciences. The project conducts action and ethnographic research into disparities in student attainment and experiences, then institutes evidence-based strategies to mitigate against and redress these disparities. I am a co-chair of the University of Kent Black, Asian and Minority Ethnic (BAME) Staff Network, which celebrates the achievement of staff of colour who identify as belonging to a BAME background and works towards impacting institutional policies and practices in order to improve their overall experiences in academia. I am also the equalities officer for the University of Kent UNISON branch.

What does effective leadership look like to me?

> A good leader can engage in a debate frankly and thoroughly, knowing that at the end he and the other side must be closer, and thus emerge stronger. You don't have that idea when you are arrogant, superficial, and uninformed.
>
> Nelson Mandela

There is no clear consensus on a single definition of effective leadership (Adair, 1979; Goleman, 1997; Astin and Astin, 2000; Kouzes and Posner, 2007). However, my perception of effective leadership represents consistency and clarity in principles, purpose, and direction that enables an individual to execute their leadership roles and responsibilities in a proactive value-driven, emotionally intelligent manner. Similar to Covey's (2004) principles of personal leadership, effective leaders generally 'begin with the end in mind' (p. 95) in establishing what they (or the team(s) that they lead) want to do, be, and become; this requires a cognitive envisioning of the values and principles upon which these actions of doing, being, and becoming are based. In this sense, for me effective leaders seek out and provide mediums through which the people they lead can engage in the act of doing; then through meaningful roles, promote a greater sense of self and improved abilities, which enables the team(s) (and its members) to achieve their goals and aspirations.

In recognising the responsibility to effect positive change, effective leadership is an interdependent process that requires collaboration, proactivity, and, through a continuous process of incremental improvement, a quest to understand in the first instance, then to be understood.

Where is effective leadership required within my field?

Contemporary contextual shifts in higher education (HE) fuelled by globalisation, internationalisation, colonialism, and neoliberalism have presented several paradigms and philosophies of leadership, often operating in parallel or tangential to established leadership theory. Within my field, effective leadership is undergirded by social justice, egalitarian and equality imperatives and seeks to challenge the philosophical underpinnings of higher education that promote structural inequalities (Ladson Billings and Tate, 1995), while equitably advocating for strategies in perusal of the organisation's corporate social responsibilities and strategic aims and objectives.

As a practitioner with both academic and professional credentials working within a 'third space environment' in HE (Whitchurch, 2015), I recognise the paradoxes and dilemmas that pose challenges to effective leadership within my field. For example, take the current phenomenon of the degree-awarding gap in HE (the so-called attainment gap). In spite of more than a decade of robust research that highlights 'race' as a statistically significant factor in promoting these inequalities in attainment (Broecke and Nicholls, 2007; Singh, 2011; Mountford-Zimdars et al., 2015; Richardson, 2015), and the implementation of various charter marks (Advance HE, 2019), metrics (Department for Education, 2016) and mandates (UUK, 2019; OfS, 2019), these inequalities persist. Worryingly, 20 years on from the landmark Stephen Lawrence enquiry (Younge, 1999), it proves difficult to deny that institutional racism is still a key feature of the academy that maintains and promotes structural inequalities. Effective leadership is often compromised in the face of conflicting social justice (public service) and market agendas, as the business of education (and that it has become) needs to remain financially viable. Initiatives such as the widening participation agenda, while satisfying market agendas to put more 'bums on seats', often promote inequalities within that cadre, with black students among those with the highest rates of non-continuation (Keohane, 2017).

Equally, structural inequalities promote differentials in academic attainment at undergraduate level (Advance HE, 2018); this contributes to the broken pipeline (Williams et al., 2019) and an underrepresentation at a macro level, where only 0.6% of professors in the UK are black (Advance HE, 2018). In terms of pay, gender pay, contracts, and workloads, universities have become seemingly complacent and reluctant to acknowledge the inconvenient truths. These truths illuminate the fact that pay of staff has dropped by 17% since 2009 (Universities & Colleges Employers Association, 2019) and that this particularly affects staff from black, Asian or minority ethnic (BAME) backgrounds intersectionally. BAME staff are often employed on precarious contracts, less likely to hold senior jobs, overrepresented in junior roles, and paid less than their white colleagues (a pay gap of 9%); black academic staff are paid 14% less than their white counterparts (HESA, 2019). In the changing landscape of HE, effective leadership is required at all levels in order to implement changes that will transform practices and policies and dismantle the established structures that promote structural inequalities for staff and students. Most importantly, redress political drivers that motivate universities to develop business models that are largely dependent on students' fees and competition for national and international research income, at the expense of the transformational potential of education.

What decisions am I most/least proud of on my journey to becoming a leader?

In developing my leadership capabilities, I am most proud of my decision to diversify my professional practice as an occupational therapist and public health specialist by working within a 'third space' environment in HE. This has seen me embark on an academic journey studying for a PhD in Higher Education, as well as adopting several leadership roles in promoting social justice and equality of opportunity, particularly for people from marginalised groups.

> What counts in life is not the mere fact that we have lived. It is what difference we have made to the lives of others that will determine the significance of the life we lead.
>
> Nelson Mandela

Within these roles, I have had the opportunity to develop my professional, personal, and interpersonal skills, while gaining valuable experience working within a multinational environment with a range of persons from varying social, cultural, and economic backgrounds. In addition to developing my professional, personal, and interpersonal skills, I have also been able to develop cultural competence (Purnell, 2000), which is a vitally important transferrable skill that is required to meet the needs of an ever-increasing multicultural society.

It proves particularly challenging to recollect a specific decision that I am least proud of in developing my leadership skills. However, I would be inclined to declare that in the past, missing opportunities to build professional, collaborative relationships with people of a different persuasion have compromised the development of my leadership capabilities. On reflection, I have adopted a stance similar to Nelson Mandela in the belief that I need to strive to be the change that I want to see.

If I had my time again...

If I had my time again I would embrace the fact that professional life is wrought with messiness, obstacles, challenges, and adversities earlier on in my career. I would view these as necessary steps towards the development of effective leadership skills, experiences, and resilience.

What questions should one ask oneself when becoming a leader?

1. What are my personal values and principles?
2. Do I have the ability to see past initial problems to a particular opportunity to get results and build, maintain, and restore relationships?
3. Am I able to be gracious to others even when we disagree about the most fundamental things?
4. Am I able to empower others to realise collective goals?
5. Am I able to conduct a genuine and honest assessment of my skills and abilities?
6. What is my circle of influence?
7. Am I able to see the 'bigger picture?'

References

Adair, J. (1979). *Action-Centred Leadership*. Aldershot, United Kingdom: Gower.
Advance HE. (2018). *Equality + Higher Education: Students Statistical Report 2018*. [Online]. London. Available at: www.advance-he.ac.uk.
Advance HE. (2019). *Equality Charters Explained [Online]*. Available at: www.ecu.ac.uk/equality-charters/charter-marks-explained/ [Accessed: 2 November 2019].

Astin, A. and Astin, H. (2000). *Leadership Reconsidered: Engaging Higher Education in Social Change*. Battle Creek, MI: W.K. Kellog Foundation. DOI: 10.4236/cus.2014.23020

Broecke, S. and Nicholls, T. (2007). Ethnicity and degree attainment. *Unassigned* 1, 1–24. Available at: www.dfes.gov.uk/research/data/uploadfiles/RW92.pdf

Covey, S. (2004). *The 8th Habit: From Effectiveness to Greatness*. London: Simon & Schuster.

Department for Education. (2016). *Policy Paper: TEF Factsheet*. Available at: https://assets.publishing.service.gov.uk/government/uploads/system/uploads/attachment_data/file/550232/Teaching-excellence-framework-factsheet.pdf (Accessed June 7, 2020).

Goleman, D. (1997). *Emotional Intelligence*. New York: Bantam. DOI: 10.1037/e538982004-001

HESA (2019). *HE Staff Data: What Are Their Salaries?* Available at: https://www.hesa.ac.uk/data-and-analysis/staff/salaries (Accessed June 7, 2020).

Keohane, N. (2017). *On Course for Success? Student Retention at University*. Social Market Foundation. Available at: https://www.smf.co.uk/publications/course-success-student-retention-university/ (Accessed June 7, 2020).

Kouzes, J. and Posner, B. (2007). *The Leadership Challenge*. 4th ed. San Francisco, CA: Josey-Bass Pubishers. DOI: 10.4236/ojl.2014.32006

Ladson Billings, G. and Tate, W. (1995). Towards a critical race theory in education. *Teachers College Record* 1. DOI: 10.4324/9781315709796-2

Mountford-Zimdars, A. et al. (2015). *Causes of Differences in Student Outcomes*. Higher Education Funding Council for England (HEFCE) [Online]:132. Available at: www.hefce.ac.uk/media/HEFCE,2014/Content/Pubs/Independentresearch/2015/Causes,of,differences,in,student,outcomes/HEFCE2015_diffout.pdf.

OfS, O. for S. (2019). *Access and Participation Plans* [Online]. Available at: www.officeforstudents.org.uk/advice-and-guidance/promoting-equal-opportunities/access-and-participation-plans/ [Accessed: 2 November 2019].

Purnell, L. (2000). A description of the purnell model for cultural competence. *Journal of Transcultural Nursing* 11, 40–46. DOI: 10.1177/104365960001100107

Richardson, J.T.E. (2015). The under-attainment of ethnic minority students in UK higher education: What we know and what we don't know. *Journal of Further and Higher Education* [Online] 39, 278–291. DOI: 10.1080/0309877X.2013.858680.

Singh, G. (2011). A synthesis of research evidence. Black and minority ethnic (BME) students' participation in higher education: Improving retention and success. 1–73.

Universities & Colleges Employers Association. (October 8, 2019). Value of university staff pay has plummeted in last decade, employers' own research reveals. Available at: https://ucu.org.uk/article/10342/Value-of-university-staff-pay-has-plummeted-in-last-decade-employers-own-research-reveals (Accessed June 7, 2020).

UUK. (2019). *Black, Asian and Minority Ethnic Student Attainment at UK Universities: #CLOSINGTHEGAP* [Online]. London. Available at: www.universitiesuk.ac.uk/policy-and-analysis/reports/Documents/2019/bame-student-attainment-uk-universities-closing-the-gap.pdf.

Whitchurch, C. (2015). The rise of third space professionals: Paradoxes and dilemmas. In: Teichler, U. & Cummings, W. (eds.) *Forming, Recruiting and Managing the Academic Profession*. Dordrecht: Springer. pp. 79–99. DOI: 10.1007/978-3-319-16080-1_5

Williams, P. et al. (2019). *The Broken Pipeline: Barriers to Black PhD Students Accessing Research Council Funding. A Leading Route report*. Available at: https://leadingroutes.org/mdocs-posts/the-broken-pipeline-barriers-to-black-students-accessing-research-council-funding (Accessed June 7, 2020).

Younge, G. (1999). The death of Stephen Lawrence: The Macpherson report. *The Political Quarterly* 70(3), 329–334. DOI: 10.1111/1467-923x.00235.

CHAPTER 13

Summary

Stephen Newton and Kendall Jarrett

The focus of this chapter was on *becoming a leader*. Despite the very different backgrounds and experiences of the three contributors, several common themes are apparent, not least the articulation of profound statements relating to awareness of leadership capabilities. For example, Dave offered us insight into his awareness that 'missing opportunities to build professional, collaborative relationships with people of a different persuasion had compromised the development of my leadership capabilities', and Rachel reflected on the need to develop a 'capacity to be nimble and agile in adapting to unforeseen events'. Further profoundness was located in statements made in relation to exploring and knowing the context within which *leadership happens*. For example, Emily suggested that 'leadership is as much about desire and preparation as it is about adaptability, being able to read your audience, and developing a sense of community and teamwork within the classroom'; and Rachel stated that 'as I am in the business of education, leadership in my field is about enabling others to lead.'

So why do such profound insights into the practice of leadership often remain unheard in HE settings? Within his reflection on where effective leadership is required in his field, Dave provides us with a critical lens through which we could begin to answer this question by recognising the 'paradoxes and dilemmas that pose challenges to effective leadership'. The value of such criticality, especially at a time when *becoming a leader* in HE brings with it a need to challenge a number of assumptions surrounding the validity and utility of HE, is vitally important. For Dave, leadership appears to revolve around combating the structural inequalities he routinely encounters that manifest as, among other things, the racial 'attainment gap' that pervades all levels of HE and of which he offers compelling examples.

For Rachel and Emily, in different ways and with different emphases, each espouses the idea of leadership as service. Rachel refers explicitly to servant leadership as a guiding principle as well as the need for 'purpose' – not simply to establish where one is leading, but why. She asks herself whether any group work in which she is involved will lead those involved to grow personally and professionally. Emily refers to 'meeting students where they are' rather than delivering teaching based on her own experiences and preconceptions.

Each contributor refers (in different ways) to the fact that they could have benefited from earlier and/or greater professional development prior to taking leadership roles. Emily refers explicitly to her wish that she had received more professional development in leadership prior to taking up her role, with a view to building a 'deeper toolkit' that would support wider engagement with students and colleagues and the development of techniques more appropriate to the type of university in which she teaches.

Also of note was that each recognised the contribution that 'other sector' leadership experiences had given them in their journeys to *becoming a leader* in HE. For example, Rachel commented on her time as a leader in the corporate and charity sectors which exposed her to different leadership styles; Dave recognised his experiences as an occupational therapist and social justice advocate as being instrumental in his development of cultural competence; and Emily highlighted her time as an athlete and the importance of reflection to determine how/where performance improvements could be made. Here, Emily alludes to a key issue in HE concerning how a leader goes about enabling the whole team to play at a higher level, rather than just enabling the success of a few individual stars.

There is a commonly held view in HE that engagement underpins learning. It stands to reason, then, that the same can be said about learning to lead – that engagement is a key element in *becoming a leader*. Rachel demonstrated an appreciation of this by suggesting that if she had her time again she would 'invest more in developing healthy working relationships' and 'volunteer to take on more responsibilities'. For her, *becoming a leader* was about *doing leadership*. For Dave it is about recognising that 'professional life is wrought with messiness, obstacles, challenges, and adversities' and the need to 'view these as necessary steps towards the development of effective leadership skills, experiences, and resilience'.

To conclude, it is important to us as authors that the idea of HE is about becoming, not having. This view extends to leadership in HE. What we do to assist colleagues in *becoming a leader* is just as important as what we do to assist those *being a leader*. *Becoming a leader* in HE is challenging and requires considerable sacrifice, grit, and vulnerability to be shown, all of which resonate within Rachel, Emily, and Dave's accounts of *becoming a leader* in HE.

CHAPTER **14A**

Being a leader
Joanne Bowen

Professional biography

I am at heart a mid-career medical researcher, passionate about finding ways to improve the treatment experience for people with cancer. I am currently Head of the Cancer Treatment Toxicities Group and Discipline Lead for Physiology within the Adelaide Medical School at the University of Adelaide. How did I get here? After completing a Bachelor of Health Sciences (Honours) and PhD in Medicine from the University of Adelaide in 2006, I received a National Health and Medical Research Council Postdoctoral Training Fellowship. In 2011 I was appointed Lecturer (Physiology), followed by promotion to Senior Lecturer in 2015 and Associate Professor in 2017.

Leadership responsibilities

Research

As Head of the Cancer Treatment Toxicities Group, I am responsible for leading highly motivated researchers across projects that broadly cover molecular mechanisms and management strategies for normal tissue toxicity in response to chemotherapy, radiation, and targeted therapies. My group includes undergraduate research placement students, Honours students, higher degree candidates (MPhil and PhD) and postdoctoral fellows. Projects are funded by philanthropic awards and industry contract research. As the Head, I am primarily responsible for securing all funding and external collaborations, maintaining research outputs, ensuring students have a high-quality training experience and achieve milestones, and support staff to obtain professional development and project-specific performance indicators.

Teaching

I am the Faculty of Health and Medical Sciences Honours Coordinator, which requires me to promote and maintain excellence in researcher training across the four Honours Programs run through the Schools of Medicine, Public Health, Dentistry, and Nursing. I have restructured the Honours Degree of the Bachelor of Health and Medical Sciences twice, and have helped to align curriculum and assessments across disciplines in conjunction with the Honours course coordinators. I am also the senior postgraduate coordinator for the School, responsible for assessing domestic and international scholarship applications, managing higher degree research student milestones, and organising student seminars.

Administration

As Discipline Lead, I steer staff within the Discipline of Physiology through teaching and workload allocation, curriculum design, and research. In addition to managing direct reports, I also lead recruitment of new appointments, negotiate service teaching arrangements across programmes external to the School, and manage vacancy and backfill teaching positions. For the past two years, I have also been Deputy Associate Dean Gender Equity and Diversity. This role includes providing guidance and consultation with the Associate Dean, and proxy reporting for the Chair at Faculty Board. During this time I have devised and led initiatives concerning the representation of female academics within grants and fellowship rounds and organised the first Adelaide Medical School Women's Development and Promotion Workshop. Data and feedback from these initiatives has helped inform strategies within the Faculty Gender Equity Action Plan to better engage female researchers.

Professional

I am a Board Member for the Multinational Society of Supportive Care in Cancer. This leadership group is responsible for instigating initiatives to increase awareness of supportive care globally through activity within specialised study groups. Key events in the calendar include organising the annual scientific meeting, attended by well over 1,000 delegates from almost 60 countries, and publication of clinical practice guidelines for the management of cancer treatment toxicities. My portfolio includes chairing the awards committee, a task that enables me to help recognise the best and brightest researchers within the field through awards and travel scholarships.

What does effective leadership look like to me?

In 2018 I participated in the Adelaide Women Leadership Development Program, run by Inkling Women (https://www.adelaide.edu.au/hr/development/programs/leading/women/). Through this programme, 13 women from across the university received focused training on becoming a leader within their area and developing skills to elevate themselves and their colleagues. It also provided an opportunity to shadow existing leaders and learn from their different styles. The insights gained during the shadowing sessions shaped what I see as truly excellent leadership that's worth aspiring too. Effective people leadership to me is feeling energised and valued by those who I report to. It is walking out of a meeting and feeling empowered to take action. Leadership during structural changes and uncertainty (which seems to be the new norm in academia) should be optimistic and support adaptability. Leadership decisions should be transparent and outcomes-focused, with leaders closing the loop once the change has been implemented. The leaders I have seen get the best out of their team are the ones that are completely authentic and self-aware of their own flaws, and are able to rally teams to work towards a shared goal. Effective leadership to me is recognising strengths in each person and helping to support growth of confidence in their unique abilities.

Where is effective leadership required within my field?

One of the most critical places for effective leadership in my field is supporting student and early career researcher development. As postgraduate coordinator, lab head, and mentor, I have a responsibility to foster a culture of excellence in researcher training, while also ensuring a supportive environment that promotes resilience. I strive to ensure all students graduating from their PhD programme have completed a range of broadening experiences in addition to the expected scientific writing and conference participation, including access to industry-based project involvement, teaching, professional society service, and international exchange. I believe it is through these additional facets of professional development that students become the next leaders, both within and outside academia.

What decisions am I most/least proud of as a leader?

The decision I am most proud of as a leader is the creation of the Cancer Treatment Toxicities Group, where in 2015 I brought together three independent research labs (and their heads) under a combined structure to increase impact. It resulted in enhanced student attraction, funding, and industry contracts. The group is now more multidisciplinary, bridging genetics, pharmacology, physiology, and microbiology, and has had sustained output growth since its inception.

It has also led to amazing successes through the group's postgraduate students winning prizes and recognition including Falling Walls Lab, Channel 9 Young Achievers, and SA Science Excellence Awards. Conversely, I am least proud of the example I set as a leader in the first 12 months of the new group. Despite wanting my students and staff to have a good work–life balance, I was guilty of working nights and weekends, sending emails at all hours, and being unable to separate work from home. My behaviour wasn't giving them permission to relax outside of working hours, even if I didn't expect them to respond immediately to my emails, they often did. I now make a concerted effort to ensure that I set a positive example of working sensible hours and maximising life away from the lab, as I hope they will emulate this in their future workplaces.

If I had my time again...

If I had my time again I would have taken a leadership course earlier in my career. I would have been more strategic about seeking mentors and coaching, and asked more questions about the inner workings of academia from the outset of my position. For the first few years I lacked clarity regarding the purpose of my role, and how I really fit into the bigger picture within the university. This meant I often felt like I was working in a silo. That way of working was not sustainable, and likely fuelled some bad habits like not relinquishing enough control or actively seeking leverage opportunities. These are poor leadership qualities and hindered growth of my team. However, once I made more connections (particularly with mentors outside of the university) and had a clear vision of how I contributed to the success of the organisation, it gave me more drive and satisfaction, and eventually made me a better leader.

Another change I would make is letting go of activities that drain energy and don't contribute to overall career progress in a much timelier manner. I think going into academia, there is a risk of taking on too many responsibilities too quickly, essentially collecting more and more duties without a clear picture of how they relate to overall performance and purpose. However, with time being allocated across too many activities, none really get the attention they deserve, especially the ones that are most critical to success. The Think Well programme (https://www.ithinkwell.com.au/) has some fantastic resources to illustrate how to be more effective and say 'no' when needed, which leads to improved focus and success.

What/who had the most impact on me and my development as a leader?

Without doubt the greatest impact on my development as a leader has to be my PhD supervisor and then later mentor, Professor Dorothy Keefe. She showed me that providing stretch opportunities and championing a junior researcher elevates their career in ways that no other research output can achieve. One such opportunity was taking on a leadership role in the Multinational Association of Supportive Care in Cancer Mucositis Study Group when I was a postdoctoral fellow. As part of the role, I was co-organiser of a systematic review and clinical practice guidelines update that involved over 70 contributors from across the globe. That experience developed skills in organisation and communication on a scale that I would have never achieved within my laboratory environment. It translated into my career when setting goals with realistic timelines, bringing together diverse groups, and having confidence to make new contacts outside my field.

What questions should one ask oneself when exercising their leadership?

The questions that I seem to ask myself most often when exercising leadership are: (1) Do I have enough information? (2) How is this going to affect my team? (3) Where does this fit into the strategic plan for the university? For me, it boils down to whether people in the team are going to feel included and valuable to the overall goal we are trying to achieve. One question I would like to ask, and act upon, more often is how I can effectively assess whether the approach is working and provide constructive feedback to individuals.

CHAPTER **14B**

Being a leader
Luke Buchanan-Hodgman

Professional biography

I am Director of Undergraduate Admissions and Outreach within the School of Economics at the University of Kent. Unusually for someone holding a key leadership position within the department, I am only two years into my academic career. That being said, the responsibilities my role requires of me are complementary, and the constituent parts of the brief align neatly with my previous experience. The leadership responsibilities required of the holder of the position are numerous, but pertain nearly exclusively to activities concerning undergraduate recruitment and school/college visits. Some of my duties are: to organise school and college visit days – both on- and off-campus – that help meet the targets we set for ourselves concerning our civic mission; develop new and exciting material in which to generate a motivation to study economics; liaise with professional service staff on a daily basis in order to keep a handle on recruitment activities such as Open Days and Applicant Days; and regularly make what can be very taxing decisions on borderline applications.

Leadership responsibilities

Professional

In order to achieve what is expected of me when carrying out these tasks, it is crucial that I remain focused on the expectations A-Level students have about university-level study. A tangential but equally important requirement is that I ensure academic colleagues, predominantly those who focus on teaching, are kept abreast of the changing nature of A-Level assessment and the background of our typical applicant. This can sometimes lead to conflicts: if recruitment is weaker than expected, and adjustments to entry tariffs are considered necessary, this can have a significant impact on the design and assessment of modules in our undergraduate suite of programmes. Therefore, a considerable degree of mapping – albeit imperfect – is undertaken: matching the support we provide in-house, both academic and pastoral, to the composition of our incoming cohort. In order for this mapping process to be effective, I must regularly consult with the senior tutor and student support officers. These members of the school are there to guide our students when they arrive with us, therefore they require to be kept informed of key recruitment developments.

Administration

Uniquely among my colleagues, I frequently liaise with our partner schools and colleges in the locality, and members of the wider staff body within the university whose remit it is to organise outreach activities. Regular discussions with local teachers and heads of department enable me to develop engaging activities to run on visit days and help determine the future direction of our outreach work. In the ever more competitive landscape of student recruitment in higher education, these activities, which draw to the fore the work we do at the University of Kent, are becoming integral to our continuing ability to attract talented local students. Although our reach is international, through our campuses in numerous other countries, we are building a strong regional presence through these activities.

What does effective leadership look like to me?

Open and honest working relationships with colleagues. In order to function as a team, and by extension to effectively lead that team in the right direction, you must have mutual respect. We can only function as a cohesive unit if colleagues feel that they are able to discuss ideas freely. Whether it concerns a new marketing strategy, a change of direction in terms of our outreach work, or the recruitment of student ambassadors, a leader must take seriously the opinions of those with whom they work. By placing considerable weight on the opinions of those there to support the task at hand, it allows them to become personally invested in ensuring our joint success, both within the department and the university at large. You have to give colleagues the space for blue sky thinking if practices are to improve and evolve over time.

Where is effective leadership required within my field?

In the delegation of duties. Although it is crucial in the ideas phase of a new strategy to ensure each member of the team knows their individual input is valued, it is equally as important that colleagues are delegated responsibilities during the implementation phase. I am incredibly lucky that I work alongside a competent and well-informed professional service staff, all of whom are free to exercise their discretion within their clearly delineated role with each of our projects. Successes and failures are shared in equal measure, but we are all aware at the outset what duties are required to be undertaken and how the details of these are to be communicated. I feel that by effectively delegating important elements of a task that you ensure colleagues more fully buy-in to what you are trying to achieve. Once completed this allows each of us to take pride in the component we uniquely contributed, alongside that of the whole.

What decisions am I most/least proud of as a leader?

At my stage in my career I do not feel I have a vast reservoir of past successes and failures to reflect upon. However, what I am most proud of achieving since taking up the position is the development of a formal 'outreach' scheme. Prior to my arrival the school did not engage fully with our partners – there were sporadic events, but these were mainly determined by the interests of those colleagues who were free at any given time. I used my previous experience as a secondary school teacher to develop a module entitled 'Personal Finance using Excel' that A-Level and GCSE students can participate in. Working very closely with a student ambassador, we also created a range of distance learning material that will allow us to scale up the reach of the course. This enables us to provide a particularly useful course not only locally but potentially internationally, too. It contributes directly to the civic mission of the university in that it formalises our engagement in the Kent and Medway region. Students learn skills in finance and computing – both in very high demand by employers. I am particularly proud that I took the initiative to set up such a course and hope that with the continued support of the University of Kent it will flourish.

When it comes to what I am least proud of, it would be that at times I can overstretch myself and it falls to my team to provide support that often goes above and beyond what can reasonably be expected. My roles are so varied that it can be difficult to ensure balance. I teach roughly 600 students over the course of the year and it is very easy to embark on too many projects simultaneously. During the most recent academic cycle this caused me to become somewhat detached from a new advertising campaign, one that was central to recruitment. I was very lucky that the professional support staff stepped in and fulfilled the role I ought to have played. Knowing when to see existing projects through before beginning new ones is a skill I still must master.

If I had my time again…

When developing the outreach programme I would have from the start engaged and consulted more widely with schools and colleges. I leant slightly too much on my own experience when developing the course material; in hindsight, an exploratory review of the precise skills demanded by the FE sector would have almost certainly led to fewer revisions. I was somewhat reticent to do this at the beginning – a camel is a horse designed by committee – but it would have been more efficient.

What/who had the most impact on me and my development as a leader?

Dr Otsu of Keio University was my research supervisor and taught me two crucial lessons: the first was the value of Socratic questioning; the second was to trust. Although seemingly contradictory, these were complementary. During the time we spent together I would often find myself explaining to him in minute detail the work I was undertaking. He would require deep explanations of the course I was plotting in my research and expected thorough, complete, and well-reasoned answers. Although initially intimidating, it taught me that to question is to know. Once I have sated his need to determine how I was progressing, he trusted that would continue and did not pursue me. This hands-off approach, coupled with periodic deep discussions, showed me how a working relationship can be both managerial but also provide space for colleagues to explore their own ideas of how to solve problems.

What questions should one ask oneself when exercising their leadership?

Is my team invested in the project? That is the key question. If they are not, either you have not allowed them the space to contribute fully, or the project, its importance, and their role in achieving your common objective have not been adequately explained. As I discovered this year, it can also be that you have simply too many projects running simultaneously and not enough bandwidth to deal effectively with each. This is why openness within a team is absolutely critical: if one member is becoming overburdened, it is the role of a leader to assess the balance of the workload. Providing colleagues with the space in which to contribute fully, and thus become invested, has to be considered when delegating in the first instance.

CHAPTER **14C**

Being a leader
Lisa Fedoruk

Professional biography

My leadership journey has taken an organic pathway rather than a traditional route. After completing my BEd at the University of Alberta and teaching in secondary public education for five years, I made a career transition into industry and became a territory manager for a global pharmaceutical company. Little did I know, the sales, corporate training, and leadership skills I accrued over six years in this role, along with my previous educative practice, would transfer into my subsequent career transitions and experiences.

Opening a new career chapter, I returned to my innate teaching roots to become an Instructor at SAIT Polytechnic while completing my MEd in Adult Learning. Looking for new leadership opportunities, my time at SAIT Polytechnic was spent in the classroom, as an International Program Coordinator, Chair, and member of numerous campus committees, and the faculty voice as a delegate on the board of governors. All of these roles led me to complete my PhD at the University of Calgary in Adult Learning.

The fluidity of my journey continued in this new institution. I was able to harness the previous knowledge I amassed and apply it to my ensuing roles at the University of Calgary as an instructor, programme coordinator, research associate, and within my current position as an educational development consultant at the Taylor Institute for Teaching and Learning. In this role I collaborate with the academic community in guiding and supporting postsecondary teaching and learning. More specifically, as a faculty leader I am a facilitator for programming and resource development in the Taylor Institute's Certificates in University Learning and Teaching, and Teaching Assistant Orientation programme. I am also a board member on the University of Calgary's Conjoint Faculties Research Ethics Board.

Leadership responsibilities

Programme coordination

I am an academic leader for the Taylor Institute's Certificates in University Teaching and Learning for Postdoctoral Scholars and Graduate Students. Made up of five individual programmes, such as *Theories and Issues in Higher Education* and the *Foundations of the Scholarship of Teaching and Learning (SoTL)*, I work in collaboration with other academic programme leaders to ensure sound pedagogical guidance and teaching excellence within our certificate programme. I also teach within these programmes, which provides me the opportunity to continually enhance my facilitation skills, build relationships with our participants, and develop communities of practice through mentorship.

Research

As an educational development consultant, part of my role is to continually engage in and promote scholarly work and research. Currently I am collaborating with my colleagues around research involving mentorship between teaching assistants and their supervising instructors. In addition, we have been investigating assessment in higher education as it relates to 'real-world contexts' through an existing framework on authentic assessment for experiential learning. Once complete, these resources (published articles, guides) are placed on our website as open resources for public dissemination and implementation.

Professional/service

I am a member of the Conjoint Faculties Research Ethics Board at the University of Calgary. In this role I serve as a research ethics consultant to faculty, postdoctoral scholars, and graduate students by way of guiding and supporting their efforts in applying for ethics certification when embarking on investigations involving human participants. Subsequently I attend monthly board meetings to engage in full board reviews of high-risk proposals and am a delegated reviewer for lower-risk interdisciplinary research ethics proposals involving humans. I take this leadership role very seriously as the university must abide by strict national rules and guidelines to remain in good standing and qualify for funding for ongoing scholarship. Of great importance to me is promoting 'ethical-mindedness' that advocates for including ethics as a key component of research project development rather than perceiving it as an add-on or a hurdle to overcome at the conclusion of a project's design. It is an approach that incorporates ethical thinking into research design in order to mitigate harm at all stages and levels of the research process.

What does effective leadership look like to me?

The greatest examples of effective leadership that I have had the privilege to observe and take part in have occurred during my memberships on academic boards. Most recently, participating as a member and delegated reviewer on the research ethics board at my university has taught me the underlying principle of 'do no harm'. From a research perspective we must protect human beings as participants in studies via ethical areas of consideration, but those ethical considerations also apply to how leaders treat people in daily life. For example, having a keen awareness of power dynamics, fairness/equality, confidentiality, and conflicts of interest by way of best practices within leadership behaviour can mitigate struggles and challenges and demonstrate respect.

Additionally, being a member of the SAIT Polytechnic Board of Governors provided me the opportunity to see the higher educational landscape from a different vantage point. Observing and participating in institutional strategic planning, decision-making surrounding disbursement and investment of a multi-million-dollar budget, and the requirement to problem-solve in diverse contexts have been some of the key skills for effectiveness, efficiency, sustainability, and adaptability of a higher educational institute in the face of economic and political uncertainty. To achieve this, I learned that the success of an institute, organization, or business depends upon the ability of a leader to collaborate, organize, and manage a team through honest and transparent communication.

Where is effective leadership required within my field?

My work encircles most realms of teaching and learning in the higher education community. One of the most important areas for effective leadership within this field of educational development is through the guidance and support of faculty, postdoctoral scholars, and students in attaining their educative goals. I strive to model pedagogical leadership within the delivery of certificate programmes surrounding teaching and learning and professional development offerings, ensure a safe and confidential space during one-on-one consultations, and contribute to the continuous enhancement of teaching and learning across the campus community through open communication, collaboration, and problem-solving.

What decisions am I most/least proud of as a leader?

The decisions I am most proud of as a leader stem from my previous experience at SAIT Polytechnic as an international project coordinator and team member delivering faculty development and teaching workshops abroad. During one sojourn our team journeyed to Kazakhstan and worked closely with Russian and Kazakh translators to deliver a Western-style teaching model (learning-centred) via plenary sessions as well as facilitated individual feedback sessions with foreign instructors. Reflecting upon my leadership skills in this situation, I used my previous international teaching experience to overcome the challenges my team felt, such as differences in language, teaching styles, and the overall culture that we experienced. As a team we took time to check our own assumptions, and be open to other ways of doing, being, and thinking. Overall, the greatest outcome of this situation was achieving our goals and the goals of the participants through communication, collaborative problem-solving, and teamwork.

I believe my least proud moments might be common experiences in leadership by way of taking on more than I should. Doing this has led to questionable examples of unbalance, poor decision-making, implementing change too quickly, and overall stress/health issues. One of my greatest mistakes was making my personal contact information available to colleagues and students and receiving communications at all hours of the day and night with an expectation of a timely response. In turn, this behaviour was modelled and created unrealistic and unfair expectations. I now make a conscious effort to promote mental and physical health and wellness through strategic ways and set boundaries on availability and response times. This certainly is a work in progress!

If I had my time again...

I would have sought out a mentor earlier in my career. Often times I felt too reliant on my own experiences and sometimes jumped too quickly before looking. The consequences were inefficient and ineffective use of time and resources. Understanding that you are not alone is key in beginning to accept and embrace your vulnerability as a leader, but more importantly as a human being. My mentor has helped me navigate the stages of developing my professional identity through encouragement of formal reflective practices, providing experiential opportunities, teaching and demonstrating humility, and offering sound advice and suggestions in times of uncertainty.

What/who had the most impact on me and my development as a leader?

My PhD supervisor has had the greatest impact on me and my development as a leader. I am very fortunate, as Dr Colleen Kawalilak was also a professor of mine when I completed my MEd. We organically connected and developed a mentor/mentee relationship, but also a friendship that has continued to this day. She provided many scholastic and professional opportunities that offered me challenges and insight into the academy and she was instrumental in strategically guiding me when I suffered overwhelmingly from imposter syndrome. The greatest gift Colleen provided as a mentor was knowing when to be available for guidance and support and when to step back to allow me to independently explore and discover.

What questions should one ask oneself when exercising their leadership?

Are the words of advice/recommendations/suggestions I am giving something I would do myself? This lends itself to an essence of authenticity. A second question to ask oneself is 'How do I feel about this?' In higher education's changing landscape, I feel our instinct/intuition is incredibly important as a precursor to decision-making and problem-solving. Finally, I recommend reflecting on ethical areas applicable to your situation, such as power, fairness, confidentiality, and conflicts of interest. These 'ethics of leadership' demonstrate respect for all people you work with and lead, resulting in behaviour that may positively transform future decisions and outcomes.

CHAPTER 14

Summary
Kendall Jarrett

For Joanne, Luke, and Lisa, the reality of *being a leader* in HE has brought with it countless opportunities to impact upon both the individual and the institution. Collectively, their understanding and appreciation of what *being a leader* means is broadly shared, with reference to a need for authenticity and to provide purpose and space for others to pursue professional endeavours. It was also intimated by all three that *being a leader* requires an appreciation of both the role they see themselves playing in/for the institution and the context within which one operates.

For Joanne and Luke, finding the right balance between work and life and between stretch and overstretch presented consistent leadership challenges. For Luke and Lisa, being over-reliant on one's own experiences when determining leadership direction and action brought with it moments of learning significant to their development as a leader.

Of significance across each *being a leader* story was the impact a research mentor had had on personal leadership development. Luke, Lisa, and Joanne spoke glowingly about the impact their PhD supervisors had on shaping them as leaders through providing stretch opportunities, championing them as junior leaders, and allowing space to develop and explore their own ideas. These opportunities for personal and professional growth provided by their research mentors had a profound and lasting effect on the manner within which each now enacts their own leadership. To that end, Joanne spoke about the legacy of involvement in a formal leadership development programme, developed in partnership with an outside agency, but at its core embracing opportunities to shadow fellow leaders *from within* the institution (a key focus of Chapter 2).

Sometimes *being a leader* requires abrasive action ahead of passive manipulation, or indeed vice versa, but at all times it requires a familiarity with the nuances of role. This nuanced requirement was evident when each was asked of what leadership decisions they were most proud of? For Lisa, it was the bringing together of peers to achieve complex and challenging goals associated with the delivery of a teaching model to colleagues in Kazakhstan. For

Joanne, it was the bringing together of three independent research labs to create the Cancer Treatment Toxicities Group, which ultimately led to improved research impact and sustained output growth. For Luke, it was bringing to life a formal outreach scheme that included development of a fit-for-purpose learning module to help achieve scheme goals.

Over time, it is inevitable that what makes a leader proud will change as more experiences of leadership begin to accrue. It follows then that the more leadership experiences one has, the more one will wish they had done things differently. When completing the sentence *If I had my time again…*, Lisa and Joanne spoke about their desire to be more strategic in finding a mentor earlier in their careers. Luke and Joanne spoke about the need to ask more questions in relation to either the task they were leading or their place/identity within the institution as a new academic. Joanne also stated a want to have earlier exposure to leadership courses and leadership development opportunities when first starting out in academia – an underpinning philosophy which informed the conception and writing of this book.

Being a leader requires consideration of a range of questions, not least the questions one should constantly be asking oneself as a leader. For Luke, Lisa, and Joanne, these questions include:

1. Do I have enough information?
2. How is this going to affect my team?
3. Have I allowed my team the space to contribute fully?
4. Where does this fit into the strategic plan for the university?
5. How I can effectively assess whether the approach/my decision is working?
6. Are we/am I spread too thin? Are too many projects running simultaneously?
7. What do I feel about the situation/the response I've received/what I have asked colleagues to do?
8. What are my moral obligations in this instance?

CHAPTER **15A**

Leaving leadership
Carlton Cooke

Professional biography

At the time of writing I am the Head of the School of Social and Health Sciences at Leeds Trinity University (LTU) in the UK and also the university lead for research and knowledge exchange. Prior to this I worked for 25 years at Leeds Beckett University (LBU). What this amounts to, amongst other things, is that I have never worked outside of HE. I went straight through from completing my BSc joint honours in physical education and mathematics in 1980 to a Post Graduate Certificate Education (which gave me Qualified Teacher Status in secondary schools), a PhD in the biomechanics and exercise physiology of running (all at the University of Birmingham), and then (after completion of research-related contracts at the University of Birmingham and Loughborough University) to my first full-time permanent appointment at LBU in 1990.

The focus of this contribution is primarily based on me leaving my leadership position at LBU after 25 years, although I am about to move back to LBU from LTU, but as a research professor, not to a faculty leadership position.

Leadership responsibilities

My leadership responsibilities began formally in 1992 at LBU when I took on a programme development role, leading on the replacement of BA (Hons) Movement Studies with BSc (Hons) Sport and Exercise Science, BA (Hons) Physical Education, and BA (Hons) Sport and Recreation Development, which all still exist in updated forms today. In 1993 I was offered a principal lectureship and readership within two days of each other. I accepted the readership, which marked the formal beginning of my contributions to leadership in research at LBU, although I had been researching and publishing since my arrival. In 1995 I was appointed as the Deputy Head of School for Leisure and Sports Studies and was awarded a chair in 1998 as the Carnegie Professor of

Sport and Exercise Science. In 2004 I became the acting head of the School of Leisure and Sports Studies and later the same year became an associate dean of the Carnegie Faculty and head of a new School of Sport, Exercise and Physical Education. In 2006 I became the Associate Dean for Research in the Carnegie Faculty. Later the same year I was seconded to be the University Director of Postgraduate Research for two years, after which I went back to my faculty role for a year before becoming the University Director of Research for a year in 2009. Again, I went back to my faculty role in 2010 until I left LBU to take up the post of Head of School at Leeds Trinity University in 2015.

In my formative years, prior to acceptance of the formal leadership responsibilities outlined above, I held a number of 'in at the deep end' leadership roles within a variety of sports teams as well as the Scout Movement. Such opportunities involved no development or training in leadership, but I always had a habit of putting myself forward for such roles or being asked to undertake them. On reflection, I would like to believe that my motivation was always to contribute something to teams, and to facilitate and effect positive change, not just for me but for others around me. However, I know others along the way would not agree, as some teachers described me as arrogant, and when I was growing up I was fiercely competitive and hated losing. For the most part, though, I was asked or invited to consider taking on most of these early leadership opportunities, so adults saw something in me as a potential leader. This allowed me lots of experiential learning, where I think I did develop a degree of unconscious competence, learning much from my formative experiences, particularly my mistakes, and observing other leaders who also stumbled along their own experiential learning curves.

What does effective leadership look like to me?

I have in recent years become acquainted with leadership literature and helped create courses to develop it, as well as completing numerous leadership development courses in HE. However, I will give a personal non-academic view of what effective leadership looks like to me. Effective leadership for me focuses on the facilitation and development of people, both as individuals and in teams. Shared clarity and good two-way communication are key components of effective leadership, with a balance between working towards, and wherever possible, achieving agreed goals and outcomes, and how you get there, which is all about the journey and the culture in your part of the organisation. Throughout my working life the nature of the culture and the journey have come to assume far more importance to me as a leader than just striving for outcomes and goals. I believe effective leadership is about providing vision and an environment in which individuals will know what is expected of them and feel confident that they will be supported to take risks and be innovative, and that they can express their own views and contribute to shaping the culture and direction of the group. They are not merely followers, but participants and co-creators in the culture and the focus of the work of the team. Effective leadership also requires attention to effective operational management.

Where is effective leadership required within my field?

There are several aspects of leadership required in my field of work and discipline area. I am a professor of sport and exercise science but have retained early influences from physical education. I have always spanned more than one discipline, working across biomechanics and exercise physiology, researching performance and health, and am an advocate of multi- and interdisciplinary work. My leadership of academic groups, research centres, departments, and schools has always reflected my own values of a balance of contributions to teaching, research, and knowledge exchange, and the overlap, synergies, and benefits there are between and across these elements. That is not to say that all academics need to work across all areas like I have chosen to do, but they need to support a culture where all these elements are valued and important for students and staff alike. This is a primary reason for me seeking to maintain leadership of groups, departments, and schools as well as in research and knowledge exchange. I have often been questioned on this by those who don't see past the workload to the value of being an academic leader and manager alongside being a research professor. This twin track of leadership has allowed me to shape the culture of groups of academics I have led, facilitating growth and development across all the aspects of academia that are in my view important to success in departments and schools that focus on sport-related HE.

Currently, as a head of school leading two departments, one of which contains subject areas I know very little about, I have found my approach transfers quite well. I believe it is because it is inclusive to all aspects of academic life and expects others to contribute to shaping and supporting a positive culture that they are part of, which is welcomed by most academics. That said, I would not claim to always take everyone along with my approach.

What decisions am I most/least proud of when looking back on my leadership?

Having worked for so long at LBU, I am most proud of my influence and legacy for the Carnegie School of Sport. Many of the leadership decisions I made that I am most and least proud of relate to the same things: staff appointments and promotions. On balance I believe I have made many more good leadership decisions than bad in terms of appointments and promotions, which is important, as decisions on other people's roles and futures and their contributions to the team are a critical part of leadership. I don't try to surround myself with like-minded people, as this is not healthy for an organisation or team, but I consider the same key question as when I decide on a job: can I see how I can make a positive difference if I take the job? So, in selection processes I have led I always make an appointment or give or support a promotion to the person I believe has evidenced their ability and desire to make the greatest positive difference in terms of culture in the workplace and potential for achievement.

Before I had even considered leaving LBU I made what I believed was an important decision in terms of succession for a key aspect of my role in research leadership, which would be better for the future of the school and the university. We had done really well in the Research Excellence Framework (REF) audit of UK universities in sport and exercise science and leisure studies in 2014, which I had led on, working with a team of very experienced professors who each ran research centres as part of the Institute for Sport, Physical Activity and Leisure. I had encouraged a younger professor to step up to be a centre lead instead of me and become part of the team, which worked very well. I then suggested that I step back as lead for the next REF in 2021 and that this younger professor take over. I was still there as associate dean and head of the Institute for support when needed, but this was an important step in the incremental process of succession. When I left LBU I was confident this professor would step up and move things to a higher level for the university, though it happened sooner than either of us expected. I left LBU nearly five years ago and evidence suggests this succession plan has proved very effective.

If I had my time again...

If I had my time again, I would make decisions on my career path with more of a focus on the activities I wanted to spend most of my time doing. Addressing this balance would probably mean I would stay closer to my subject area; this is where I feel I am at my best as I can be a more effective leader in facilitating the development of staff and students who share my interests in the study of sport, physical activity, and health and physical education.

I would try to curb my enthusiasm for new challenges in leadership, but this perspective only comes with the benefit of hindsight, as you don't really know until you try. An example would be taking on leadership across academic areas which were a long way from my own academic home. There are both benefits and costs to doing this and I don't regret my decisions, but curbing my enthusiasm would have allowed me to keep a better balance of activities that I enjoy in my work. Enjoyment of work is critical to generating a positive culture and, in my view, effective leadership. In terms of my leadership of others, I would work harder at understanding different types of leadership and certainly place a very high value on culture over strategy and outcomes right from the start.

What/who had the most impact on me and my effectiveness as a leader?

Different people have influenced my approach to leadership at different times in my career. I was privileged to be taught as an undergraduate and supervised for my PhD by Professor Craig Sharp. Craig was, amongst many other things, a brilliant scientist with a great love of sport. He was a warm, generous, and modest man, with a great sense of humour as well as being a gifted communicator. He led by example and with great humility. My tutor at university was George Cooper, who had the knack of extracting the best from people, including me, by setting high expectations but making them appear eminently achievable, something which past students of mine have told me about my style of supervision. I am reminded from time to time that I once said in response to the team of postgraduate researchers working on a demanding lab protocol 'that my 9 year old son could do it' (which was probably true), to which the immediate response was 'yes, but could an ageing professor!'

I spent six months at Loughborough under the leadership of Professor Clyde Williams, when working as a research associate on the national fitness survey. Clyde is a very strong leader, and everyone knew what the vision was for the group he led and how, as young academics, we could develop as researchers based on his no-nonsense approach. I benefitted hugely from Clyde's leadership in that short period of time and he has continued to offer guidance and support throughout my career when I have requested it. His model and practices for leading a research group and developing young academics had a major influence on me and I have applied much of what I learned from Clyde's leadership during my leadership roles related to research, especially when I set about growing research at LBU in sport and exercise science.

More recently I have worked with ex-military leaders; the two who have had most impact on my views on leadership are Dave Bunting OBE and Stevan Jackson, both mountaineers and great leaders but who go about it in different ways. One is quiet, calm, supportive, and loyal, who has so much in the way of exemplary leadership through unconscious competence and is brilliant at selecting, building, and leading teams. The other is loud, a great storyteller and entertainer, an aspiring academic, who is also supportive and loyal and also builds and leads great teams. Both of them get the best out of their team members, neither gives out orders, but they help ordinary people achieve great things. It would be remiss of me not to give credit to my wife Belinda, who has taught me much about effective leadership throughout my career. She is calm, careful, considerate, and very supportive as a leader and values actions more than fine words.

What questions should one ask oneself when considering their legacy as a leader?

Without ducking the question, I believe it is for others to judge the legacy of a leader. However, my questions would focus on evidence of efficacy as a leader in terms of the culture and achievements of the groups that I have led. Did I leave the group in a better place than when I started to lead them? Have I facilitated and developed others in the team who can take over as leaders, doing it in their own way, but mindful of the importance of culture and shared vision and values? Do individuals I have led still keep in touch with me and ask me for guidance?

Achievements can be assessed using various metrics in HE, some in the form of key performance indicators and some as national surveys and audits of university performance, and these have their uses as well as limitations. Much more difficult is any assessment of culture. Local ways of gathering staff opinions and feedback are just as important as those for students and can focus on academic leadership at different levels of the organisation, which can also give an insight into your legacy as a leader in terms of outcomes and culture. When I left LBU I was surprised and humbled by the number of people who came along to see me off and the unsolicited kind words they said about me as well as the messages I received from people not able to make the event. I also hear from time to time mention of my legacy by those in leadership positions now that filter back through various ways and means as I apply myself to my leadership roles at Leeds Trinity University. I am equally confident I still get the blame for past actions, some of them possibly appropriate, but that comes with the territory.

CHAPTER **15B**

Leaving leadership
Fran Beaton

Professional biography

I started teaching in HE in 1980, having previously taught English to speakers of other languages (ESOL) in the voluntary and private sectors. My first HE job involved teaching English for academic purposes and ESOL to adult learners, later mentoring student teachers preparing to teach ESOL, and subsequently (1988–1994) working as a teacher educator at Goldsmiths, University of London, preparing students to teach their mother tongue as a foreign language. My work throughout this period was combined with bringing up a young family. In 2004 I moved to the University of Kent to lead Kent's PG Certificate in Higher Education (PGCHE).

Leadership responsibilities

In 1994 I moved into a full-time leadership role at Goldsmiths as programme coordinator and lecturer in charge of languages. I was responsible for 35–40 part-time teachers and cohorts of between 700 and 900 part-time learners each year. Although I was familiar with the institution in many respects, this role represented a step change and there was an awful lot to learn: financial modelling, feeding into/responding to institutional policies and decision-making, curriculum development, staff recruitment and retention. There were three particular challenges. First, attracting and supporting part-time students, who were not necessarily working towards a certificate or other qualification, in an institution primarily geared to full-time undergraduate and postgraduate students. Second, expanding the languages portfolio to include professional qualifications in interpreting and translating and to expand teacher education through partnership with other organisations, such as Instituto Cervantes, the Foreign and Commonwealth Office Language Centre, and other universities. Finally, creating opportunities for our part-time teachers for systematic professional development, both to support their students and student teachers and to enable good practice to be celebrated and shared.

Although I was then unfamiliar with the term, my aim was to build a community of practice among these part-time teachers, all teaching on different days (mostly in the evenings) and with few opportunities to gather as a group. I set up a series of professional development events, predominantly on Friday evenings when there was no teaching, focused on themes identified by the teachers themselves and complemented by termly professional development days held on a Saturday. These combined talks by invited speakers on topics of general interest, such as approaches to teaching grammar or using video, with language-specific discussion groups and world cafe style mixed language groups. As these initiatives bedded down, part-time teachers increasingly proposed and led sessions and facilitated the discussion groups. Many taught in several institutions and spread the word about these events, enabling external participants to join in. This generated a rich repertoire of resources and strategies to tackle common problems.

My leadership role as a teacher educator expanded through two opportunities. The first was involvement in a national project (led by Professor John Klapper) training language assistants teaching in UK universities. Two colleagues from the London School of Economics (LSE) and the School of Slavonic and Eastern European Studies (SSEES) and I extended this languages-specific provision to include a more general orientation into UK HE. I became more involved in teaching on Goldsmiths' MA in Education, working with students who were educators (in adult, further, and higher education) across a range of disciplines. Both initiatives gave me crucial experience in interdisciplinary teaching, so when the opportunity arose to move to an institution-wide interdisciplinary role at the University of Kent, it was irresistible.

I joined Kent in 2004 and led Kent's PG Certificate in Higher Education (PGCHE) until 2014. Central to my initial task of leading a curriculum review of the PGCHE was building a team of experienced research-active education academics, both to reshape the PGCert and to cope with rapidly rising student numbers. By the time I relinquished the leadership role, our team comprised five full-time lecturers and student numbers had risen to over 300. Crucially, we had built a collective ethos about the role of the programme in supporting academic development in the round, driven by and exemplifying research-led teaching as the academics taking the programme did in their own disciplinary practices.

What does effective leadership look like to me?

Reflecting on these experiences, and of being led, I believe characteristics of effective leadership include:

- Having a clear vision of what you want to achieve and why – this may start with a hunch but should be evidence-informed and principled.
- Understanding contextual constraints and opportunities – leaders need to be proactive, but initiatives are sometimes, of necessity, reactive.
- Humility – having a clear vision does not mean others' ideas are not equally valid; accept there are other points of view.
- Interpersonal skills – it's no good trying to lead in a vacuum; you need to persuade, involve, and empower others.
- Self-awareness – take time, periodically, to identify and reflect on your own strengths and weaknesses as a leader. Learn both from your mistakes and other people's feedback.

Where is effective leadership required within my discipline?

Everywhere! But particularly when someone is in a pivotal role and can influence policies and practices upwards, sideways, and downwards. Disciplinary leadership is important in justifying and defending the discipline, securing its future without perpetuating a narrow view of the discipline – the echo chamber that is a potential hazard of community of practice theory.

What decisions am I most/least proud of when looking back on my leadership?

My responses to these questions are informed by the beliefs articulated above. The decisions of which I am least proud were generally taken without attending sufficiently to other people's perspectives and contextual constraints. For example, the programme expansion I oversaw at Goldsmiths began at a time when the notion of lifelong learning for personal satisfaction and growth was supported politically and practically through low fees being charged. This relatively benign climate changed abruptly in the early 1990s, shifting to a model where funding would only be allocated to courses leading to a qualification. Furthermore, individuals would only be funded if they were studying for a qualification above ones they had already gained. While the decisions I took secured the future of languages provision, I paid insufficient attention to the implications for the day-to-day work of the languages teachers themselves in handling the demands of the new regime. These were both bureaucratic, contributing to a termly paper trail on the retention, progression, and achievement of each of their students, and philosophical. The majority of teachers were passionately committed to the notion of lifelong learning as a personal and public good and were disturbed at the abrupt shift of emphasis to certification.

The decision of which I am most proud relates to my leadership of the PGCert at Kent, particularly the shift towards making it research-led and taught by a core team of specialist academics. The rationale for doing this needed to be carefully and thoroughly argued, particularly justifying the importance of making new appointments. I took time to talk to previous participants about their experiences of the PGCert, to more experienced members of academic staff about their perceptions of the programme and to staff who had taught or were still teaching on the PGCert. I reviewed feedback from previous cohorts and external examiners. These conversations informed a consideration of the strengths and areas for development of the PGCert, how it related to academic professional development and future directions, particularly in overhauling curriculum content. There were also significant contextual developments throughout this time (e.g. a drive for institutional provision to align to the UK Professional Standards Framework and enable participants to gain HEA Fellowship). This combination of circumstances enabled a successful case to be made for expanding the team, shifting the focus beyond 'How we do things at Kent' to a more pedagogically rigorous approach, aligned to nationally recognised standards. This both enhanced the quality of the programme and contributed to institutional imperatives.

If I had my time again…

If I had my time again, I would be more aware of external factors before they become acute. For example, in the Goldsmiths situation, I had not seen the change in the funding model coming; with hindsight, the direction of travel had been clear in various government policy documents, which I had simply not thought to read. Had I known, I would have thought through the implications, prepared the ground more carefully for my part-time teachers, and fought sooner to make sure they were properly paid for the extra work the move to certification entailed – they were in the end, but it took a while. I would also have developed more sensitive political antennae earlier to identify the constraints and possibilities of different contexts and changes. Finally, I would hope to be braver about having difficult conversations with challenging people.

What/who had the most impact on me and my effectiveness as a leader?

Unquestionably, the greatest impact has been from colleagues who have mentored me (in some cases for many years) and colleagues with whom I am working or have worked. In the former instance, this mentoring has often been informal, originating in a specific context but permeating more widely and deeply, triggering reflection on how I articulate my approach to leadership. In the second, ongoing and open-minded dialogue with my colleagues has been central, both as my leadership role has changed and as others have taken on new leadership roles themselves.

What questions should one ask oneself when considering their legacy as a leader?

The idea of legacy has long dominated other discourses and, in my view, is potentially problematic if individuals think about their legacy while they are in the present, rather than retrospective reflection. With that proviso, I would distil the key questions to something like this:

- Why do you think your legacy matters?
- When you took on a leadership role, what did you hope to bring to it? What did you hope to achieve?
- As you leave, or prepare to leave, a leadership role, of what are you most proud?
- Which critical incidents have been most influential in your conception of leadership?
- What do you think current and previous colleagues would say about your role as a leader?
- Community of practice (CoP) literature refers to an 'outbound' trajectory: 'directed out of a CoP but seeing the world and oneself in different ways' (Wenger 2010, p. 134). What does this look like to you?

Reference

Wenger, E. (2010) Conceptual tools for CoPs as social learning systems: Boundaries, identity, trajectories and participation, in: Blackmore, C. (ed) *Social Learning Systems and Communities of Practice*, (pp. 125144). London: Springer. DOI: 10.1007/978-1-84996-133-2_8.

CHAPTER **15C**

Leaving leadership
David Hopkins

Introductory note

When I am asked to contribute a chapter to a book or a paper for publication, I always respond positively, which probably tells you more about me than the discernment of the commissioning editors! So it was with this chapter. However, as I write I feel an unease as I recognise the many questions I need to consider: had I really 'left' leadership when, at just over 50, I moved from being a dean to join the Blair government for its second term? Is there something so distinctive about leadership in HE that it does not apply to other professions? Am I now so over the hill that all I have left to recount is the past? Perhaps I will begin to resolve this unease in the pages that follow...

Professional biography

I am currently Chair of Educational Leadership at the University of Bolton, as well as being Professor Emeritus at the Institute of Education, University College London and the University of Nottingham, whilst still consulting globally on school and system reform. Among a range of previous educational roles, I have been Chief Adviser to three Secretaries of State on School Standards in the UK, Dean of Education at the University of Nottingham, long-term consultant to the OECD, a secondary school teacher, Outward Bound instructor, and International Mountain Guide.

Leadership experience

As I review my professional life, there are four areas where I have exercised leadership. Although the leadership contexts that I have been involved with are at first glance quite dramatically different, the skill sets they draw on are very similar. The four contexts are:

1. *Adventure leadership* – Born and brought up in South Wales, at the age of 17 I was sent on a course at the Eskdale Outward Bound Mountain School. My schoolteachers hoped that this experience would 'make a man of me'! It is for others to say whether the course was successful in that respect, but what it did do was to generate a lifelong love affair with the mountains and instil in me a deep belief in the power of experiential learning (Hopkins and Putnam 1993, 2012). It also set me on a journey of leadership that embraced not just Outward Bound (I became an instructor two years later), but also an International Mountain Guide when, in 1978, I was one of the first ten British guides to receive the International Carnet. Over the years I have led 12 expeditions to the greater ranges and chaired the Guides' Professional Standards Committee.
2. *School improvement activism* – At the age of 35 I had to make a decision between becoming the director of the National Mountaineering Centre in North Wales or becoming a tutor at the Institute of Education, Cambridge. I chose the latter and have no regrets, particularly as I could continue to guide during what were then the long Cambridge vacations. That enabled me with colleagues at Cambridge and many others in the 'invisible college', particularly those associated with the OECD, to develop and nurture the emerging field of 'school improvement' (Hopkins et al. 2014). We did this in two ways: by leading the international research/policy community on the one hand and working intensively with networks of school leaders and their colleagues in their local situations on the other. The extent that I was successful in this regard has recently been documented by Hallinger and Kovačević (2019). Leadership of an emerging field of study stands in contrast to that of mountain guiding, but still draws on skills of sustaining narrative, careful navigation, and maintaining collaborative relationships.
3. *Academic leadership* – After 11 years at Cambridge, I left to become Dean of Education at the University of Nottingham. I was becoming restless and was concerned by a degree of insularity and frustrated by some lost opportunities caused by poor decision-making. I used to joke that 'I left to re-join the real world'. In retrospect, the motivation was more to leave Cambridge than to join Nottingham, but I was very impressed by the university – its provision, ambition, and the leadership of the then Vice Chancellor, Sir Colin Campbell. To my surprise I immediately became Head of School and shortly after Dean of the Faculty. My task, I was told, was to 'modernise' the school and faculty and bring it up to national and international standards. I was one of a small number of strategic appointments across the university with a similar brief. We supported each other, were on reflection moderately successful, and each of us went on to other successful careers.

4. *System leadership* – During my time at Nottingham, besides my increasing engagement with international projects and consultancy, I also became more involved with the national education scene. For example, we won the competition to host the National College for School Leadership on the Jubilee Campus at Nottingham, where I was significantly involved in programme design; and also in 1999 was asked by the Secretary of State for Education, on one day a week, to lead the Partnership Board tasked with improving Leicester City LEA. It was natural then, when Sir Michael Barber left the Department for Education (DfE) to establish the Prime Minister's Delivery Unit, that I applied for his position. Leaving a university for a senior position in government – Chief Adviser to the Secretary of State on School Standards and Director of the Standards and Effectiveness Unit (SEU) – in one's early 50s was a greater challenge than I had anticipated and necessitated a massive upswing in my learning curve. Not only was I responsible for continuing to raise standards nationally through a reconfiguration of the policy agenda, but also as a neophyte I had to negotiate and survive in the civil service and political culture, which was quite another mountain to climb! Having said that, I was very fortunate in middle age to have had the opportunity to play a minor role in one of our great reforming governments, and to work with political colleagues of such passion, commitment, and intelligence was an enormous privilege.

What does effective leadership look like to me?

At first glance these are four very different leadership roles, but for me in living through them they have all been part of a whole. The skills required were also very similar from context to context. This unity has been greatly assisted by two commitments or characteristics that I have tried to hold onto irrespective of the role that I was currently in. The first is an unrelenting belief in moral purpose, and in terms of leadership and education, it is manifest in the creation of learning conditions that enable every person to reach their potential, whatever that potential may be. As I write this, I am reminded of the words of Amitai Etzioni (2000, pp. 11–13) in *The Third Way to a Good Society*:

> We aspire to a society that is not merely civil but is good. A good society is one in which people treat one another as ends in themselves. ... The Third Way is a road that leads us toward the good society. ... it points to the directions that we ought to follow but is neither doctrinaire nor a rigid ideological system.

The second is that throughout my professional life I have deliberately attempted to situate myself at the confluence of policy, practice, and research. This includes mountain guiding as well as the more traditional educational leadership roles. It has, however, not always been a comfortable position to hold and, sadly, on occasions, has led to opposition from those who I would normally have regarded as allies in the quest for establishing the 'Good Society'. But no worry, here we stand, and one can do little else. In essence, I tried over the years in my own way to transcend policy, practice, and research, to unify all three in the pursuit of educational excellence and the realisation of human potential.

Where is effective leadership required within my field?

In 2008 we published an article entitled 'Seven Strong Claims about Successful School Leadership'. The article was based on a major literature review and proved to be far more popular than we anticipated, having been extensively cited over the past ten years. Recently, ten years after the original paper, we revisited each of the seven claims, weighing each of them against the recent empirical evidence, and proposing revisions or refinements as warranted (see Leithwood, Harris, and Hopkins 2019). One of our original claims that has been resoundingly supported by the more recent research is that almost all successful leaders draw on the same repertoire of basic leadership practices. I mention this because this basic repertoire of practices neatly encapsulates the leadership activities that I have tried to follow across all the roles described above and spanning a 50-year time horizon.

The five leadership practices that appear to be particularly important when student outcomes and learning (broadly defined) are taken as the dependent variable are:

1. *Establishing narrative* – The ability to generate an inclusive and empowering vision for participants, that combines values and moral purpose on the one hand and operational strategies on the other, is imperative.
2. *Keeping the focus on teaching and learning* – Ensuring that pedagogic expertise is the core professional skill is crucial. It is the consistency of teaching and learning practices that is the critical independent variable. These are best expressed as protocols that contain practical best evidence strategies.
3. *Developing people* – The expansion of professional repertoire becomes the key staff development activity, that involves every member of staff in peer coaching. The model follows a theory, demonstration, practice, feedback, and coaching sequence that uses the protocols as a basis for observation, feedback, and skill development.

4. *Re-designing the organisation* – Creating a work culture and norms that support and enhance the previous three practices is essential. Establishing working conditions that are empowering, allocate sufficient time for professional development and peer coaching ensures that positive change is sustained into the medium term.
5. *Refining personality traits* – It is becoming increasingly apparent that the personal characteristics of the leader has significant impact. The ability to generate trust, enhance intrinsic motivation, be flexible rather than dogmatic, as well as resilient and optimistic, would appear to be the qualities that characterise leadership across a range of successful organisations.

What decisions am I most/least proud of when looking back on my leadership?

At a general level, it is exceedingly clear that when I did not focus on all of the five practices (outlined above) and the interactions between them, I was not very successful. There is a paradox here: in most situations one or two of these practices need most emphasis, but without a realization that all are important and interact in often predictable ways, sustainability and culture change will not occur. For as Edgar Schein (1985, p. 2) once memorably said: 'The only thing of real importance that leaders do is to shape and manage culture.'

So, let me give an example of success and failure from each of my four leadership areas:

- *Mountaineering* – As a guide, I have been most successful when I have managed to combine the power of narrative, focusing on the goal, with skill development and the provision of infrastructure support. As the leader of the Nanda Devi Traverse expedition in 1978, where my close friend Ben Beattie died, I underestimated dramatically (as sadly did so many of our generation at the time) the skill set required to climb such mountains in 'alpine style'.
- *School improvement* – As an 'invisible college' we have obviously been successful at establishing school improvement as a movement through a compelling narrative, identification of key skills and strategies, and empowering colleagues in schools and the 'middle tier' to take control (Hopkins 2013, 2017). Where we have been unsuccessful is counteracting the insidious and ubiquitous GERM virus, as Pasi Sahlberg (2012) terms it, that focus on quick-fix, top–down, accountability-driven tactics that are having such a detrimental effect on the life chances of so many students globally.
- *Dean* – At Nottingham I did try to establish a narrative and a vision that focused on core purpose together with engendering collaborative

practices, and it did have some impact. I am not sure, however, how sustained the impact was. External standards constrained some developments and whether I left too early before culture change was embedded still worries me.
- *Government* – Michael Barber was a hard act to follow, especially when the initial energy behind public sector reform was beginning to be spent and the spectre of Iraq began to loom. There was also a feeling within the civil service that the infrastructure that Michael had created, that was initially so effective at delivery, had to be cut down to size. Working with outstanding ministers such as Estelle Morris and David Miliband, however, we were able to create a new and compelling narrative that was welcomed by the profession and had some major policy successes, such as *Excellence and Enjoyment* and the *New Relationship with Schools*. We were never able, though, to ensure sustainability into the long term, by our inability to manage the conformist civil service ethos or control the political cycle (Hopkins 2007).

What/who had the most impact on me and my effectiveness as a leader?

My debt to so many is enormous, and I stand in awe of those, who through their example, taught me. There are so many more than those few mentioned below:

- *Mountaineering* – In Outward Bound it was Tom Price, Roger Putnam, and Art Rogers who, through their inspiration and trust in me, provided the space and opportunity to grow. As a guide, it was John Brailsford, Peter Alison, and Barbara Roscoe (nee Sparks), who set the bar high and would not let me falter. As a mountaineer, it was Peter Boardman, Sir Chris Bonington, Leo Houlding, Howie Richardson, and Doug Scott, who were and are powerful role models. Once again it was their inspiration, although they may not recognise it, through narrative, the assiduous development of skill, and the emphasis on collaboration and resilience, that made the difference.
- *School improvement* – Members of the previously mentioned 'invisible college' have been instrumental in my development. I was privileged to have been mentored by the likes of Michael Fullan, Bruce Joyce, and Lawrence Stenhouse, whose understanding and exemplification of the holy trinity of research, policy, and practice continues to inspire and direct me. There are also my companions on the 'Journey of School Improvement', such as Mel Ainscow, Pasi Sahlberg, Andreas Schleicher, Ray Shostak, and Mel West. Of the many outstanding school leaders that I have learned from, I

will just mention four – Trish Franey (Bristol), Sir Paul Grant (London), John Baumber (Sweden), and Kevan Naughton (Bolton). In different ways and contexts, each transformed their schools through the application of the practices already discussed and through themselves blossoming as system leaders.
- *Dean* – At Nottingham, as noted earlier, Sir Colin Campbell was an outstanding leader, combining as he did clear vision, an understanding of core purpose, and sustaining infrastructure together with an unrelenting commitment to excellence.
- *Government* – I have already mentioned the two outstanding politicians that I worked with: David Miliband and Estelle (Baroness) Morris. Once again it was their ability to apply the core leadership practices that made all the difference. The fact that over three winters the ministerial team in Education travelled around the country and spoke each year to at least half of the secondary heads and a quarter of the primary heads about the policy agenda and its impact on practice speaks for itself.

What questions should one ask oneself when considering their legacy as a leader?

I am going to cheat here and suggest two sets of questions, initially designed for different audiences but with clear overlap, as they both reflect the importance of the five basic leadership practices.

After I left government, I took a funded Chair in International Leadership based at the Institute of Education (now UCL) London. Whilst there I was invited to speak at a national conference on leadership. Conscious of my own biography, I wanted to link adventure and leadership. So, I sought the collaboration of Sir Chris Bonington. He shared with me his experience as the leader of the expedition that in 1976 first climbed the Southwest Face of Everest and placed the first two UK citizens – Dougal Haston and Doug Scott – on the summit of Everest. After telling the story of the expedition and using Chris's slides, I made the comparison with school leadership and then said the following:

On first appearance, leading a team up the Southwest Face of Everest may not be similar to leading your school, but do you:

- Expose yourself to risk and challenge complacency?
- Have a clear objective, develop a plan, then tell the story?
- Carefully allocate roles and develop people within and beyond them?
- Manage core purpose and create the conditions where every learner can achieve their potential and achieve high standards?
- Have clear operating systems, but being open to innovation?

- Set objectives and then trust colleagues?
- Cultivate the energy that direct experience and trust generates?
- Open yourself up to awareness, adventure, and challenge?

Whilst in government, as part of the attempts we were making to transform the education system and move it to another level, I developed the concept of 'system leadership' (Hopkins 2009). System leaders are those heads who are willing to shoulder system-wide roles in order to support the improvement of other schools as well as their own. As such, system leadership is a new and emerging practice that embraces a variety of responsibilities but are responsive to the following questions. As a system leader, do you:

- Measure your success in terms of improving student learning and increasing achievement?
- Fundamentally commit yourself to the improvement of teaching and learning?
- Develop your schools as personal and professional learning communities?
- Strive for equity and inclusion through acting on context and culture?
- Realise in a deep way that the classroom, school, and system levels all impact on each other?
- Understand that in order to change the larger system, you have to engage with it meaningfully?

Concluding note

Having now responded to the brief given to me by the editors, I need in concluding to respond to the question I set myself at the outset. I must say that I am happier now than when I began. The reason – well, I have convinced myself that leadership is not restricted to a role but spreads across the range of human endeavour. It is a lifelong skill that embraces moral purpose and narrative, the development of skill in oneself and others, the importance of collaborative learning, the establishing of appropriate learning conditions, and the continuing enhancement of personal qualities. You can never leave leadership!

References

Etzioni, A. (2000) *The Third Way to a Good Society*, London: Demos.
Hallinger, P. and Kovačević, J. (2019) A bibliometric review of research on educational administration: Science Mapping the literature, 1960 to 2018. *Review of Educational Research*, 89(3), 335–369. DOI: 10.3102/0034654319830380

Hopkins, D. (2007) *Every School a Great School*, Maidenhead: McGraw-Hill/Open University Press.

Hopkins, D. (2009) *The Emergence of System Leadership*, Nottingham: National College for School Leadership.

Hopkins, D. (2013) *Exploding the Myths of School Reform*, Berkshire: Open University Press, McGraw Hill Education.

Hopkins, D. (2017) The past, present and future of school improvement and system reform (The William Walker Oration). *ACEL Monograph*, 56. 1–23. [Online] Available at: http://profdavidhopkins.com/assets/docs/Future%20of%20School%20and%20Ststem%20Reform%20ACEL%20Monograph.pdf (Accessed June 8, 2020).

Hopkins, D. and Putnam, R. (1993 & 2012) *Personal Growth through Adventure*, Abingdon, OX: Routledge.

Hopkins, D., Stringfield, S., Harris, A., Stoll, L., and Mackay, A. (2014) School and system improvement: A narrative state of the art review. *School Effectiveness and School Improvement*, 25(2): 257–281.

Leithwood, K., Harris, A., and Hopkins, D., (2019) Seven strong claims about successful school leadership revisited, *School Leadership & Management*. DOI: 10.1080/13632434.2019.1596077

Sahlberg, P. (2012) *Global Reform Is Here!* https://parsisahlberg/global-educational-reform-movement-is-here!

Schein, E. (1985). *Organizational Culture and Leadership: A dynamic view*. San Francisco: Jossey-Bass.

CHAPTER **15**

Summary
Stephen Newton

In 2018, I was delighted to have the opportunity to work with an old friend, Dr Nigel Spencer (who kindly provided the Foreword to this book) to co-author a series of papers on the broad topic of creating competitive advantage in professional services through the strategic use of learning and development.[1] Nigel had held roles as global head of learning and development in major professional firms and was moving to work at Oxford University's Said Business School. In the final paper in the series, we examined career pathways for senior leaders.

In revisiting that paper, I found that, as in other aspects of this book, similarities between leadership in HE and in the professions (and elsewhere) seem to outweigh the differences, even allowing for the variation in context. It appeared that those about to leave leadership roles in the professions face two main types of challenge: practical and philosophical, which appear to be linked.

The practical challenges revolve around succession and transition planning as they affect client relationships and, hence, securing ongoing revenue. Separately, organisations need to secure the knowledge and experience of departing seniors, regardless of their role.

Leadership departures can offer an opportunity to free up space within the organisation for the development and advancement of others. However, there is a need to manage expectations internally as to who will take on the various roles held by the departing leader. That in turn indicates a need for an objective understanding of the capabilities of candidates and the relationships they have with relevant clients and colleagues (i.e. 'stakeholders' as we described them in Chapter 1). All of these factors go together to contribute to the maintenance or change of the culture of the organisation. Culture can of course be real (experienced by individuals) or perceived.

Whilst the partnership deeds of many professional firms include a 'normal' retirement date (something not now typically found in the field of HE or in industry), we found that a surprising number of professional firms lacked robust succession plans. Indeed, many did not begin to address the question of retirement planning (let alone the possibility of an unexpected exit due to, for example, illness) until a late stage. The paper made a number of recommendations to address the practical issues identified, including the development of a toolkit of leadership succession questions to discuss periodically within the leadership team.

The philosophical challenges were mostly around the willingness or otherwise of senior leaders to contemplate their own departure from an organisation in which they may well have worked for many years and which, for many, defined them. Firms often struggled to make retirement an 'okay' topic of conversation and it was necessary to create a broadly based initiative, led actively from the top, to work on achieving such transitions smoothly. A key problem for many senior individuals was the fear that, in leaving leadership and transitioning to retirement, they would lose not only status but relevance – hence the felt importance of legacy.

In this chapter, David, Fran, and Carlton outline their own career progressions and reflect on both their learnings from becoming and being leaders and then from the idea of leaving leadership.

Having described four distinct careers as a mountain guide, a leader in education, a government policymaker in education, and as an academic, David describes himself as seeking to work at the confluence of policy, practice, and research, then to unify them in the pursuit of educational excellence and the realisation of human potential. He notes that almost all leaders draw on the same basic repertoire of leadership practices: establishing a narrative/vision, developing people, refining personality traits, and maintaining focus on learning. In the practice of leadership, he highlights the comparisons with mountaineering: exposing oneself to risk, setting clear objectives, allocating roles, and delegating whilst developing people to excel in their roles, managing a core purpose, and creating an enabling, supportive environment.

In conclusion, David notes that the most important thing that leaders do is to shape and manage culture. He concludes that leadership is a lifelong skill that is not restricted to a role but spreads across the range of human endeavour requiring the continuing development of personal qualities and that, as such, one can never truly leave leadership.

Carlton focuses on leadership in terms of developing people and experiential learning, having himself received no formal leadership training. His focus has been on the leadership journey rather than goals – working on a twin track of leadership as an academic and manager alongside his research. Like David, Carlton highlights the importance of a clear vision and an enabling, supportive environment, where individuals are encouraged to be innovative. He indicates that colleagues should feel empowered to co-create the culture of the organisation, which he feels is crucial to success in leadership.

In terms of leaving leadership, he describes a masterfully planned succession initiated some years in advance for his own role. This not only ensured continuity and organisational success, but as a by-product cemented his own legacy. In retrospect, Carlton indicates that he could have focused more on activities on which he preferred to spend time, curbed his enthusiasm for new challenges in leadership, and focused more on organisational culture over strategy and outcomes.

Fran's contribution is dense and reflects two main streams of work. It outlines an interesting and clearly successful career path, working initially within an organisation (Goldsmiths, London) that was built to deliver full-time undergraduate and postgraduate courses but within which she led a cadre of 35–40 part-time teachers and 700–900 part-time students. The changes of funding model that occurred in the early 1990s shook up that successful model at a fundamental level, not only financially but in terms of the paper trail required to track retention, progression, and achievement of students. Fran's leadership role changed significantly as a result, perhaps acting as a catalyst for her move to lead the Postgraduate Certificate in HE (PGCHE) programme at the University of Kent. She observes that she would have wished to be more aware of external factors before they became acute.

Whilst her professional biography is impressive, to my mind some of her most interesting observations in this piece are regarding legacy. She makes the point that it can be potentially problematic for individuals to think about their legacy whilst they are in the present rather than in retrospect. A key question, she observes, is 'Why do you think your legacy matters?' One might suggest that if leadership requires a vision and that leaders need to start their professional journeys with the end in mind, a view of possible legacy is essential.

Note

1 https://www.sbs.ox.ac.uk/programmes/custom-executive-education/creating-competitive-advantage

In conclusion
Stephen Newton and Kendall Jarrett

It seems ambitious to attempt to encapsulate the rich learnings on the topic of leadership that appear throughout this book. However, in bringing together the many contributions from individuals who have deep practical experience of leadership, it has become clearer to us that there are some common threads running through the various personal stories and examples. There seems not to be great variance by professional context. In other words, there is more in common in terms of what leadership 'is' in practice between HE, the professions, corporates, sport, public and third sectors, and the military than there are significant distinctions. However, there are nuances depending on cultural/geographic context.

What do we feel have been standout points for us from compiling these personal stories of leadership in action and overlaying them with our own experiences?

First, the traits and characteristics of effective leaders that are mentioned consistently are largely common, regardless of context. They include self-awareness, honesty, integrity, trustworthiness, and taking a genuine interest in others as well as being able to articulate clearly a vision around which the group can coalesce. Linked to this articulation of vision is encouraging individuals within the group to contribute to developing the delivery plan and to believe that they are able to fulfil their part in achieving it.

Some contributors appear less comfortable with this narrative of leadership in terms of a 'vision, plan, delivery' process, which they feel to be transactional and to rely too greatly on some kind of 'hero leader' to deliver. For them leadership is more to do with co-creating a culture in which individuals can thrive and in which things are achieved in an almost organic manner. Leadership in this context is as much about individual growth as task completion. These ideas are often referred to as 'servant leadership' or 'leadership as service', although it is clear that this means subtly different things to each person. In each case, the building of strong relationships between leaders and those they seek to lead was emphasised.

Almost all of our contributors indicate that they would have preferred to receive (more) professional training and development in leadership skills prior to taking on leadership roles. They also see such development as an ongoing process. The importance of effective mentoring to their professional success is mentioned time and again – also, the positive impact of particular academic supervisors. In many cases, the mentoring relationship has translated into one of friendship.

The issue of patience (or lack of it) arises in several narratives, especially where a newly appointed leader fails to understand the strength of an embedded culture or structure and seeks to effect change too swiftly or without adequate consultation. If such a failure occurs, contributors comment on the need for, and benefit of, deep reflection to ensure their success in the future.

Some contributors who have worked within larger systems (such as multi-site organisations) comment on the need to establish what is non-negotiable in terms of culture and operations and what can be left to local management. They also note the need for sometimes brutal honesty with staff around their capabilities and willingness/reluctance to change and grow within the system. That may lead to a need for 'fast failure' – in other words, removing an individual who is simply not suited to work in the new context and who might become a block to progress.

Communication comes up time and again as a required skill for leaders. However, rather than being viewed as the ability to make set-piece speeches to rally the group, it is more often viewed as encouraging constructive conversations and as a means of collaboration. Linked to communication is the felt need to exercise influence with colleagues rather than relying on hierarchy to give instructions and expect them to be followed. This need to influence effectively is also commonly found in the professions, where leaders may in fact be *primus inter pares* seeking to gain agreement on a course of action from a group of bright and opinionated people who see themselves as peers, rather than acting as a more or less benevolent despot.

Something which many of our contributors have pondered is the idea of legacy. Views vary quite widely. One felt that it would be invidious to carry out a role with one eye on one's legacy and that legacy could only be considered after the event in light of the facts. Another observed that legacy was inevitably impermanent, as any project would become someone else's responsibility after your departure. Another felt that it would be inevitable to leave a legacy of some kind when leaving a leadership role: however, the actual nature of that legacy would depend on the perceptions and experiences of others. Part of an HE leader's legacy to themselves would of course be a set of skills that are inherently valuable outside HE.

One observation that struck home for us was to the effect that success in leadership is not simply in being appointed to a role and doing a job. Real success in HE leadership, as is the case in sports, entails genuine passion to perform and willingness to do the hard work of training and self-development needed to achieve excellence. Linked to that was discussion of the performance of education – how leaders can engender improvements in the delivery of education and learning and then both embed these and sustain them. Success in delivering holistic student learning would depend on intentionality and aligning culture, curriculum, co-curriculum, and a sense of community.

Our work on this book has emphasised for us that there is no single 'right' approach to designing or even to understanding leadership in HE. There are too many variables, not least the individuality of leaders and those they seek to lead, leaving aside geographic and organisational culture issues. We can only hope that readers will be able to extract ideas that will help them in their own search for success in becoming leaders, being leaders, or eventually leaving leadership. However, as one contributor observed, one may (arguably) never actually leave leadership.

Index

ableism 26–27
academics in exile 102–104, 184–185
acceptance of reality 14–15
accountability 14, 66, 167, 237
accounting firms 145
Adair, John 33
Adams, Tony 158
adaptability 50–51, 132, 149, 155, 183; academics in exile 103; effective leadership 191; leaders' stories 195, 208; military leadership 185; public sector leadership 170; system leadership 92; *see also* flexibility
Adelaide Football Club 156
administration 207, 212
Advance HE 45
adventure leadership 234
advocacy 74
Africa 173
Afridi, F. 172
after-action reports 146–147, 185
agreeableness 13
Ainscow, Mel 238
Alison, Peter 238
Amazon 134

Anderson, M. 94
Android 132
Anglican Communion 174–175
Apple 131, 132, 133–134
appointments 47, 48, 224–225
Armentrout, J. 32
Armstrong, P. 89
Arnold, R. 157
Arthur Andersen 127–129
Ashkenas, Ron 122
Asian Productivity Organisation 173, 180n10
assumptions 132
attainment gap 199–200, 204
audit profession 127–129
austerity 92, 174
Australia 62–63, 64–65, 156–157, 170–171, 184
authenticity 14, 141; cultural creatives 177; holistic learning model 76; leaders' stories 193, 208, 219, 220; self-leadership 6, 57; sport leadership 155, 156, 159, 185–186
authority 22–23
autocratic leadership 15–16, 18
autonomy 73, 88, 93–94, 170

Index

'bad' leadership 122–123
Baghurst, T. 179
Bandura, C. 155
Barber, Michael 235, 238
Baumber, John 87–101, 184, 238–239
Beaton, Fran 228–232, 243–244
Beddow, A. 5
Beer, Janet 28
Beer, M. 179
behaviours 44, 55
belonging 63, 122
Bennie, A. 154
bespoke workshops 31
Beveridge, H. 149
Bezos, Jeff 134
black, Asian or minority ethnic (BAME) background 25–26, 198, 200
Black, S. 23–24
Blackberry 130, 132–133
Boardman, Peter 238
Bonington, Chris 238, 239
Bonner, J. M. 24
book editing 111
Booms, Emily Rumschlag 194–197, 204–205
Boston Consulting Group (BCG) 173
Bowen, F. 87
Bowen, Joanne 206–210, 220–221
Box, M. 31
BP *Deepwater Horizon* disaster 123, 125–127
Bradman, Don 151
Brady, Tom 155–156
Brailsford, John 238
Braskamp, L. A. 80–81
Brexit 28
Brgoch, S. 153
Brodbeck, F. 43
Brown, N. 27
Brown, Sally 105–117, 185
Brydon, Donald 167
Buchanan-Hodgman, Luke 211–214, 220–221
budgets 30
Buffet, Warren 106
Bunting, Dave 226
bureaucratic constraints 82–83
Burton, L. 156
business schools 46
buy-in 81, 213

calmness 66
Campbell, Colin 234, 239
Carbone, G. 179
career breaks 112
Carnefeldt, Cecilia 95–98
Carnegie School of Sport 222–223, 224–225
Carton, A. M. 25–26
chain of command 137
challenge 170
Chandler, D. E. 110
change 17–18, 30, 122–123, 179, 199, 246
character 13
charities *see* third sector leadership
Clack, L. A. 23
Clark, N. 5
Close, P. 98–99
co-curriculum 80–81, 247
coaches 153, 154–155
coaching 46, 142; feedback 49; leaders' stories 209, 236; peer coaching 31, 237
Colaiacomo, Silvia 35
Coll, J. 20
collaboration 14, 74; collaborative research 107; communication 246; leaders' stories 196, 199, 201, 216, 217, 237–238; public sector leadership 170; system leadership 92; third sector organisations 174, 177; upwards leadership 7
collegiality 29–30, 73
Collin, Jim 93, 145
'Commander's intent' 138, 148
commitment 13, 196
Committee on Standards in Public Life 167
communication 14, 66, 246; clear 53; credible 50; emotional intelligence 190; 'good' leadership 122; inconsistent 179; leaders' stories 217, 223; military leadership 140–141; public sector leadership 170; sport leadership 153, 163; system leadership 96; third sector leadership 175, 176
communities of practice 216, 229, 230, 232
community 80–81, 195–196, 247
competency 13
competition 17, 191
conferences 64–65, 67, 113
confidentiality 11, 217, 219

250 Index

conflicts of interest 217, 219
conformity 93–94, 184
connection 122
conscientiousness 13, 157
consistency 53, 54, 92, 96, 198–199, 236
Constandt, B. 155
consultancy 98–99, 107
context 43, 83, 178, 183
contingent leadership 189, 190
continuing professional development (CPD) 29; leaving leadership 110, 112; public sector leadership 170–171; system leadership 98–99; *see also* professional development
continuous improvement 53, 199
contracts 176–177
contribution 170
control 23–24
Cooke, Carlton 222–227, 243–244
Cooper, George 226
corporate leadership 52–53, 121–135, 185, 189, 191
corruption 168, 172
costs 18
Cotterill, S. 151
Council of At-Risk Academics (CARA) 102–103
courage 14, 163
Covey, S. 199
CPD *see* continuing professional development
creativity 94, 134
credibility 6, 14, 50, 54, 55, 141, 159
Creelman, D. 22
Crossan, Mary 13–14, 43, 51
Crouch, A. 22
cultural competence 201, 205
cultural creatives 177
culture 66–67, 69, 190, 227, 237, 247; *see also* organisational culture
culture bearers 97
Cummins, P. 150
Curiosity and Power Learning programme 99
curriculum 37, 80–81, 247
Curry, Christina 170–171
customer leadership 5, 8–10

Daniel, C. 167
Davies, Gareth 65–66

Deakin University 89
decision-making 22, 29, 183; collegial 23; instinct 219; public sector leadership 170; sport leadership 151, 153, 159, 161
Deepwater Horizon 123
delegation 24, 53, 68, 243; leaders' stories 212–213, 214; military leadership 140; system leadership 92
democracy 179
Department for Education (DfE) 235
design thinking (DT) 36–37
devolved leadership 171, 180n7
Dewey, John 69–70
disability 27
DISC 49
disciplinary leadership 230
discretionary effort 4
discussion driven leadership 16
distributed leadership 73–74, 184, 190, 193
Doz, Yves 131
Drucker, Peter 129

economies of scale 87–88, 91–92
effectiveness 30, 53, 190–191
Eisenhower, Dwight D. 54
elected leadership 171, 172–173
elites 147–148
Elkind, Peter 128
Eloi, Serge 160–161
emeritus professorships 114–115
emotional control 163
emotional intelligence 159, 189, 190, 199
emotions 77
empathy 143, 151
empowerment 66, 153, 189, 237, 243
energy trading 127–130
engagement 205
enjoyment 225
Enron 127–130
equality 199, 200, 217
ethics 216, 217, 219; ethical frameworks 78; ethical leadership 155, 156, 177; 'good' leadership 121
Etzioni, Amitai 235
EvoLLLution 88, 99n3
exiles 102–104, 184–185
exit strategies 108–109
expectations 95, 121, 153, 157
experience 61–70

experiential learning 223
expertise 21–22, 71–72, 236
extroversion 13, 23, 49
Exxon Valdez 123, 124–125

failure 95, 123–133, 134, 246; *see also* mistakes
fairness 53, 217, 219
familiarity 29–30
Fastow, Andrew 128
Favaloro, D. 154
Fedoruk, Lisa 215–219, 220–221
feedback 49–50, 196, 210, 230, 236
Ferguson, J. 167
field trips 32
financial viability 17
Finneström, M. 179
Five Factor Model (FFM) 13
Fletcher, D. 157
flexibility 14, 110, 122, 139, 144, 237; *see also* adaptability
Franey, Trish 238–239
Fransen, K. 151, 152
Fraser, D. 88
Frawley, S. 154
Frazer, James George 24
freelancers 18
Fullan, Michael 77, 89, 238
funding 17, 68, 145; changes in 167; leaders' stories 206, 230, 231, 244; third sector 176–177
Furner, A. 5

Gallup Strengths Finder 49, 50
Gardner, P. 177
Gates, Bill 23, 133
gender equity 207
Gibbs, G. 23–24
'gig economy' 17
Giles, Sunnie 121–122
globalisation 199
Glowinkowski, Steve 44
goals 4, 122, 157, 190, 192, 199; *see also* objectives
Golden State Warriors (GSW) 155
Goldsmiths, University of London 228, 229, 230, 231, 244
'good' leadership 121–122
governance 88

Grant, Paul 238–239
grit 205
Groenwald, S. L. 87, 88
growth 122
Gurdjian, P. 178

Halford, G. 141
Hallinger, P. 33, 234
Hambling, Glynn 95–98
Hamilton, Tyler 158
Harding, C. 31
Hardy, J. H. III 24
Harvard Institutes for Higher Education 45
Hawkes, Jan 169–170, 171
Hayward, Tony 126
Health and Care Professions Council (HCPC) 198
Heck, R. H. 33
Hehir, Thomas 26–27
hero leadership 73, 93, 184, 245
Higham, R. 89
Higher Education Academy (HEA) 33, 34–35, 38n3, 38n6, 78, 231
Higher Education Funding Council of England (HEFCE) 73
higher education institutions (HEIs) 3; changing world 17, 18, 21–22; consultancy 107; elites 147–148; leadership appointments 47; peer leadership 9; system leadership 87–101; women leaders 28
hiring 44, 174; *see also* recruitment
Hobbs, Matthew 161–163
Hobson, J. 157
Hodges, J. 177, 178
The Hogan suite 49
holistic learning 71–72, 75–84, 247
Holloway, M. 177
honesty 14, 15, 55, 66, 245, 246; military leadership 136, 185; public sector 167; sport leadership 155, 185–186
Hope, Julia 35
Hopkins, David 89, 99, 233–241, 243
Houlding, Leo 238
Howieson, B. 177, 178
humanity 14
humility 14, 93, 159, 218, 230
Hunt-Davis, Ben 149, 158
Huy, Qui 131

252 Index

identity 71; academics in exile 104; cultural creatives 177; holistic learning model 76; transition 112–113
immersion 53–54
India 172
individual consideration 157
induction training 52
inequalities 27, 199–200, 204
influence 7–8, 23, 38n1, 51, 246; credible communication 50; leaders' stories 193; military leadership 140–141
informal leaders 151, 152, 162
informality 29–30
Inkling Women 208
innovation 37, 82, 122, 134, 223–224, 239
instinct 219
Institute of Education, Cambridge 234
institutional racism 199
instructional leadership 79–80, 81, 184
integrity 6, 14, 57, 66, 77, 167, 245
intellectual stimulation 157
intentional leadership 108
intentionality 76, 77, 80–81, 247
international partnerships 91
internationalisation 18
interpersonal skills 230
introversion 23, 49
iPhone 131, 132
Ives, Jonathan 133
Ivy League 147–148, 149n1

Jackson, Stevan 226
James, William 44
Japan 63–64, 183
Jarrett, Kendall 20–42, 57–58, 87–101, 183–186, 245–247; academics in exile 102–104; becoming a leader 204–205; being a leader 220–221; public and third sectors 166–182, 186; sport leadership 150–165, 185–186; system leadership 184
Jobs, Steve 133–134
John, Gus 25, 26
Johns, Alison 31
journals 111
Joyce, Bruce 238
judgement 14
Juncker, Jean-Claude 172
justice 14

Kahnweiler, Jennifer 13
Katzenbach, Jon 145
Kavussanu, M. 155
Kawalilak, Colleen 218–219
Kaz, S. 98
Keefe, Dorothy 209–210
Keirsey Temperament Sorter 49
Kent, B. 5
Kerr, Steve 155
Klapper, John 229
Knapper, C. 23–24
Kneale, Pauline 105–117, 185
knowledge 71–72, 76, 79–80, 83, 183
Kodak 130–131
Kovačević, J. 234
Kram, K. E. 110
Krøtel, S. 168
Kubicek, J. 108
Kunda, Z. 26
Kunskapsskolan 91, 93, 94, 95

Lasthuizen, K. 168
Lawrence, Stephen 199
Lay, Ken 127–128, 129–130
leadership: approaches/style 15–16, 55; becoming a leader 189–193, 194–197, 198–203, 204–205; being a leader 206–210, 211–214, 215–219, 220–221; changing world 17–18; characteristics 12–15, 71, 76–78, 143–144, 157, 237, 245; concept of 3–10; corporate 52–53, 121–135, 185, 189, 191; definitions of 4, 35, 36, 73–75; experience and culture 61–70; failures 123–133; holistic learning model 75–84; leadership jacket 166–167, 179n3; learning to be a leader 43–55; leaving 105–117, 185, 222–227, 228–232, 233–241, 242–244; management distinction 16–17; myths 21–25; Nolan Principles 167; public and third sectors 166–182, 186; realities of 25–29; sport 150–165, 185–186; system 87–101, 184, 235, 240; see also military leadership
leadership development 20–21, 29–37, 57–58, 246; barriers to success 178–179; leaders' stories 192; mentoring 46; military leadership 45, 142–143; opportunities for 221; public sector 173,

178; sport leadership 152–153; system leadership 98–99, 184; third sector 176–177; women 208; *see also* professional development
learning: core leadership skills 122; by doing 53; engagement 205; experiential 223; 'good' leadership 122; holistic 71–72, 75–84; leaders' stories 236, 243; learning culture 82; lifelong 113; military leadership 146–147; from mistakes 68, 134, 157, 223, 230; prior experiences 69–70; sport leadership 156–157; students 196; system leadership 92, 96, 97, 240
learning communities 113
leaving leadership 105–117, 185, 222–227, 228–232, 233–241, 242–244
Leberman, S. 156
Lee, E. 87
Leeds Beckett University (LBU, formerly Leeds Metropolitan University) 65–66, 184, 222–223, 225, 227
Leeds Trinity University (LTU) 222, 223, 227
legacy, leaving a 105–117, 227, 232, 239–240, 244, 246
Leicester City Football Club 150, 155
Leigh, Jen 27
lifelong learning 113
lifetime fellowships 113
Light, Richard L. 61–70, 183–184
likability 51, 53
local government 168–169, 170–171
Løkke, A.-K. 168
Long, Jessica 158
Lopez, Victor 160
Lower, L. 153
loyalty 51, 53, 63; leaders' stories 226; military leadership 136, 137, 185

Maccoby, Michael 144
MacGregor, Gabriel 168–169, 171
macro level 75, 80
management 16–17, 47–48
Manchester United 156
Mandela, Nelson 23, 198, 200, 201
Manville, Brook 122
Mardini, Yusra 150
Marek, Lukas 161–163

Marshall, Thurgood 22–23
martial arts 62–63, 183
Maskia, Rachel 189–193, 204–205
Matusitz, J. 155
McLean, Bethany 128
measurement/metrics 122–123, 129, 199, 227
mentoring 20, 37, 46, 108, 110, 142; distributed leadership 74; feedback 49; importance of 246; informal 31; leaders' stories 209, 216, 218–219, 220, 231–232; military leadership 141; Peter Principle 168; public sector leadership 171; SFHEA 34
meso level 75, 80, 82
Mickahail, B. 37
micro level 75
micro-management 10, 53
Microsoft 131, 133
Miliband, David 238, 239
military leadership 4, 43, 136–149; autocratic leadership 16; changing world 17–18; 'customers' 9–10; influence 51; leadership appointments 48; leadership characteristics 13; leadership development 45; preparation for leadership 52; servant leadership 15
millennials 170
Miller, George 141
mistakes 68, 134, 157, 223, 230; *see also* failure
models/theories/literature (M/T/L) 33
Moody's Investor Service 87–88, 99n1
Morley, L. 27
Morris, Estelle 238, 239
Moss, S. 174, 177
motivation 94, 151, 157, 163, 237
mountaineering 233, 234, 237, 238, 239, 243
multi-site institutions/multi-institution systems 87–88, 184
mutual respect 4
Myers Briggs Type Indicator (MBTI) 15, 49
myths 21–25

Napoleon Bonaparte 143
narcissism 143–144
narrative 61, 236, 237–238, 243

254   Index

National College of School Leadership 91
National Leadership Centre (NLC) 173
Naughton, Kevin 238–239
neoliberalism 199
Networked Learning Community project 91
networking 74
networks 96, 157
Neumann, Anna 78
neuroticism 13
New England Patriots 150, 155–156
New Zealand 66–68, 161–162, 184
Newman, T. 153
Newton, Stephen 3–19, 57–58, 183–186, 245–247; academics in exile 102–104; becoming a leader 204–205; corporate leadership 121–135, 185; leadership development 30, 32; learning to be a leader 43–55; leaving leadership 242–244; military leadership 136–149, 185
Nokia 130, 131–132
Nolan Principles 167
non-commissioned officers (NCOs) 45, 136, 141
Nordstrand Berg, L. 87
norms 190, 237
Northeastern Illinois University 194

Oancea, Alis 74, 75
objectives 122, 137, 240, 243; *see also* goals
objectivity 167
obsessive personality 143–144
O'Connor, D. 154
off-field leadership 153–154
oil and gas industry 123–127
on-field leadership 151, 153
openness 53, 122, 157, 167
openness to experience 13
opportunities 29, 183, 192, 221
organisational conditions 71, 72, 76, 80–83
organisational culture 10, 55, 80–81, 242, 243; adapting knowledge 183; corporate failures 123; leaders' stories 237; military leadership 137; Nokia 131; shared culture 4; standards 139; understanding 193
organisational structures 18, 24
Otsu, Dr 214

outreach 212, 213
Outward Bound 233, 234, 238

Parkinson, Tom 102
Parks, Rosa 23
Parrish, D. 24
partnerships 51, 91–95, 98, 184
patience 246
peer coaching 31, 237
peer leadership 5, 8–10
peer observations 32
Peinaar, Thana 95–98
Pellegata, A. 179
pensions 107
performance evaluation 143
personal characteristics 12–15, 71, 76–78, 143–144, 157, 237, 245
personal experience narrative approach 61–62
personality traits 13, 143–144, 157, 237, 243, 245
Peter Principle 168
Peterson, D. R. 24
Peterson, Randall S. 144
PGCHE *see* Postgraduate Certificate of Higher Education
Phillips, Erin 156
Picinnin, S. 23–24
Pigni, D. 167
Pinheiro, R. 87
planning 108–109, 139
politicians 172
Postgraduate Certificate of Higher Education (PGCHE) 33–34, 38n4, 228, 229, 231, 244
postgraduate courses 31
power 23, 219
preparation for leadership 45–47, 52, 58
Price, Tom 238
private sector 169
process driven leadership 16
'productive narcissists' 143, 144
professional development 20, 29, 81, 196; leaders' stories 205, 206, 228–229, 236, 237; public sector leadership 171; researchers 208; *see also* continuing professional development; leadership development; training
professional ethics frameworks 78

professional responsibilities 207, 211–212, 216, 222–223, 228–229
professionalism 192
professions 45–46, 47–48, 52–53, 142, 246
professorships 114–115
promotion 28, 47–48, 52, 139–140, 143, 168, 224–225
psychometric instruments 49–50
public sector leadership 166–182, 186
purpose 71, 77, 79, 83, 243; common 4, 145; leaders' stories 237–238, 239; sport leadership 150
Putnam, Roger 238

Quinlan, Kathleen M. 71–86, 184

race 25–26, 199–200, 204
racism 26, 199
Railo, Willi 151
Ranieri, Claudio 155
Razak, Mohammad Shah 66
recruitment 122, 207, 211; *see also* hiring
'red brick' universities 147–148, 149n1
reflection 153, 159, 205, 232, 246
refugees 102–104, 184–185
Reh, F. 168
relationships 73, 112, 153, 170, 192, 212, 245
reliability 192
religious organisations 174–175
Remedios, S. 167
research: centres of excellence 148; collaborative 107; leaders' stories 206, 216, 224, 236, 238; research ethics 216, 217; research leadership 84n1, 190, 192; researcher development 208; researchers' vision 75; retirement 106, 111
resilience 50–51, 149, 183, 237; academics in exile 103, 104; leaders' stories 238; public sector leadership 170; Special Forces 144; sport leadership 151, 162
respect 4, 51, 53, 136, 153, 193
retirement 106–115, 185, 242–243; *see also* leaving leadership
reverse mentoring 110, 141
Richardson, Howie 238
risk-aversion 123
Rock, David 33

Rogers, Art 238
role-modelling 74, 75, 153, 157
Ronayne, P. 167
Roscoe, Barbara 238
Rosette, A. S. 25–26
Route to Recognition for Experienced Staff (RRES) 34–36
Royal Military Academy Sandhurst 138
rugby 63–64, 183
Russell Group 147–148, 149n1
Rybacki, M. 167

sabbaticals 112
sacrifice 205
safety 4, 121, 138
Sahlberg, Pasi 237, 238
SAIT Polytechnic 215, 217
Salazar, Ken 127
Sanchex, Alexis 156
scepticism, constructive 139
Schein, Edgar 237
Schleicher, Andreas 238
school improvement 234, 237, 238–239
school leadership 89–98, 99n7, 184, 236
Schrader, D. 179
Schulenkorf, N. 154
Scott, Doug 238
Scott, G. 77
selection 52, 147
self-awareness 48–50, 183, 245; leaders' stories 192–193, 208, 230; resilience 50–51; sport leadership 155, 157, 185–186
self-care 111–112
self-knowledge 55
self-leadership 5–6, 18, 57, 103, 122, 129, 183
self-organisation 122
self-reflection 183
self-regulation 73
selflessness 167
Senior Fellow of the Higher Education Academy (SFHEA) 33, 34–36, 38n6, 71, 72, 84n2
servant leadership 15, 18, 171, 180n8, 189, 204–205, 245
shared culture 4
Sharp, Craig 226
Shepherd, S. 27–28
'shock of immersion' 53–54

256 Index

short-term roles 54
Shostak, Ray 238
Siddall, Andy 158–159
Silvester, J. 172
Simi, D. 155
situational awareness 191, 193
situational leadership 10, 189, 190, 193
skill sets 109–110
Skilling, Jeffrey 127, 128, 129–130
Slim, Bill 138, 141
Smith, M. 157
Smith, Tim 174–175
social contract 138–139
social justice 199, 200
social media 141, 171
Society for Teaching and Learning in Higher Education 78
Socratic questioning 214
Sofianos, L. 31
soft skills 46, 142, 170
South Africa 91, 95, 184
span of decision 7–8
Special Forces 140, 144, 147, 148
Spencer, J. 150
Spencer, Nigel 30, 32, 48, 242
Spencer, S. 26
sport leadership 150–165, 185–186
Staff and Educational Development Association 78
staff/team leadership 5, 10
stakeholders 9, 10–12, 57; list of 12; public sector leadership 170, 171; stakeholder mapping 5, 8, 11, 54
standards 139
Stanford, P. 174, 176
stasis 122
State University of New York 87
Stenhouse, Lawrence 238
stereotypes 25–26, 27
Stormzy 25
Stott, K. 88
strategy 122
strengths 50, 140, 208
stress 139, 140, 148
succession 225, 242–243, 244
support 112, 139, 196
Svansberg, Carl-Henric 126
Svechin, A. 138
Sweden 91, 93, 99n7, 184

Syrian academics 102–104
system leadership 87–101, 184, 235, 240

targets 122–123
Taylor Institute for Teaching and Learning 215–216
teaching: knowledge about 71–72, 76, 79–80, 83; leaders' stories 195–197, 207, 224, 236; leaving leadership 112–113; multi-site institutions 88; organisational conditions 81–82; system leadership 240; teachers as role models 75
team leadership 5
teamwork 145–146, 212; leaders' stories 195; military leadership 137–138, 145; Special Forces 144; upwards leadership 7
technology sector 130–133
temperament 16, 18
temperance 14
Thiel, C. E. 24
Think Well programme 209
third sector leadership 166, 173–178, 186
Third Way 235
Thomas, Dave 198–203, 204–205
Thomas, Gareth 158
Thomas Kilmann (TKI) 49
Thompson, P. 27
Thunberg, Greta 22
Times Higher Education 88, 99n2
Toronto Raptors 156
Toyota 147
training 45, 246; Anglican Communion 174–175; 'good' leadership 122; military 52, 137–138, 142–143; Peter Principle 168; public sector leadership 170; sport leadership 153; see also professional development
traits 13, 157, 237, 243, 245
transcendence 14
transformational leadership 79, 157, 171, 180n9, 191
transition planning 242
travel 113
trust 8, 141, 237; leaders' stories 192, 193; military leadership 4, 136, 137, 185; sport leadership 153, 155, 159, 185–186; trustworthiness 77, 245
tuition fees 3, 191, 200, 230
Turney, M. 168

turnover 123

U3A (University of the Third Age) 113
Ujiri, Masai 156
UK Professional Standards Framework (UKPSF) 33, 38n5, 78, 84n2, 231
Ulster University 89
uncertainty 18, 179, 208, 218
University College London (UCL) 45, 233, 239
University of Adelaide 206–210
University of Bolton 233
University of Calgary 215, 216
University of Canterbury, New Zealand 66–68
University of Kent 72, 198, 211, 212, 213, 228, 229, 231, 244
University of London 87, 228
University of Melbourne 64–65
University of Nottingham 89, 233, 234–235, 237–238, 239
upwards leadership 5, 7–8

values 14, 71, 73; distributed leadership 74; emotional intelligence 190; environmental context 83; holistic learning model 76–78; leaders' stories 236; military leadership 137; professional ethics frameworks 78; public sector leadership 171; self-leadership 183; sport leadership 159; system leadership 92, 95, 97–98, 99
van Eeden Jones, I. 168
VIA (Values in Action) 49, 50

vision 74, 75, 78, 191–192, 245; Anglican Communion 175; core leadership skills 122; holistic learning model 76; leaders' stories 223, 230, 236, 237–238, 243; leaving a legacy 244; 'productive narcissists' 143; sport leadership 159; system leadership 96
volunteering 110, 166
von Clausewitz, Carl 138
vulnerability 22, 141, 159, 205, 218
Vuori, Tim 131

Waddell, Karl 175–176
Wakeman, S. Wiley 144
Walker, Sam 163
Wallace, W. 22
'war for talent' 18
Watkins, Sherron 128, 129–130
Weiss, E. 20
wellbeing 111–112
Welsh, D. T. 24
West, Mel 238
Wiedeman, T. 32
Wilcox, M. 98
Wilde, Oscar 6
Willem, A. 155
Williams, Clyde 226
Williams, M. 179
women 27–28, 207, 208
work-life balance 209, 220
working groups 145
workload 213, 214
workshops 31
Wyatt, M. 172